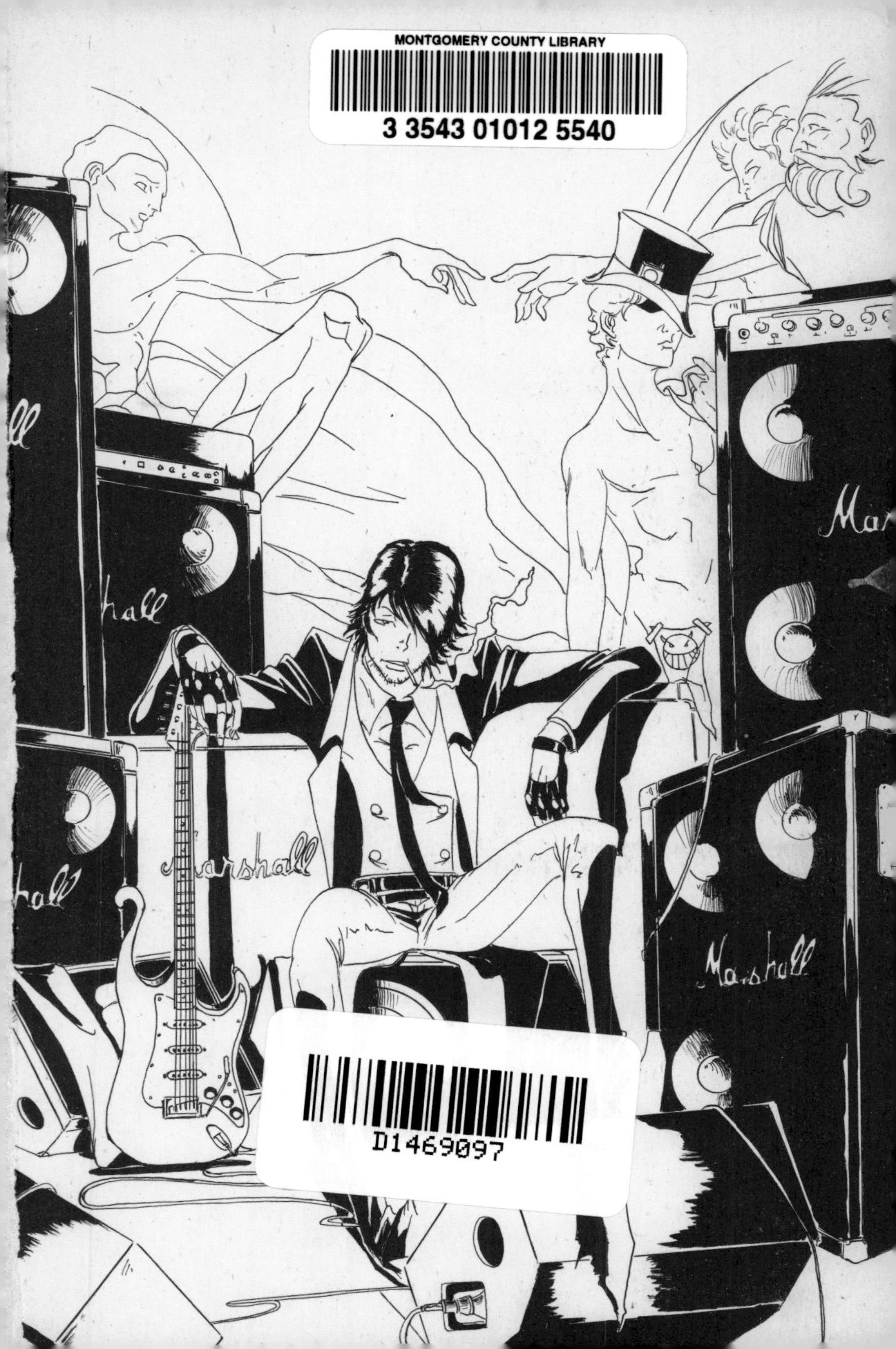
Marshall
Marshall

# *A Midnight Opera Act 1*
## created by Hans "Hanzo" Steinbach

Associate Editor - Lillian Diaz-Przybyl
Lettering, Layout and Pre-Press - James Lee
Cover Art - Hans Steinbach
Cover Color - Al-Insan Lashley
Cover Design - Thea Willis

Editor - Luis Reyes
Digital Imaging Manager - Chris Buford
Production Managers - Jennifer Miller and Mutsumi Miyazaki
Managing Editor - Lindsey Johnston
VP of Production - Ron Klamert
Editorial Director - Jeremy Ross
Publisher and E.I.C. - Mike Kiley
President and C.O.O. - John Parker
C.E.O. - Stuart Levy

A  Manga

TOKYOPOP Inc.
5900 Wilshire Blvd. Suite 2000
Los Angeles, CA 90036

E-mail: info@TOKYOPOP.com
Come visit us online at www.TOKYOPOP.com

ISBN: 1-59816-265-9

First TOKYOPOP printing: November 2005
10  9  8  7  6  5  4  3  2
Printed in the USA

# A MIDNIGHT OPERA

## ACT 1

CREATED BY
HANS "HANZO" STEINBACH

TOKYOPOP®

HAMBURG // LONDON // LOS ANGELES // TOKYO

I sing.

I sang.

I song.

I song deep.

I song deep pain.

I song deep love.

I have songed since song was sung.

Each song a separate piece...

In a longer song...

# A Midnight Opera...

...of my lovely, painful life.

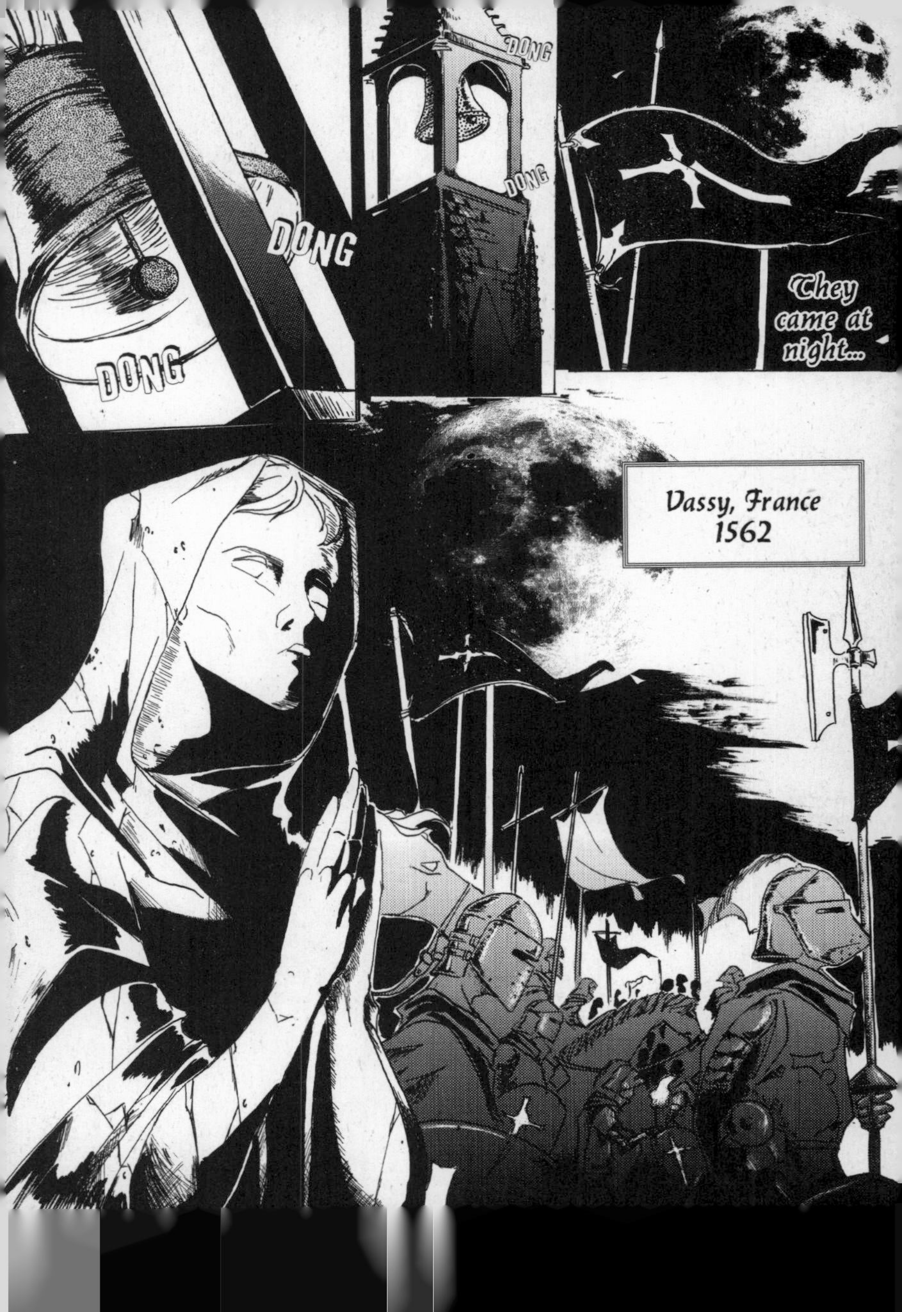
They came at night...
DONG
DONG
DONG
DONG
Vassy, France
1562

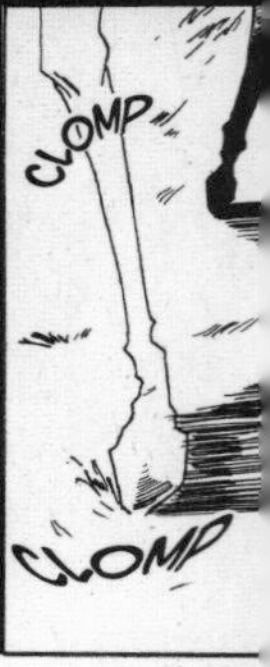
CLOMP
CLOMP
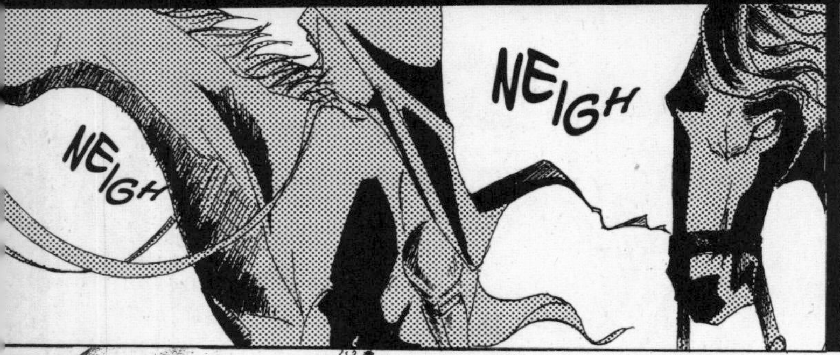
NEIGH
NEIGH
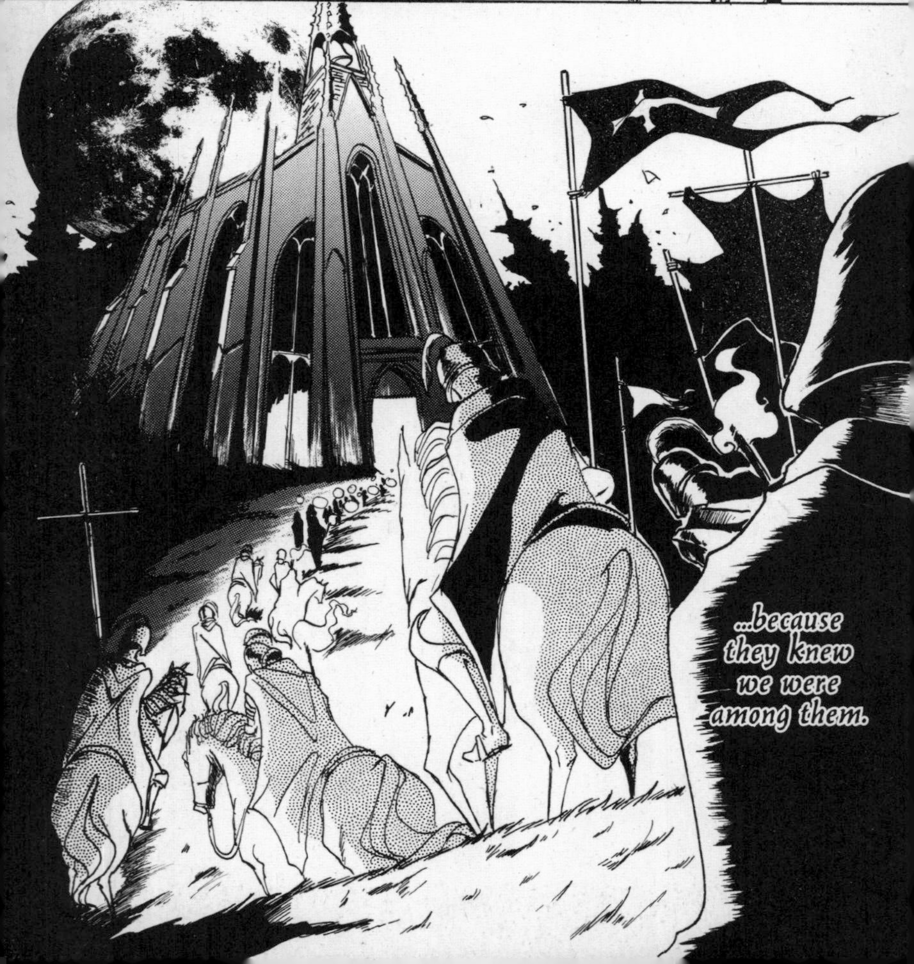
...because they knew we were among them.

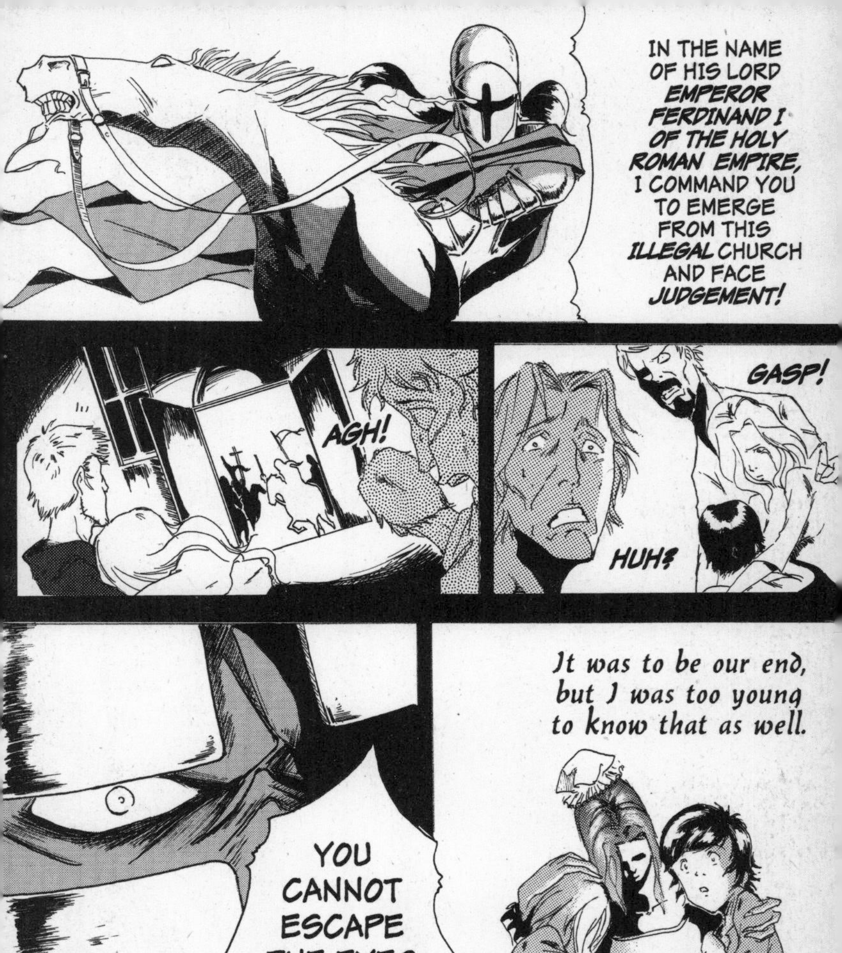
IN THE NAME OF HIS LORD EMPEROR FERDINAND I OF THE HOLY ROMAN EMPIRE, I COMMAND YOU TO EMERGE FROM THIS ILLEGAL CHURCH AND FACE JUDGEMENT!
AGH!
GASP!
HUH?
YOU CANNOT ESCAPE THE EYES OF GOD, NOR THE SERVANTS WHO FOLLOW HIS WORD!
It was to be our end, but I was too young to know that as well.

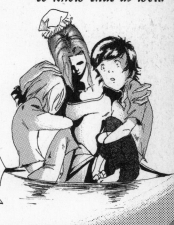

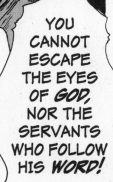

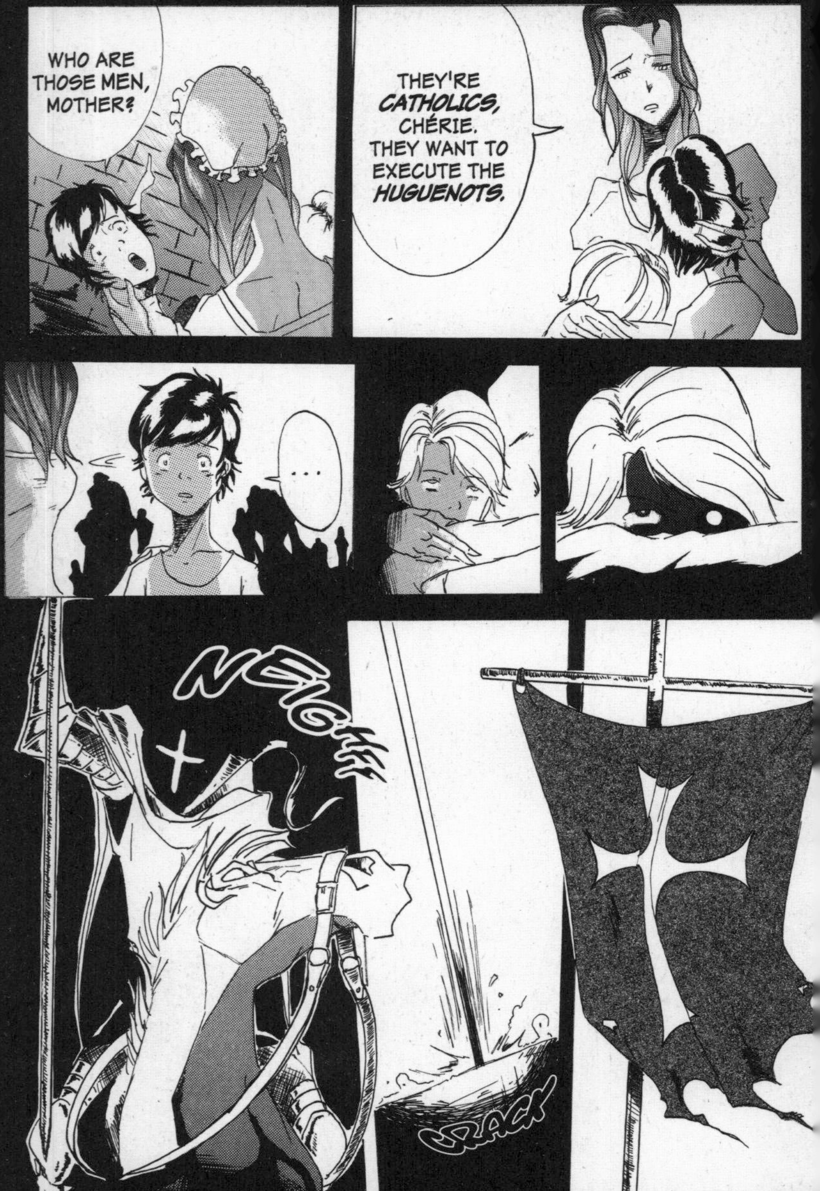
WHO ARE THOSE MEN, MOTHER?
THEY'RE CATHOLICS, CHÉRIE. THEY WANT TO EXECUTE THE HUGUENOTS.
...
NEIGHH
CRACK

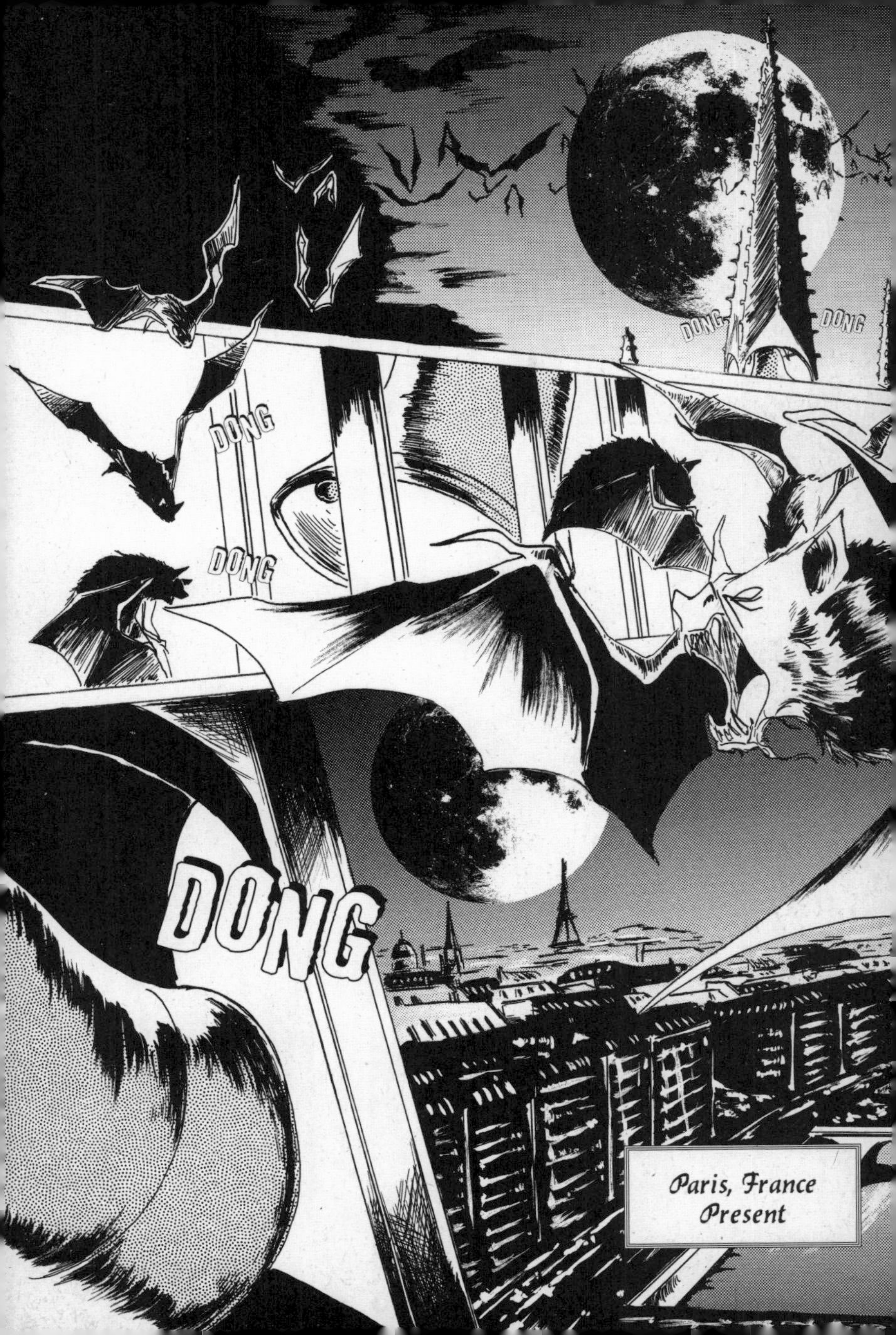
DONG
DONG
DONG
DONG
DONG
Paris, France
Present

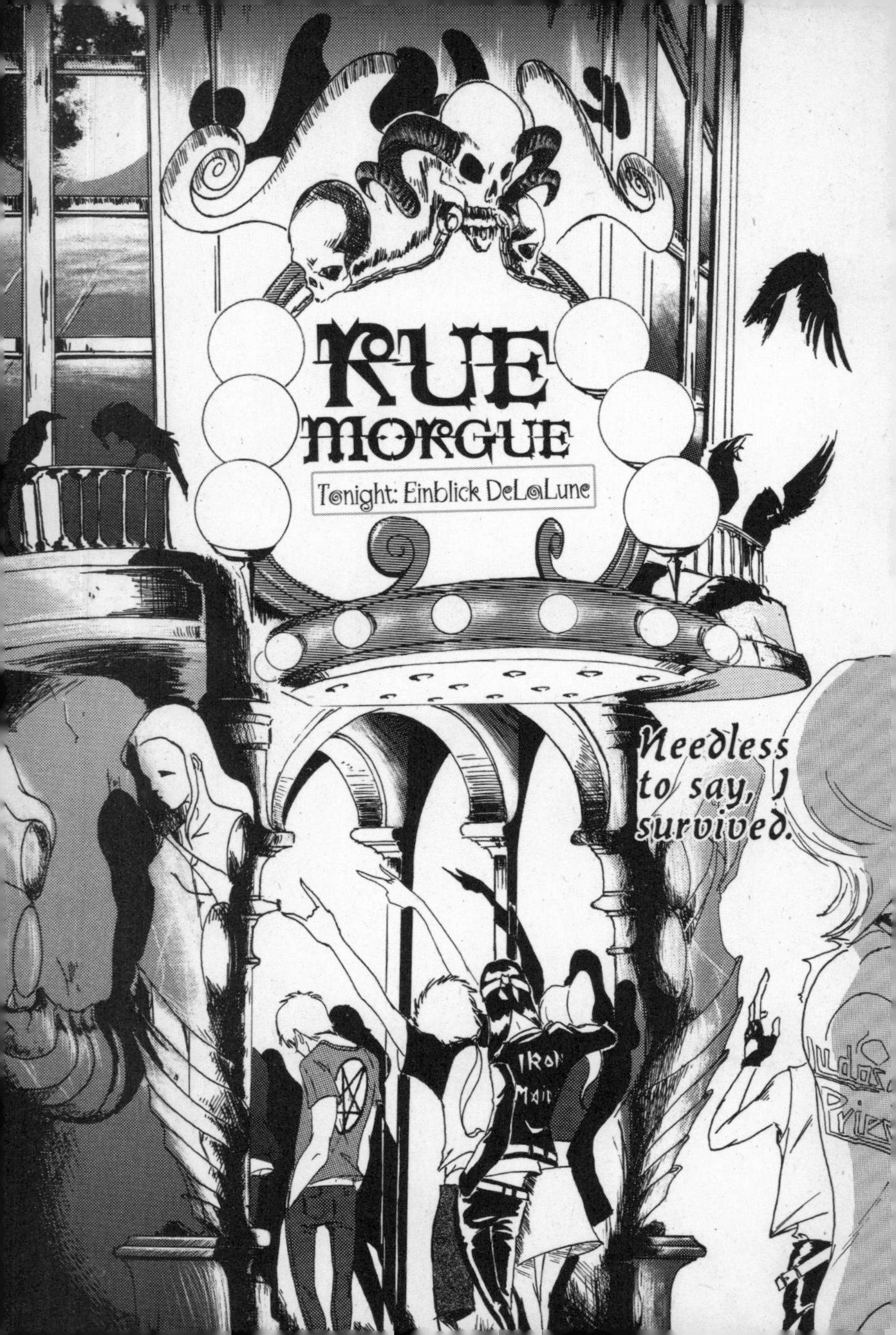
RUE MORGUE
Tonight: Einblick DeLaLune
Needless to say, I survived.

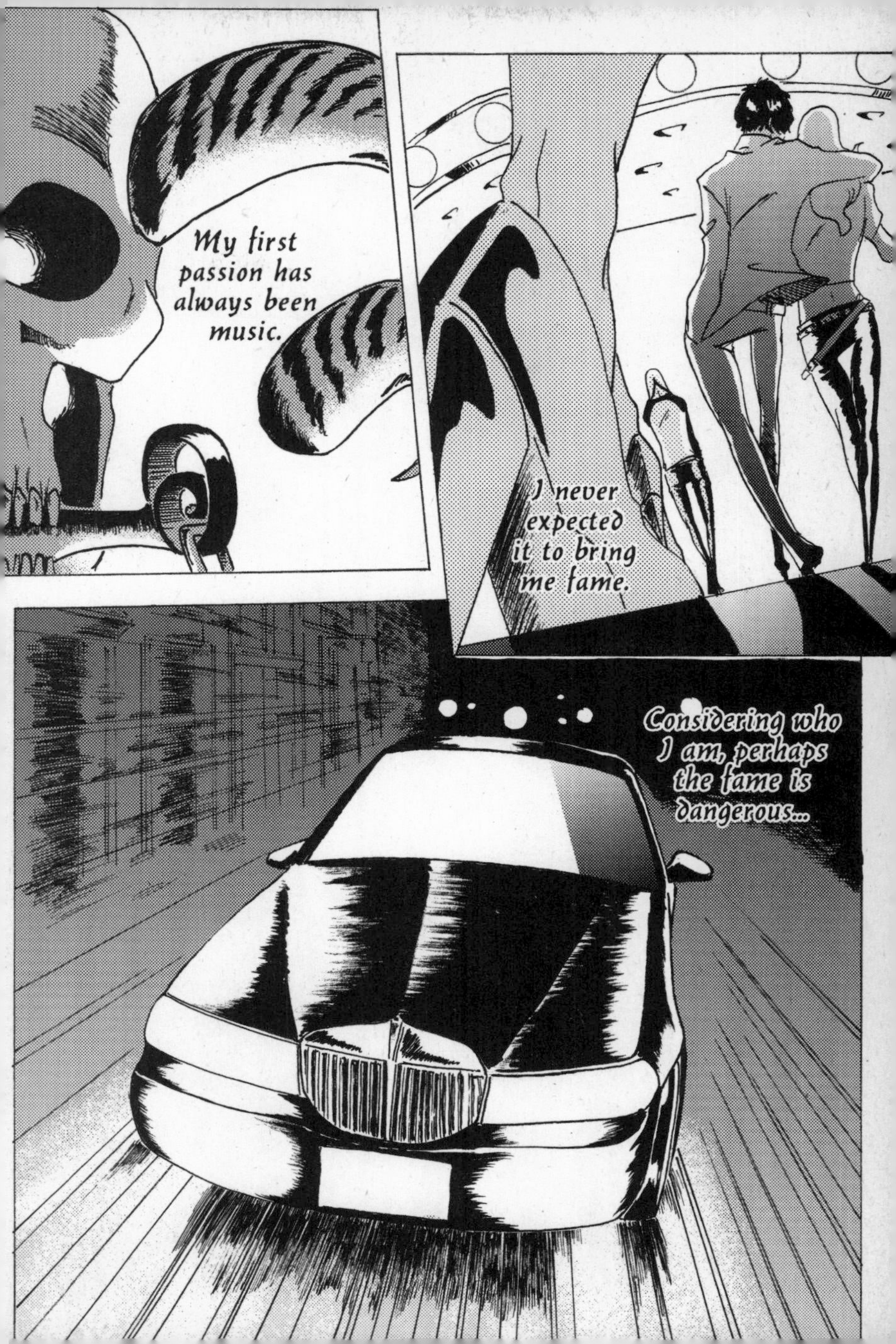
My first passion has always been music.
I never expected it to bring me fame.
Considering who I am, perhaps the fame is dangerous...

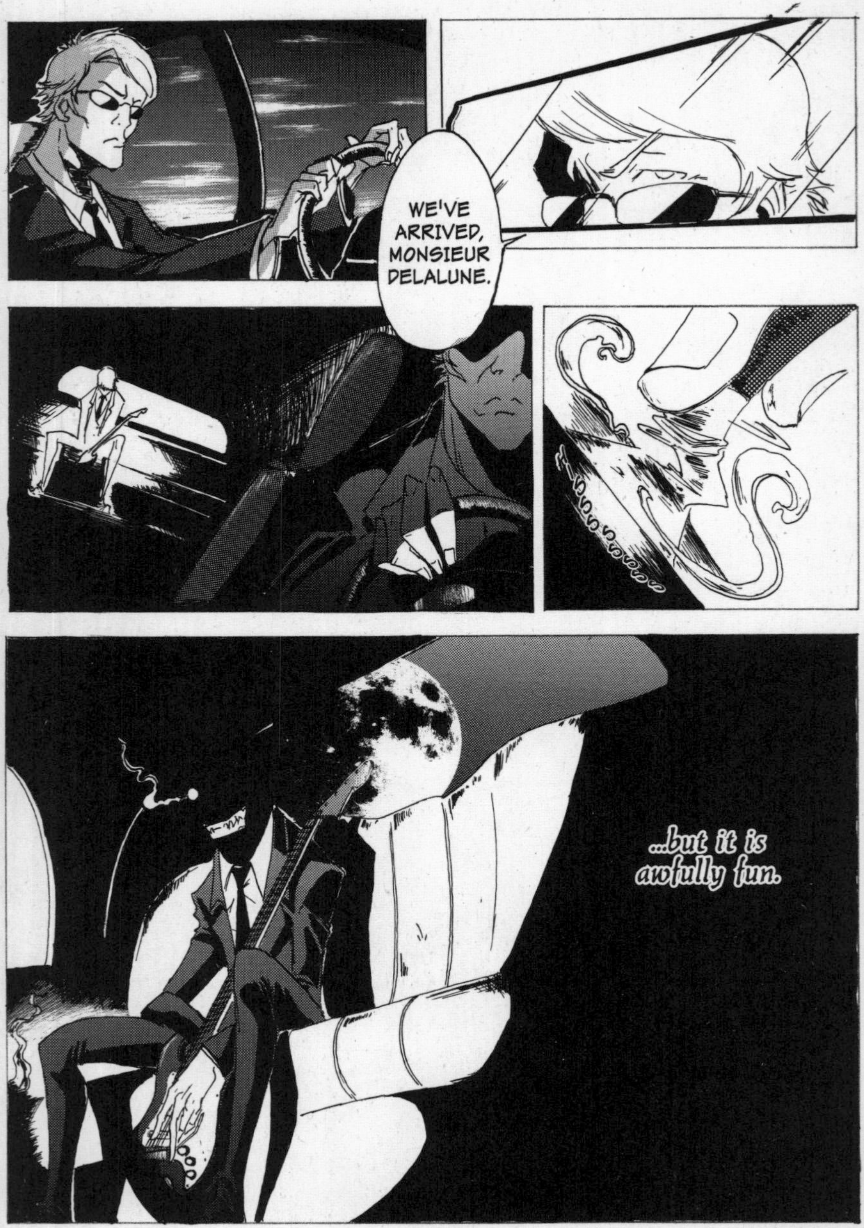
WE'VE ARRIVED, MONSIEUR DELALUNE.
...but it is awfully fun.

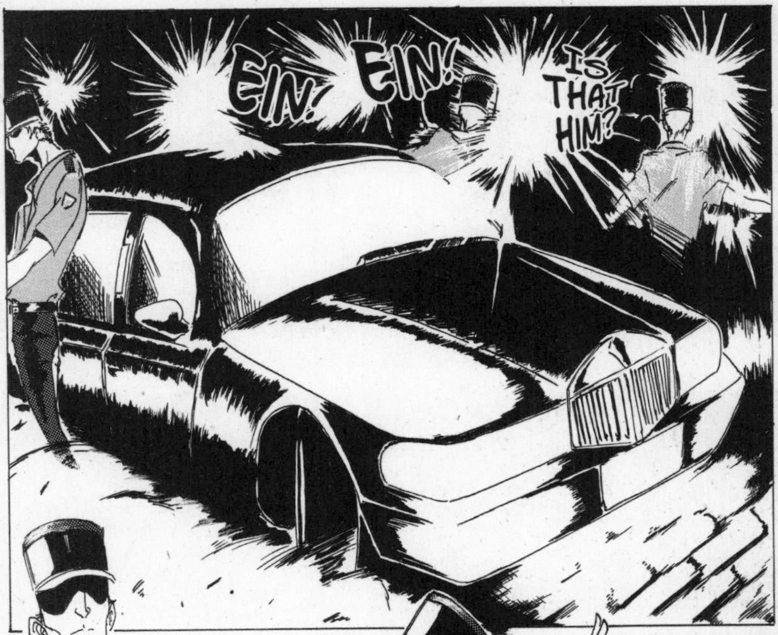
IS THAT HIM?
EIN! EIN!

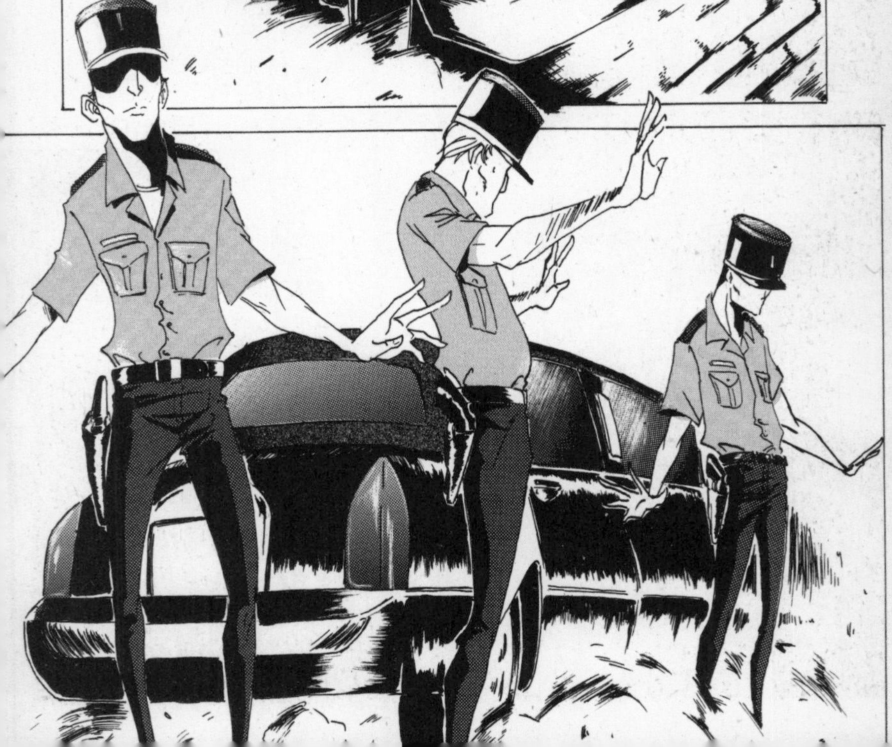

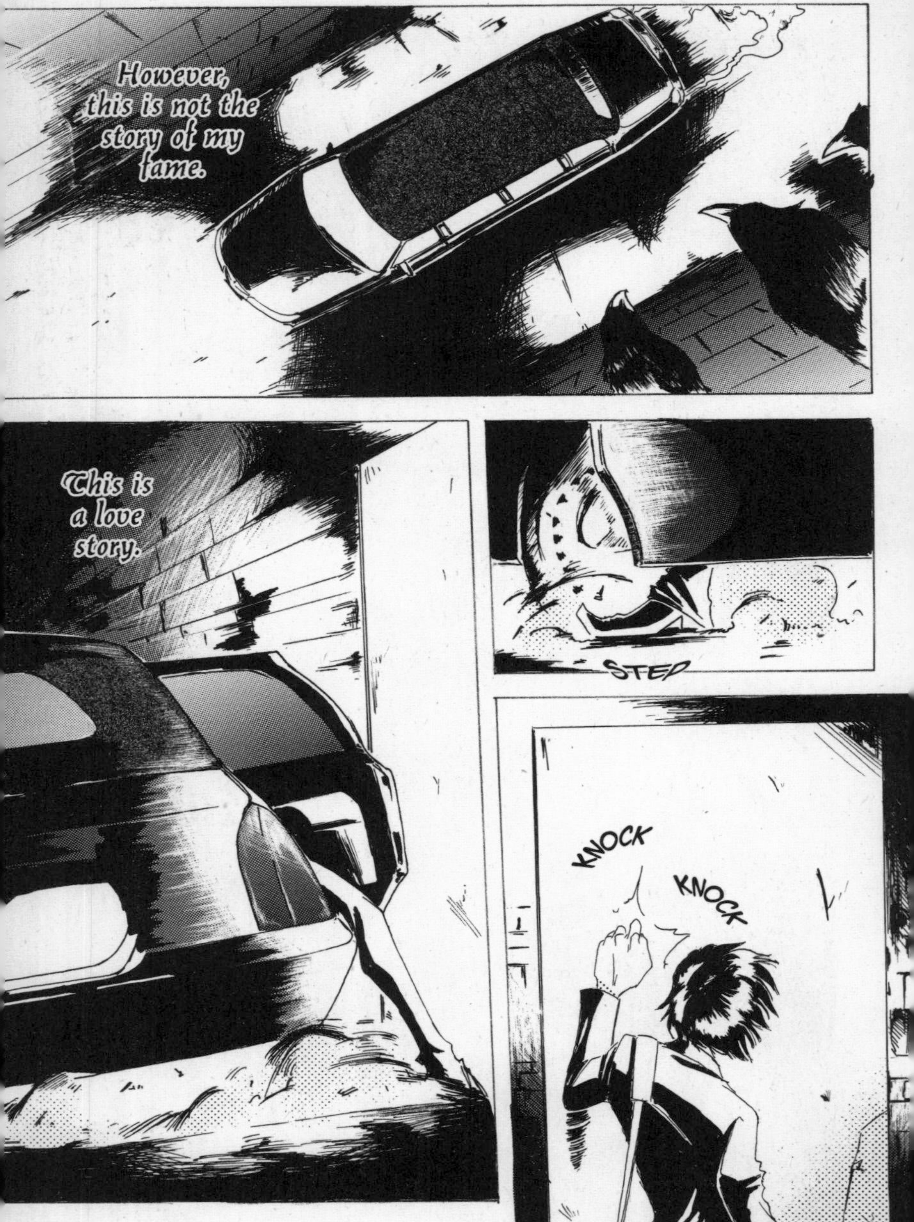
However, this is not the story of my fame.
This is a love story.
STEP
KNOCK
KNOCK

CREAK

KLIK          KLAK

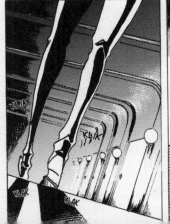

KLIK

KLIK

KLAK          KLAK

Einblick

De L.d.une

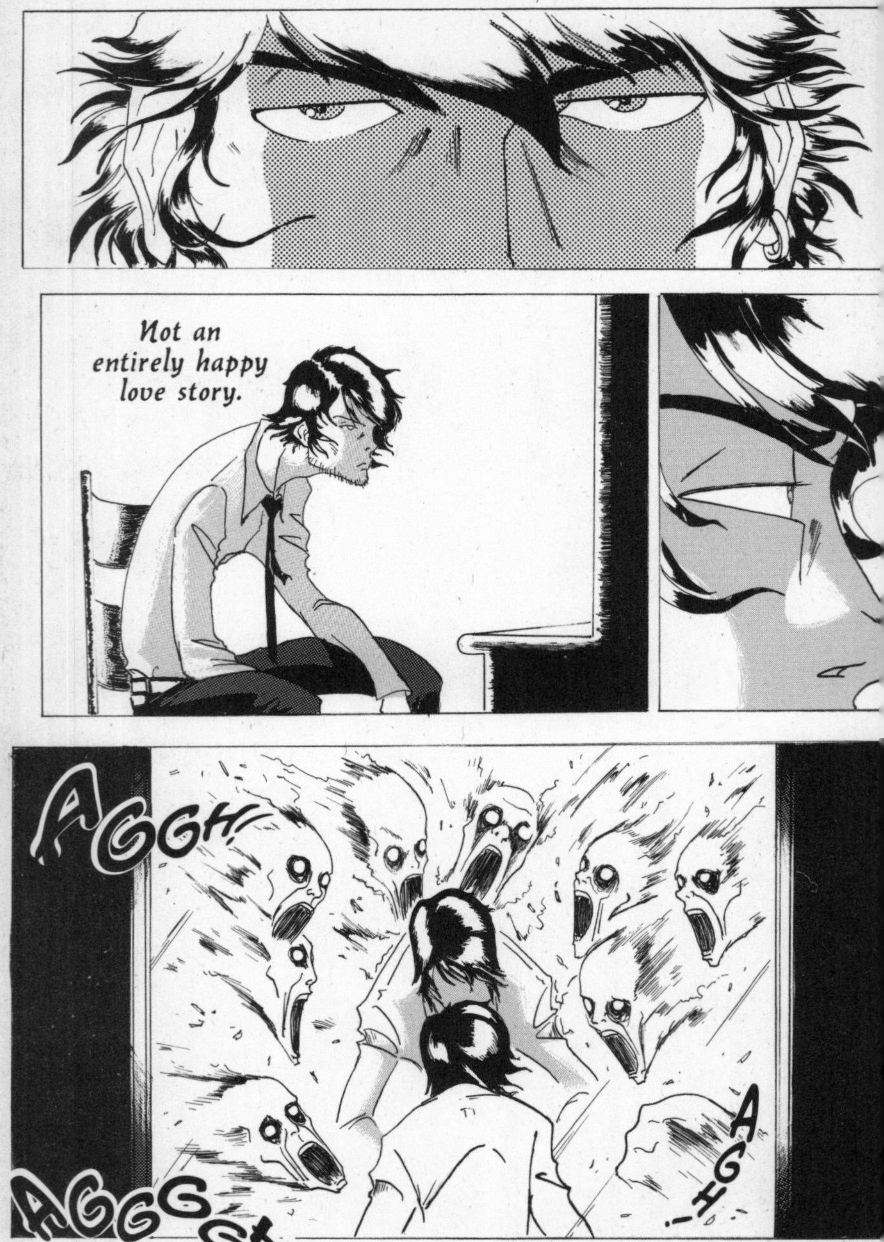
Not an entirely happy love story.
AGGH!
AGH!
AGGGH!

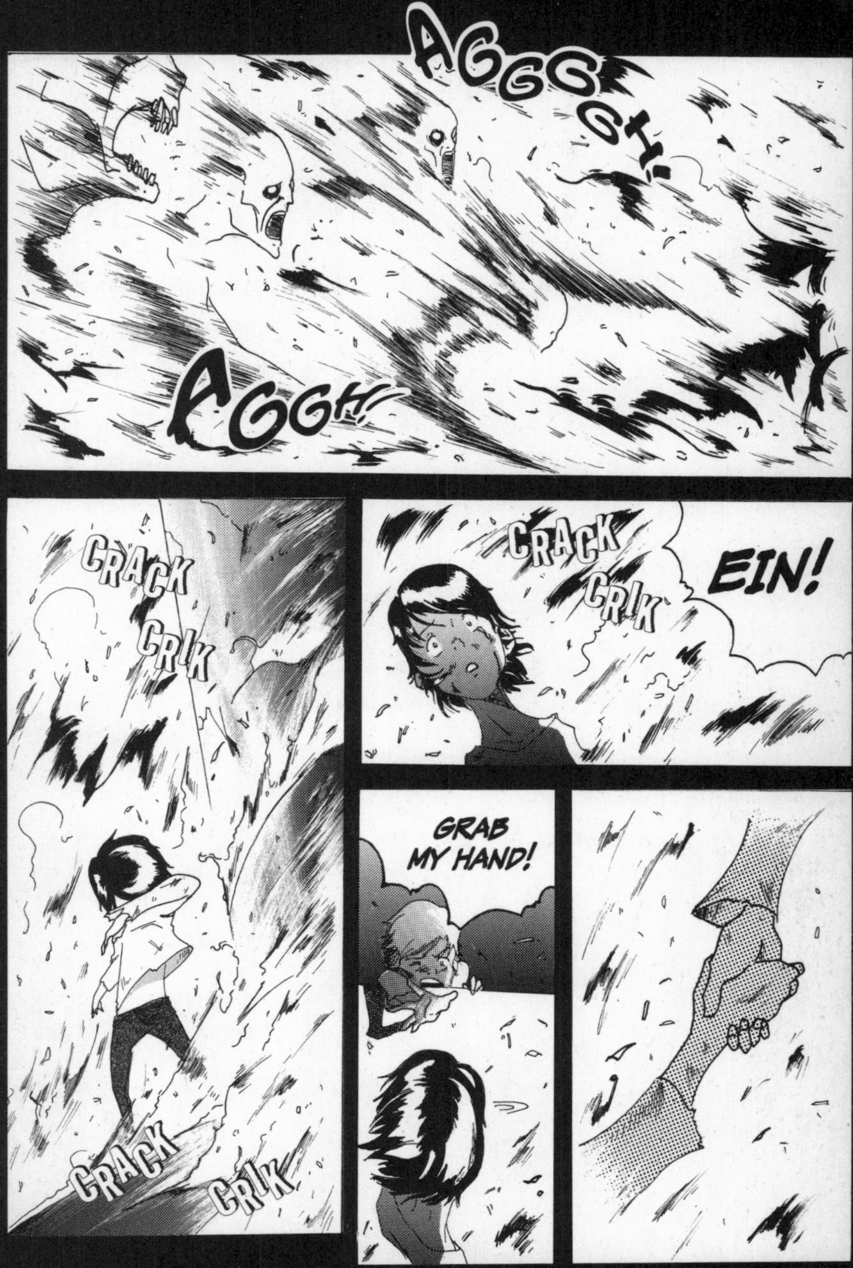
AGGGGH!
AGGH!
CRACK
CRIK
EIN!
GRAB MY HAND!
CRACK
CRIK
CRACK
CRIK

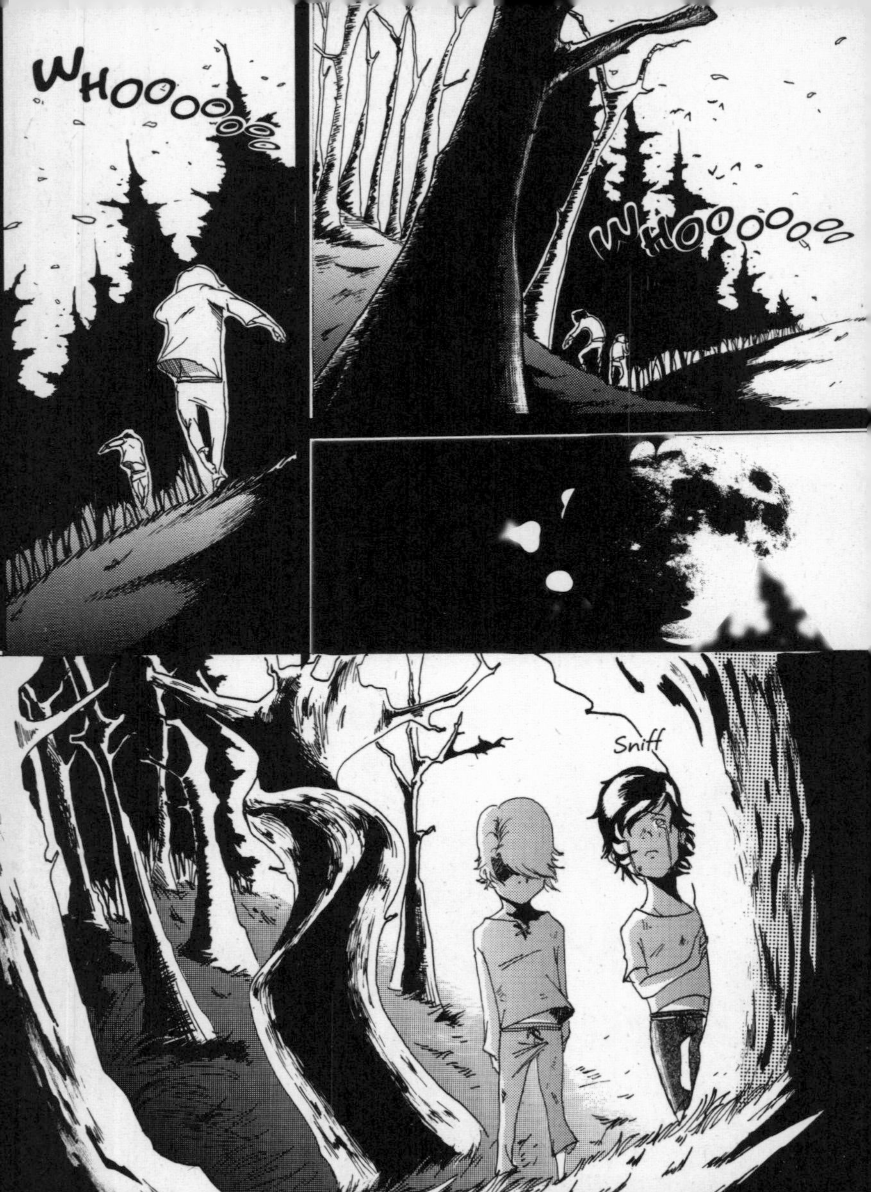
WHOOOOOOO
WHOOOOOOO
Sniff

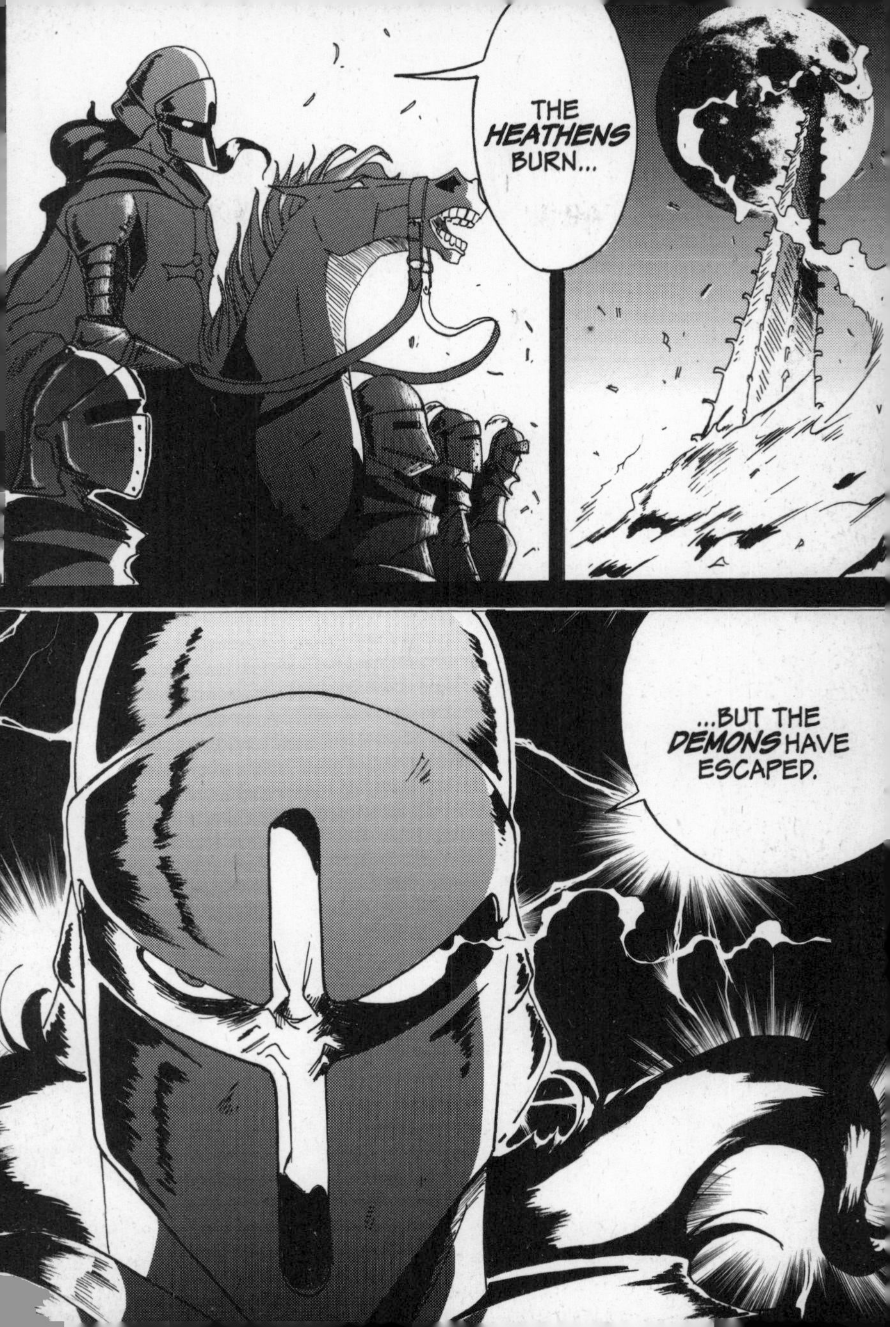
THE HEATHENS BURN...
...BUT THE DEMONS HAVE ESCAPED.

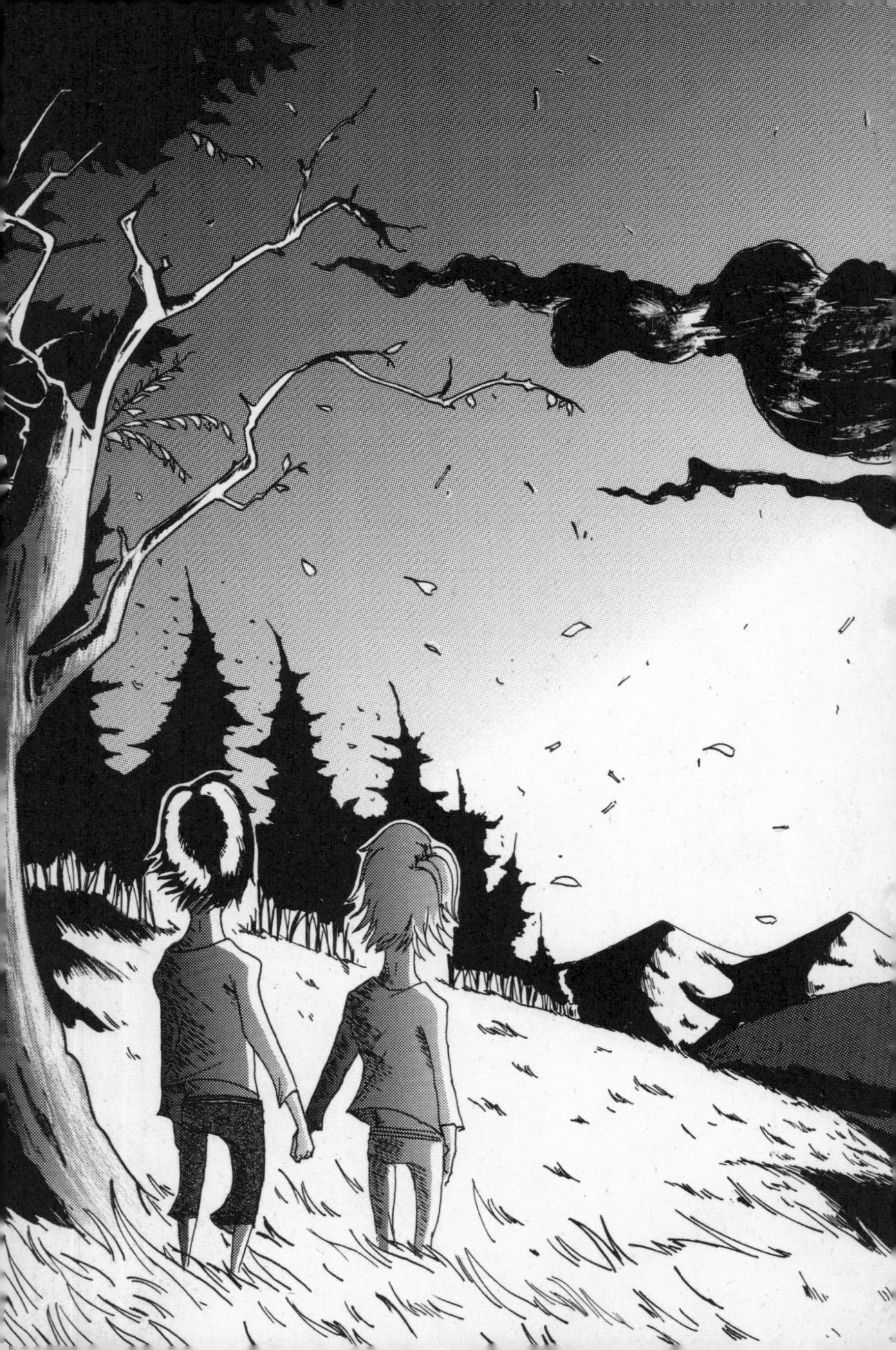

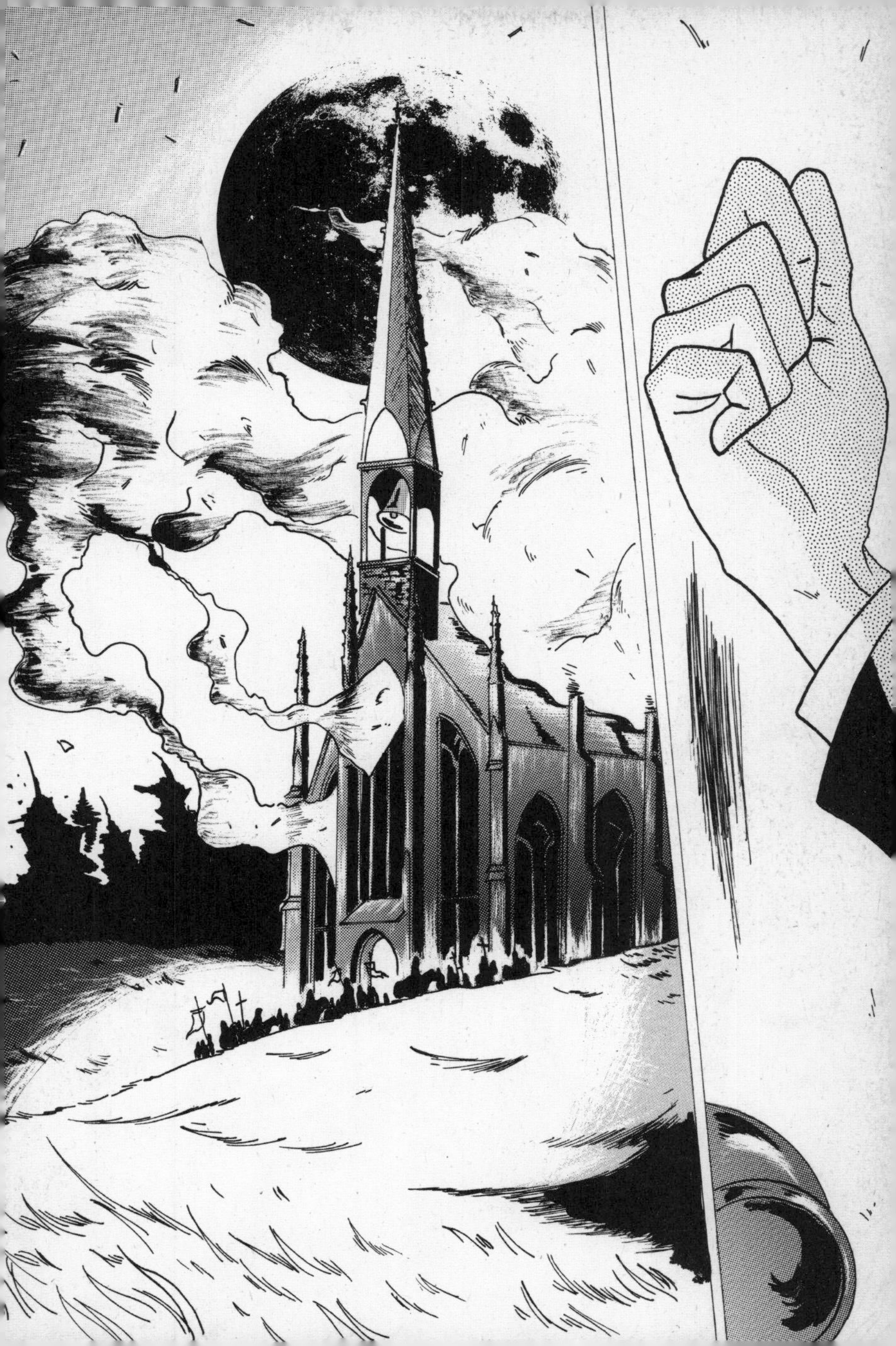

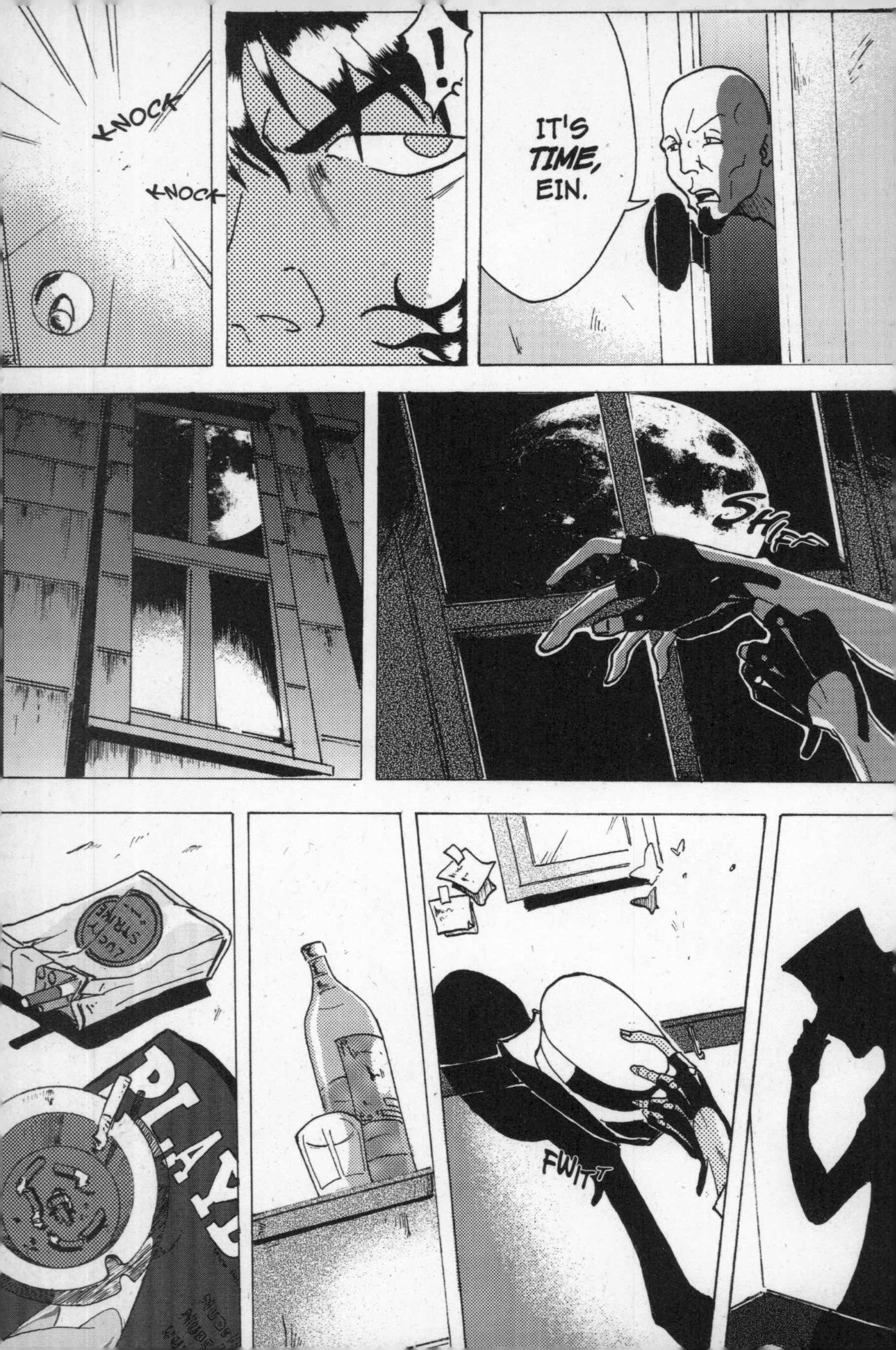
KNOCK
KNOCK
!
IT'S TIME, EIN.
SHIFF
LUCKY STRIKE
PLAY
FWITT

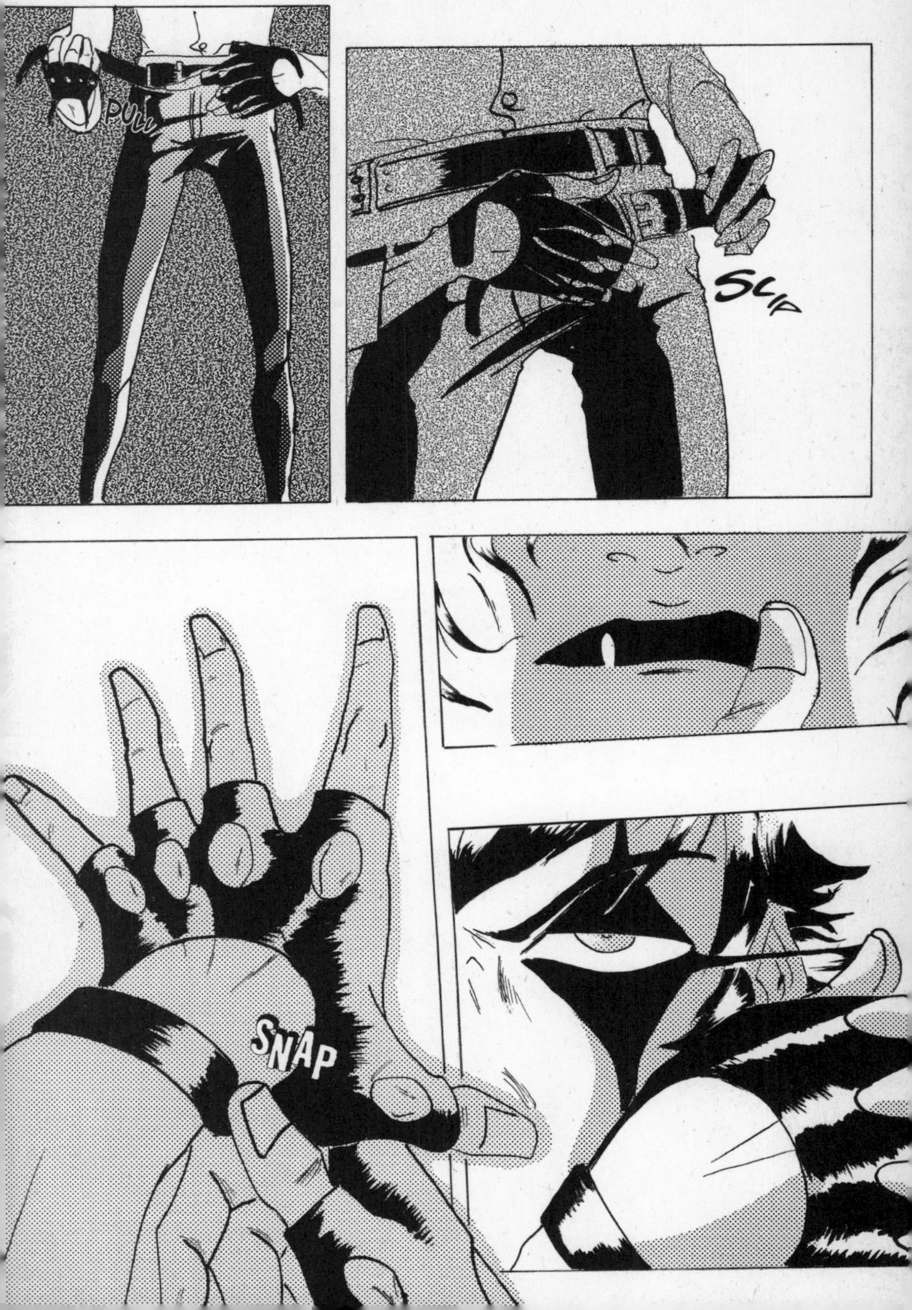
SLIP
PULL
SNAP

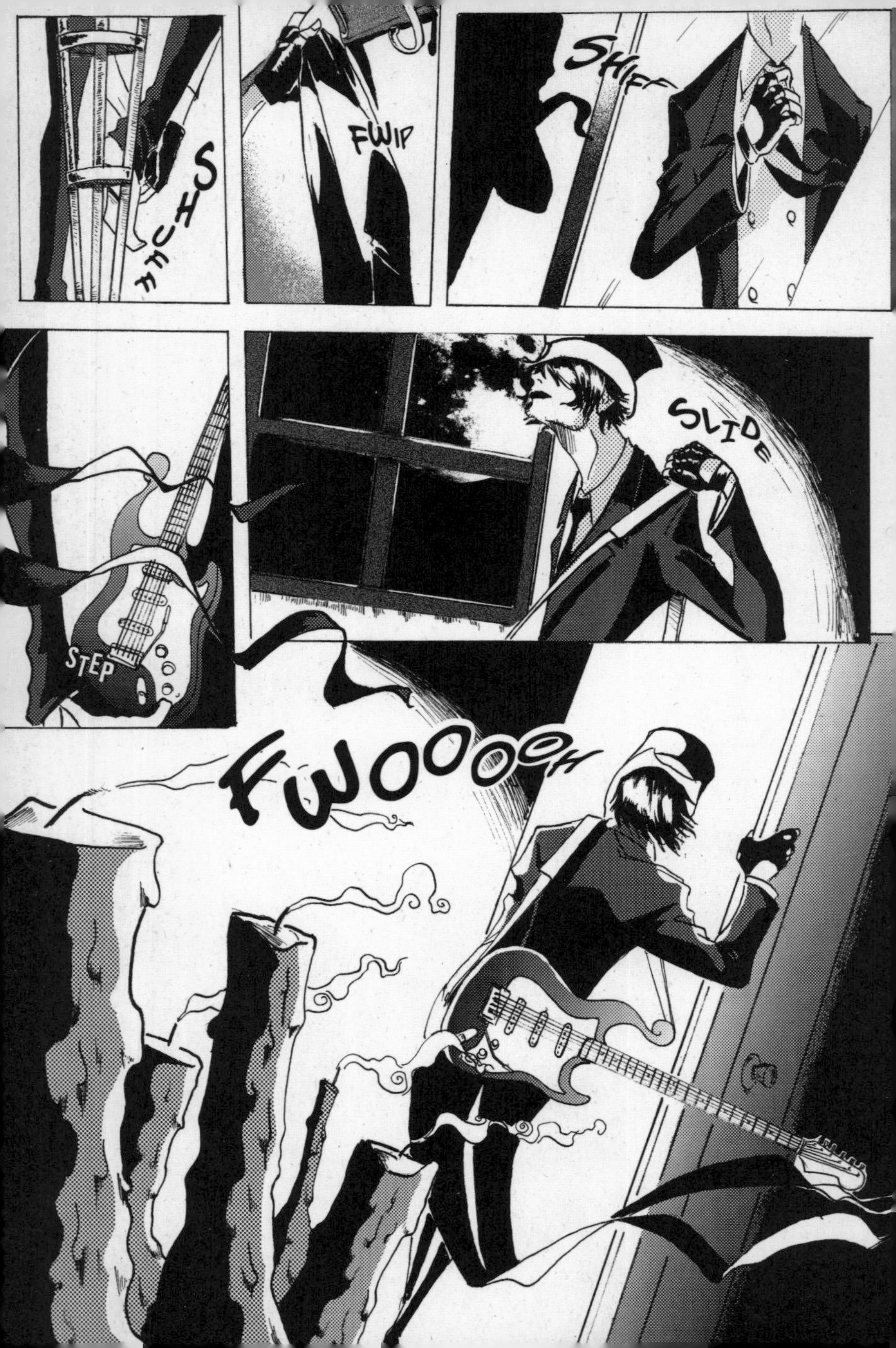
SHIFF
FWIP
SHUFF
SLIDE
STEP
FWOOOOH

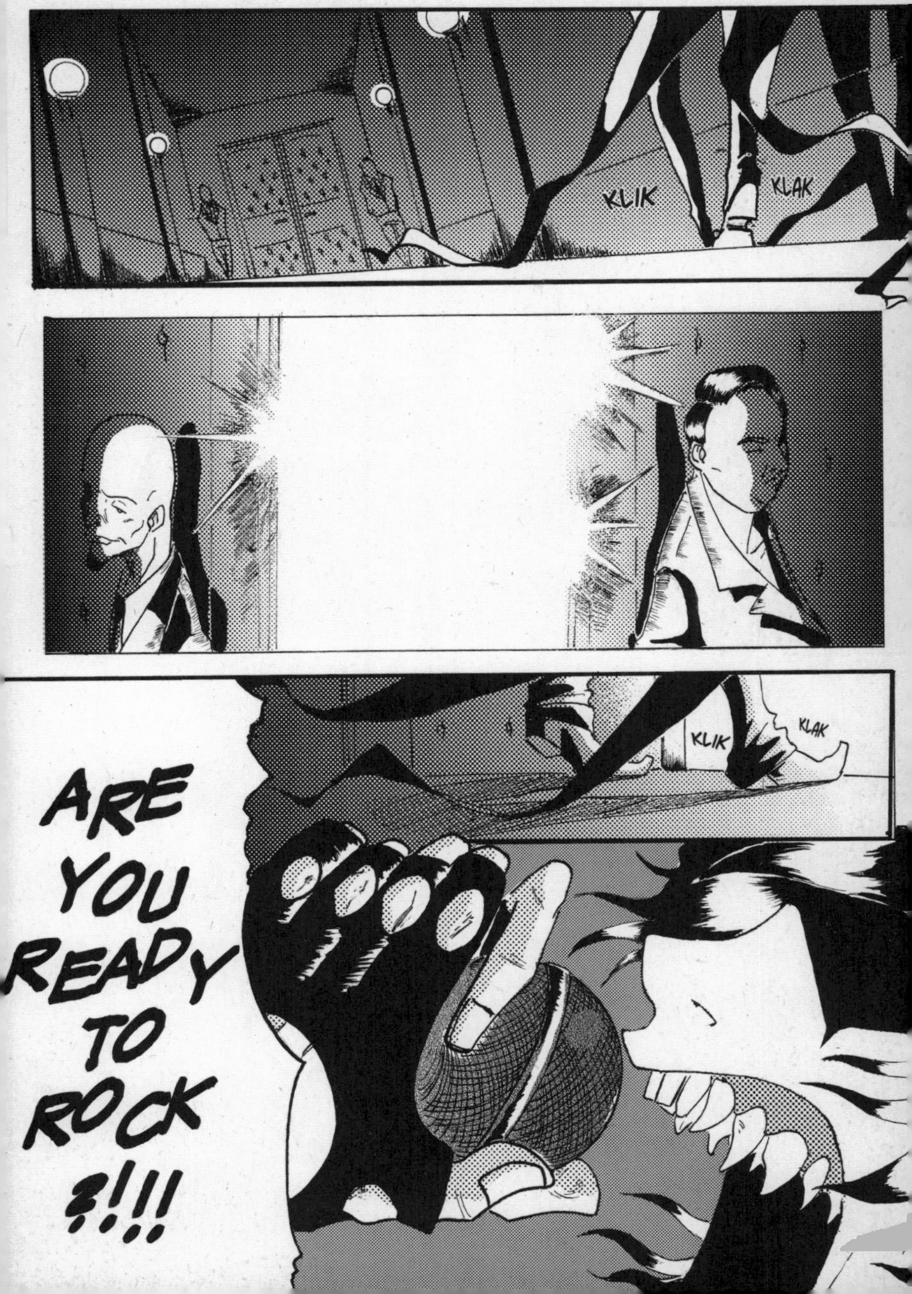
KLIK
KLAK
KLIK
KLAK
ARE YOU READY TO ROCK ?!!!

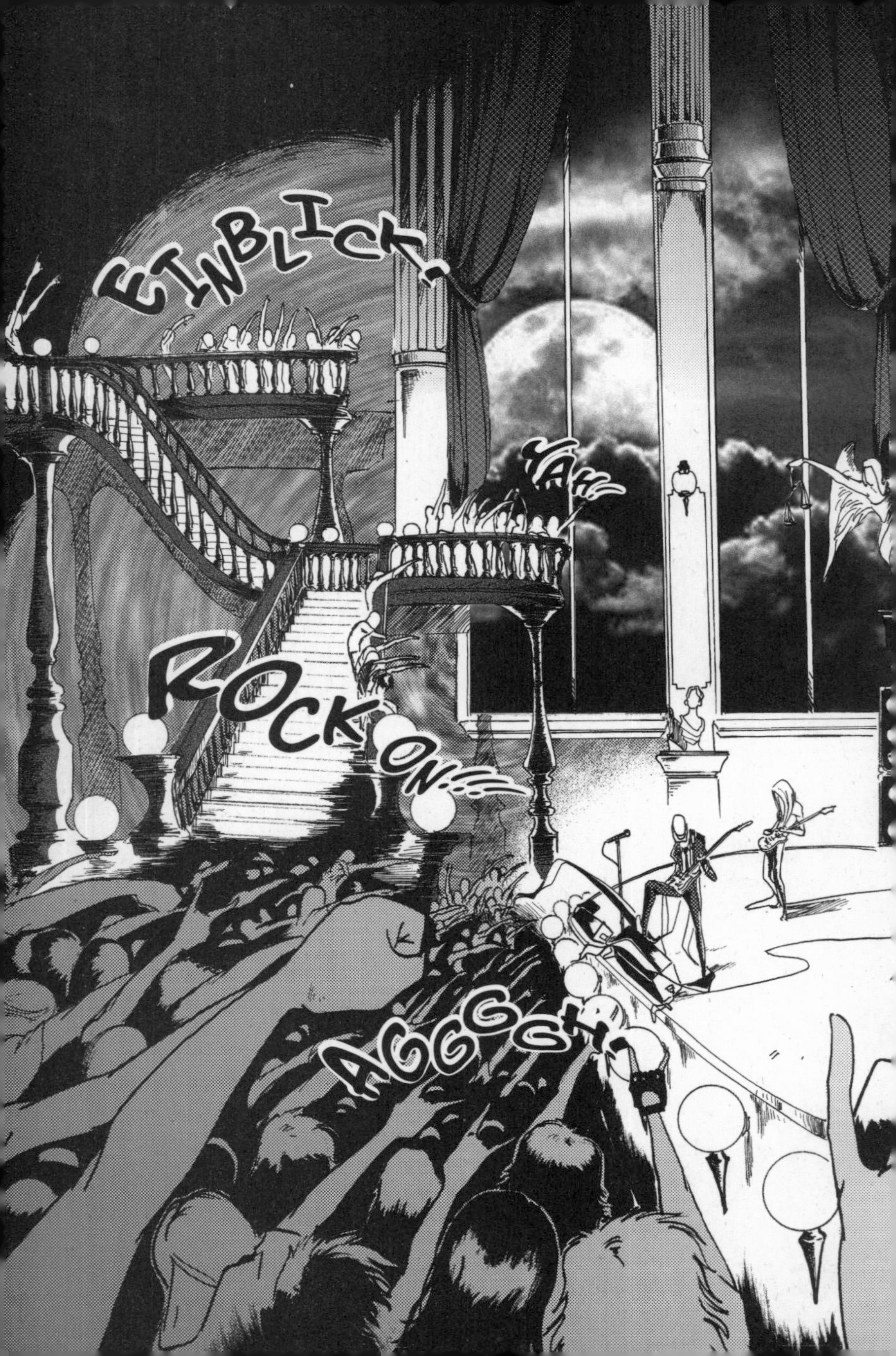

EINBLICK!
YAH!
ROCK ON!
AGGGH!

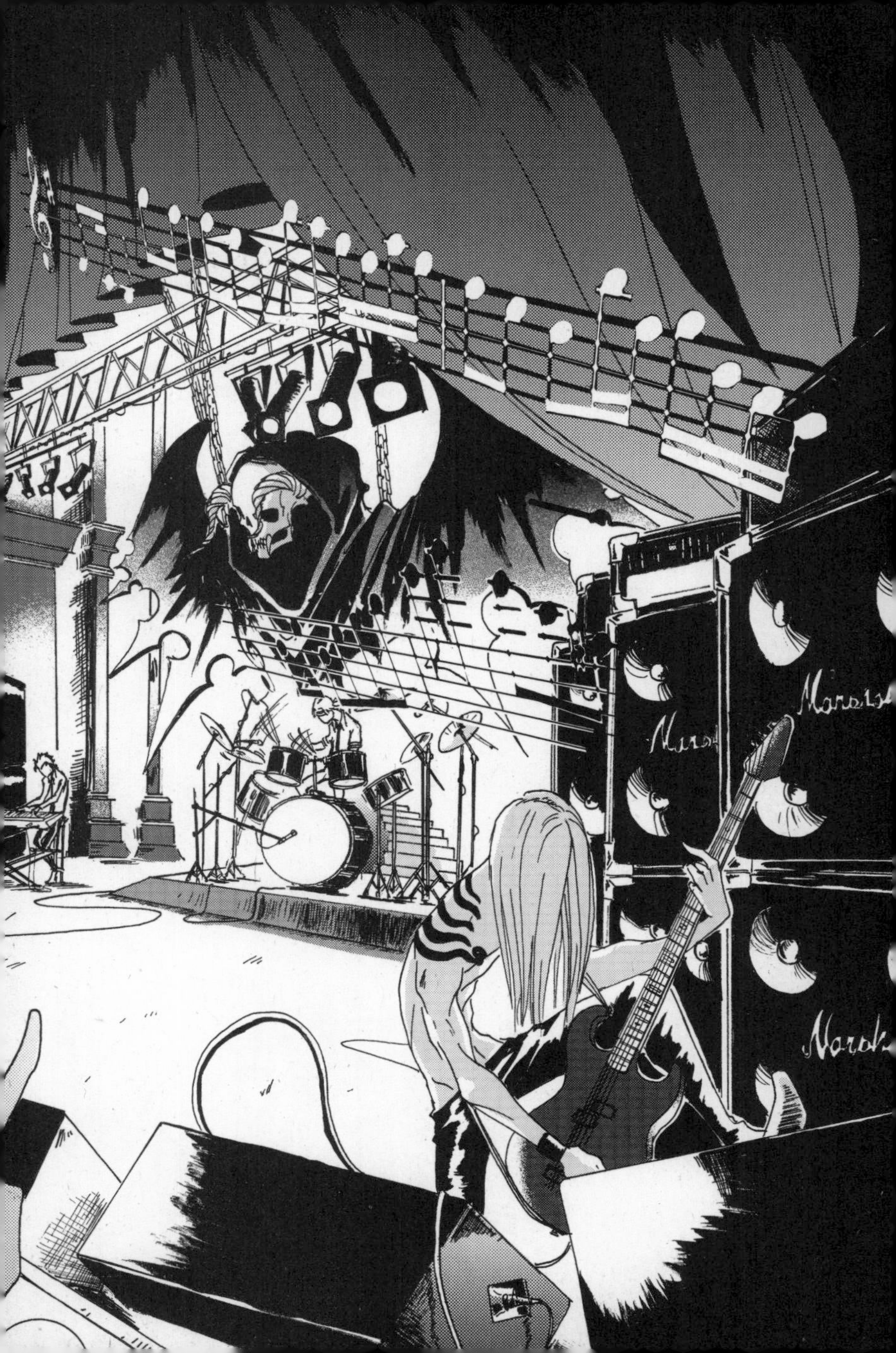

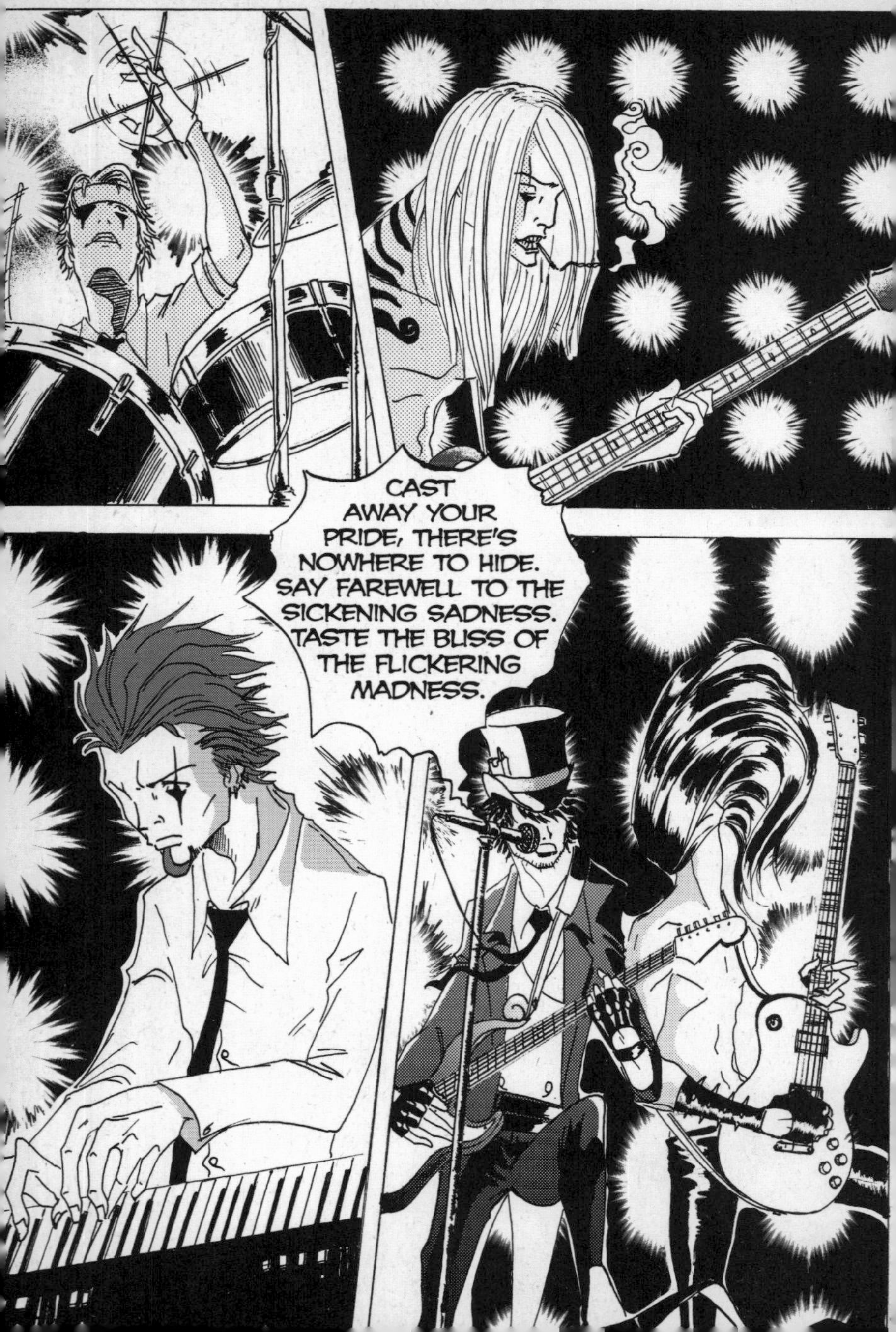
CAST AWAY YOUR PRIDE, THERE'S NOWHERE TO HIDE. SAY FAREWELL TO THE SICKENING SADNESS. TASTE THE BLISS OF THE FLICKERING MADNESS.

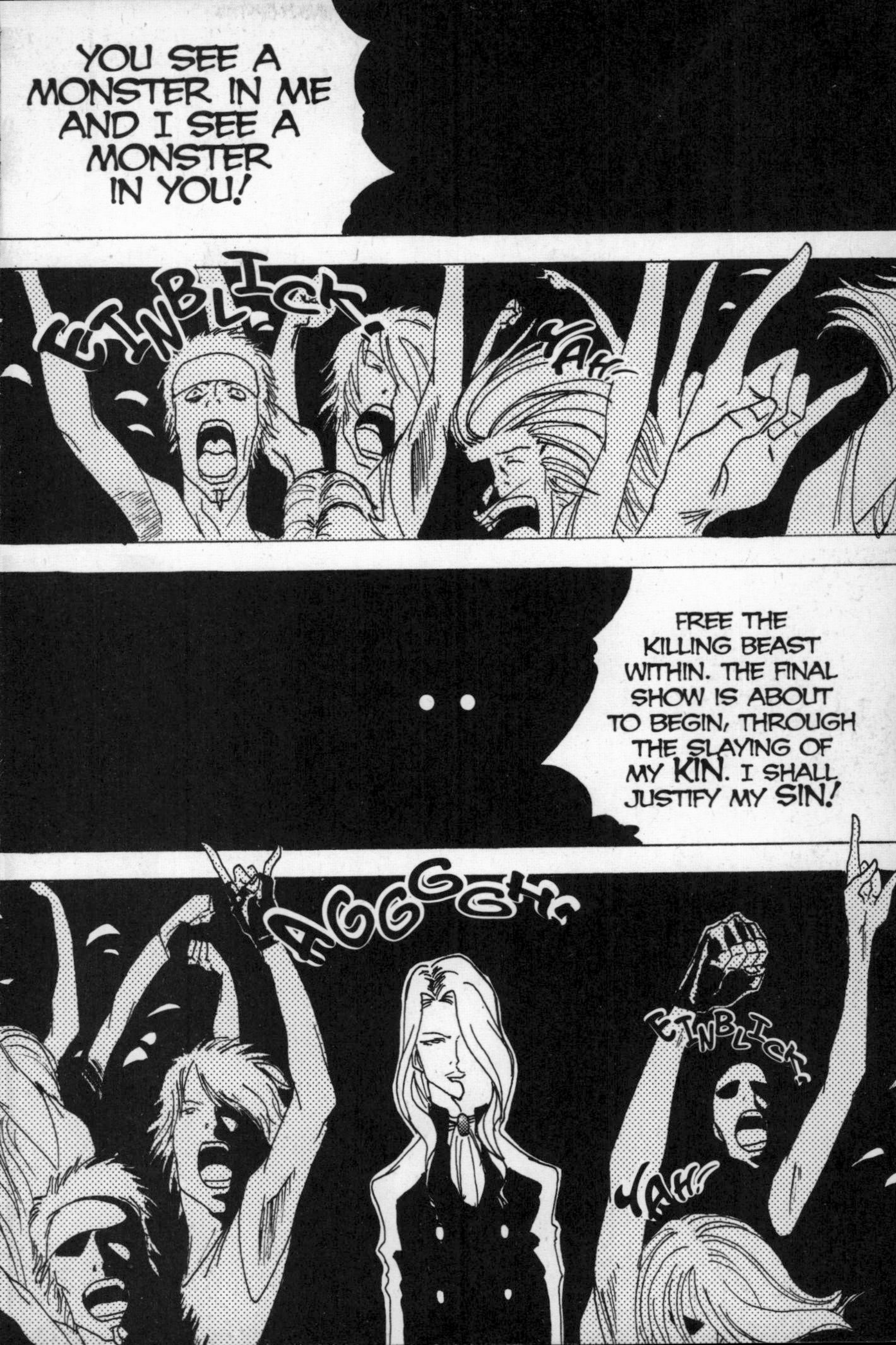
YOU SEE A MONSTER IN ME AND I SEE A MONSTER IN YOU!
EINBLICK!
YAH
FREE THE KILLING BEAST WITHIN. THE FINAL SHOW IS ABOUT TO BEGIN, THROUGH THE SLAYING OF MY KIN. I SHALL JUSTIFY MY SIN!
AGGGGH!
EINBLICK!
YAH!

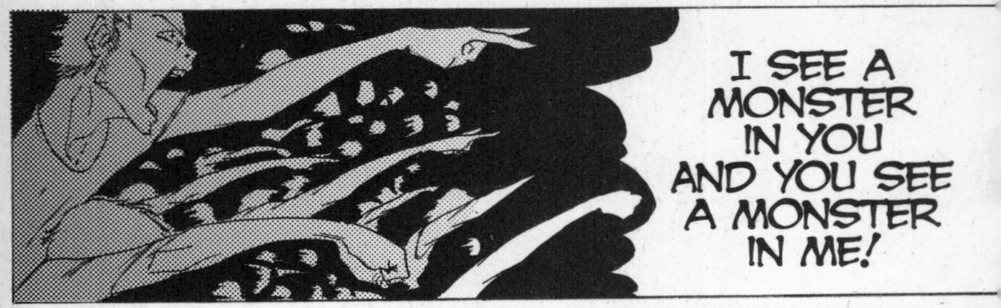
I SEE A MONSTER IN YOU AND YOU SEE A MONSTER IN ME!

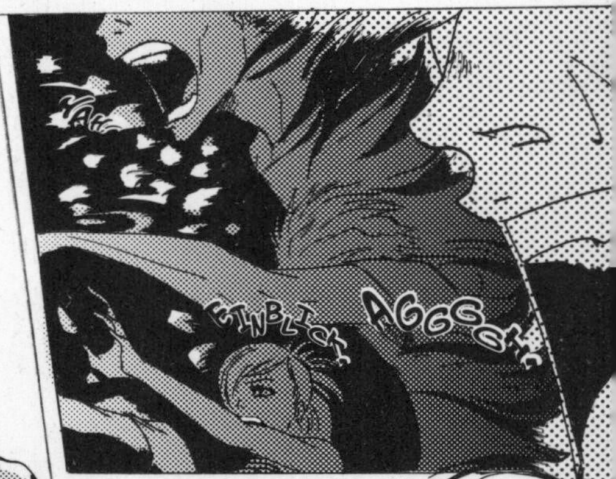
AGGGGH!

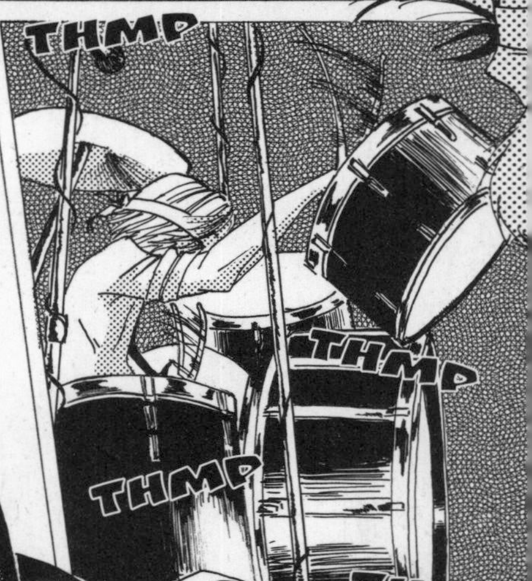
THMP
THMP
THMP
THMP

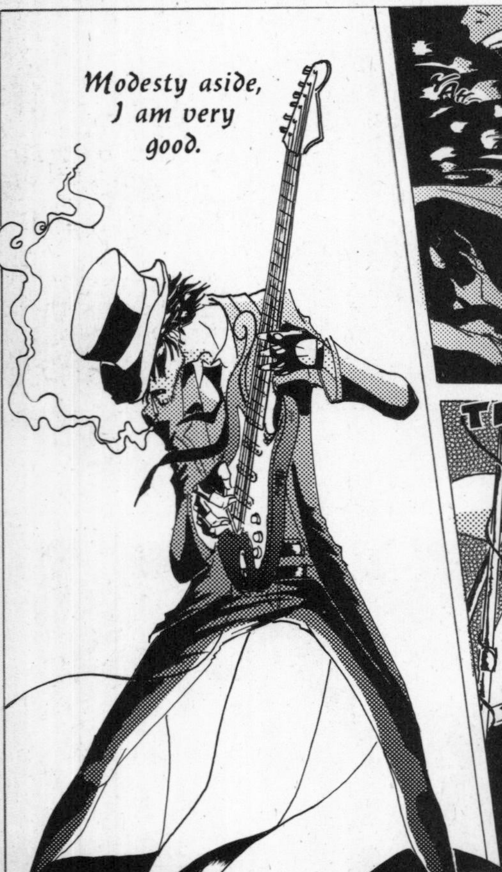
Modesty aside, I am very good.

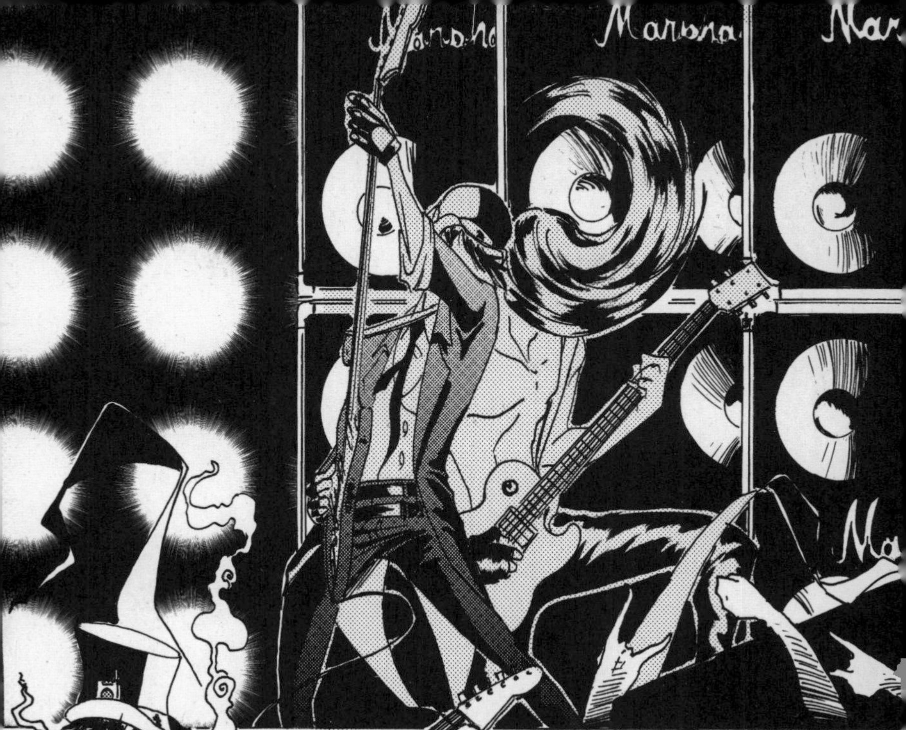
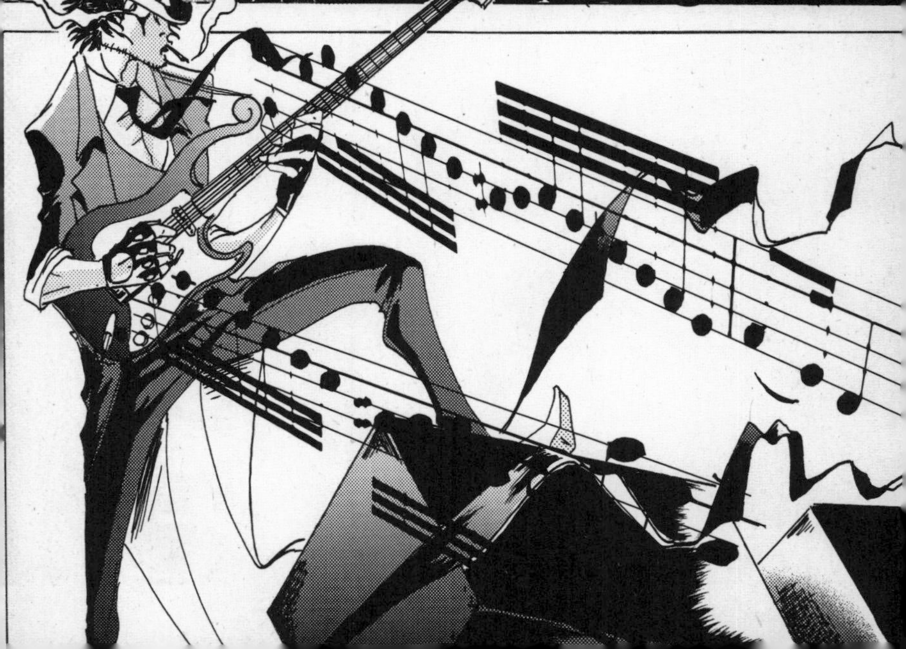

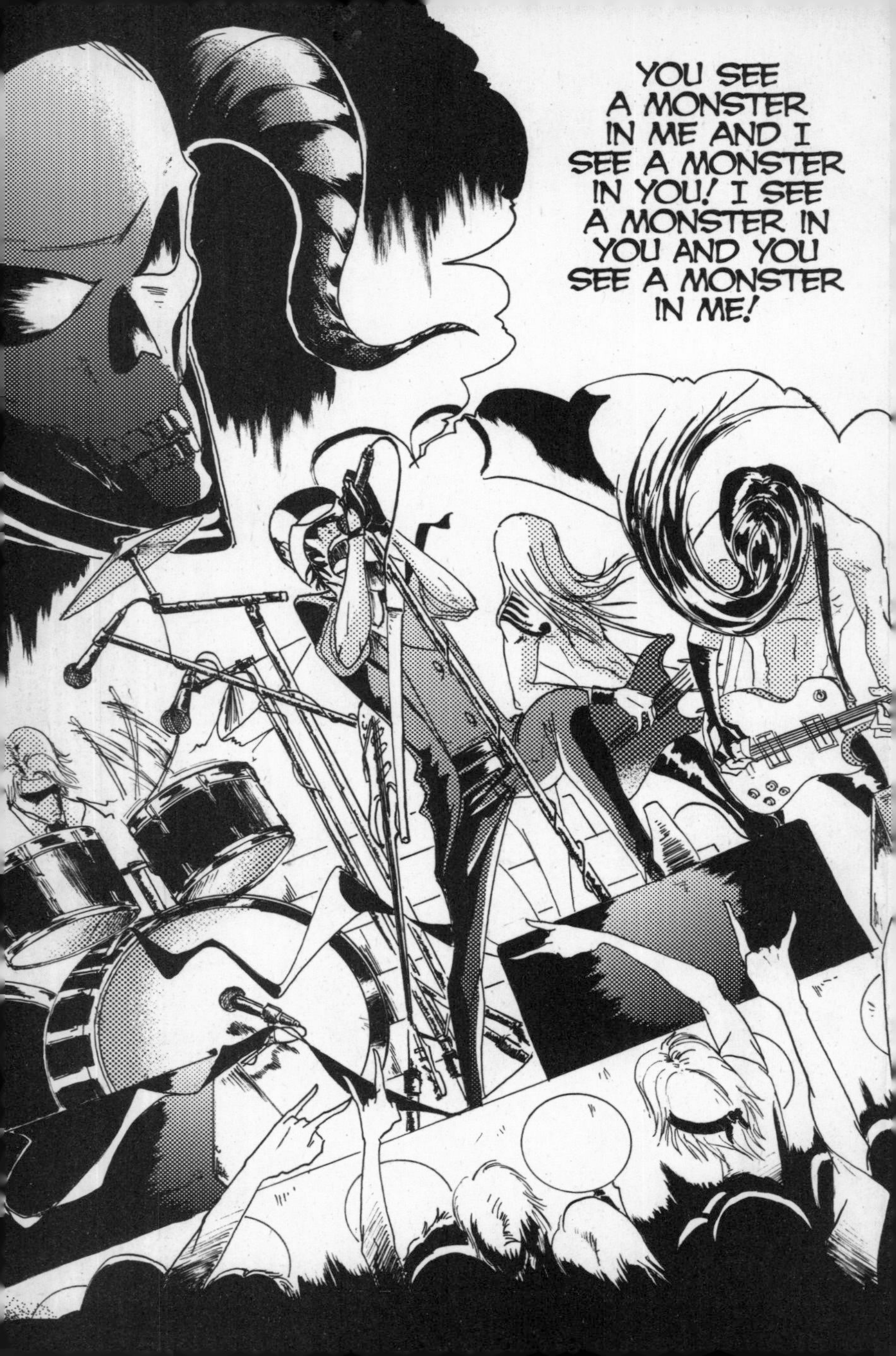
YOU SEE A MONSTER IN ME AND I SEE A MONSTER IN YOU! I SEE A MONSTER IN YOU AND YOU SEE A MONSTER IN ME!

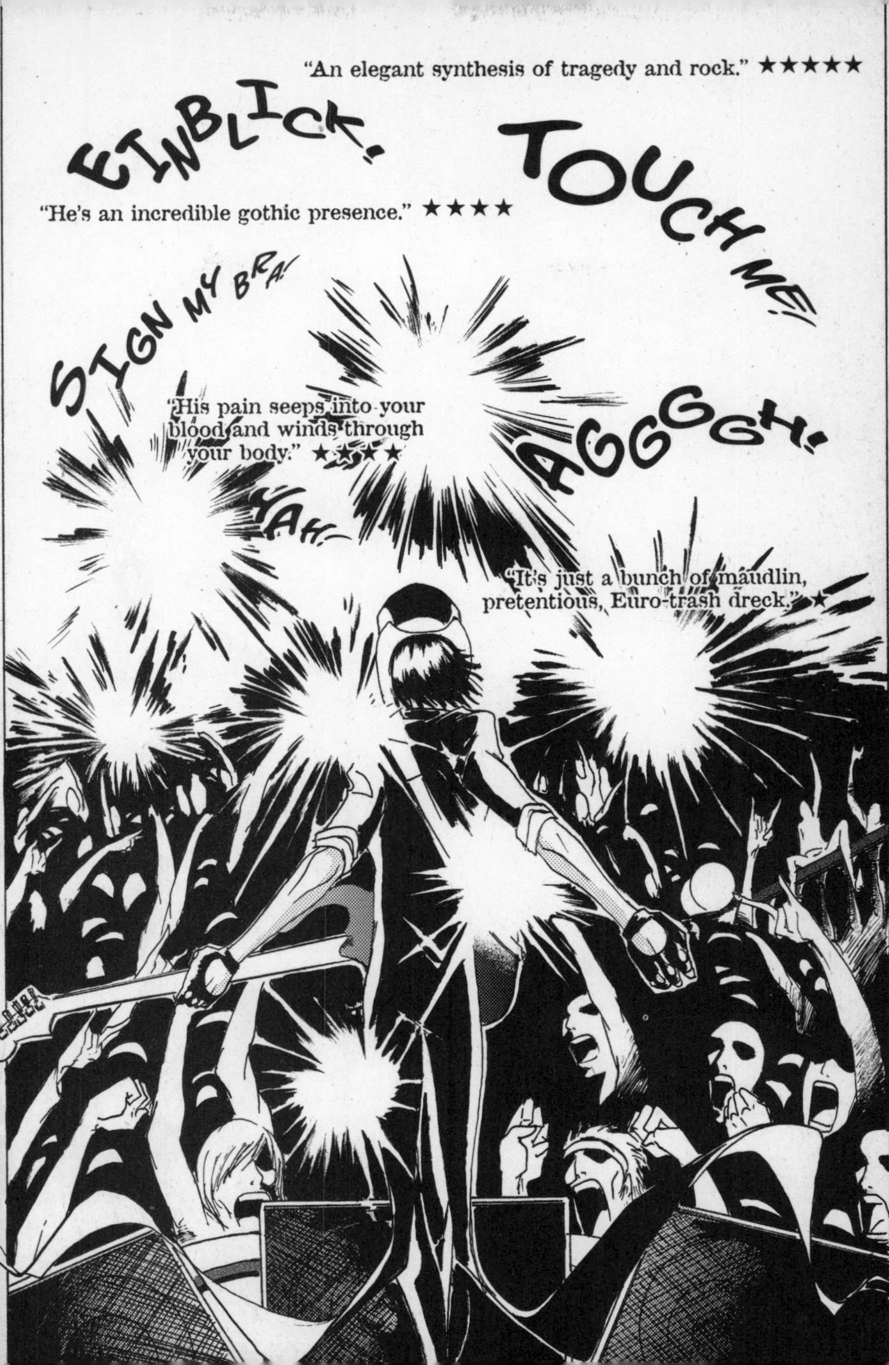

"An elegant synthesis of tragedy and rock." ★★★★★
TOUCH ME!
EINBLICK!
"He's an incredible gothic presence." ★★★★
SIGN MY BRA!
AGGGGH!
"His pain seeps into your blood and winds through your body." ★★★★
YAH!
"It's just a bunch of maudlin, pretentious, Euro-trash dreck." ★

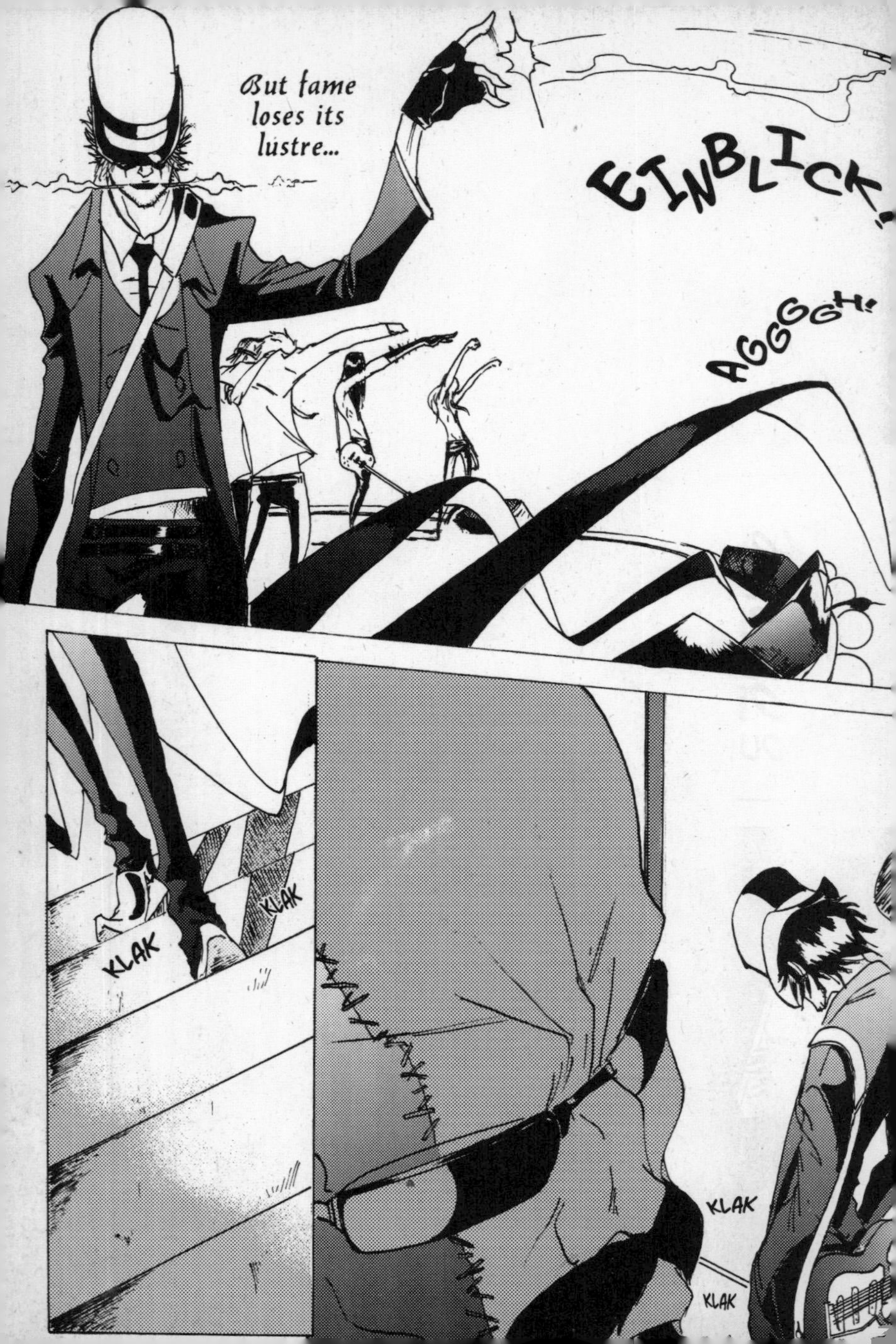
But fame loses its lustre...
EINBLICK!
AGGGGH!
KLAK
KLAK
KLAK
KLAK

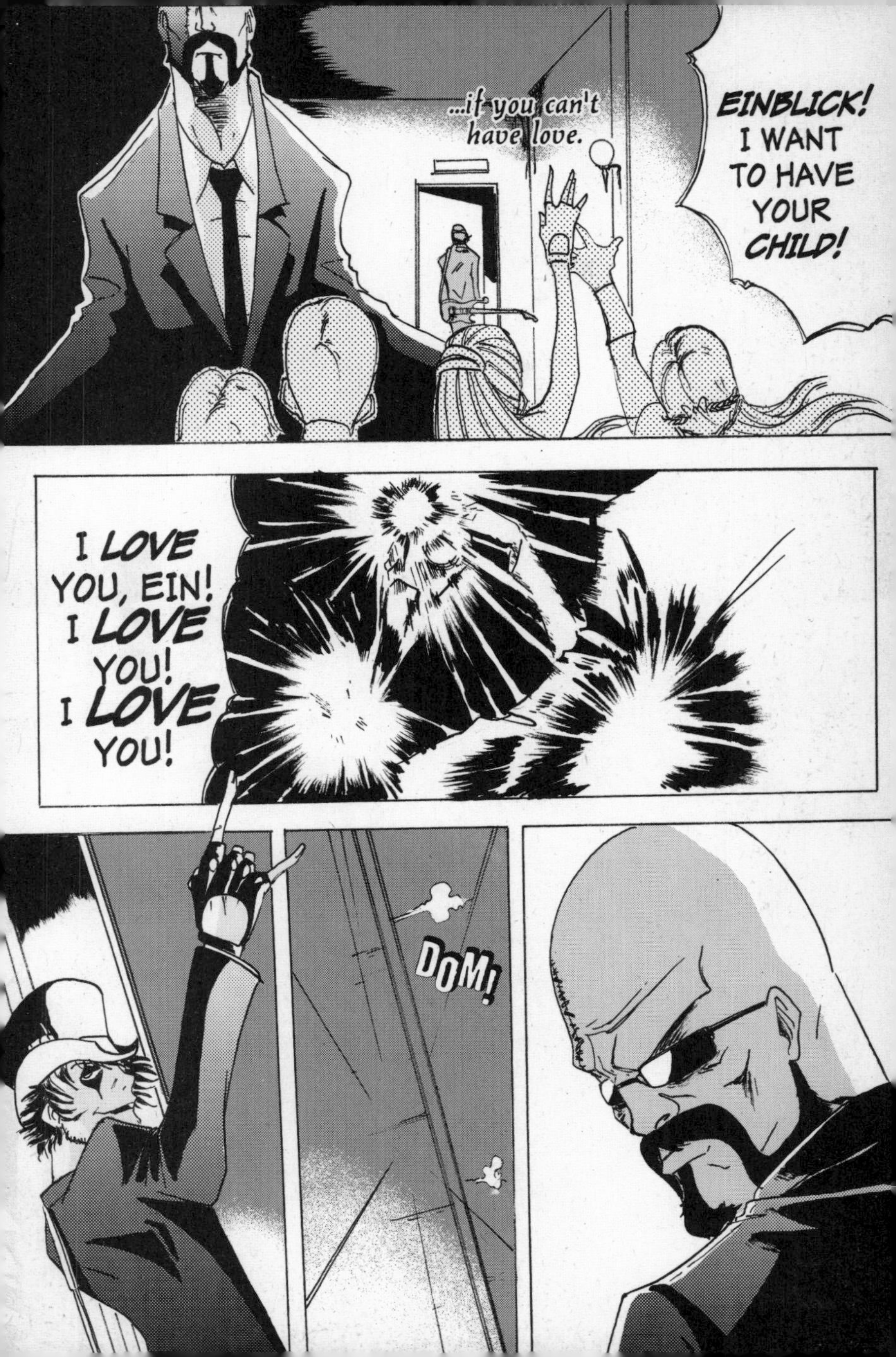
EINBLICK! I WANT TO HAVE YOUR CHILD!
...if you can't have love.
I LOVE YOU, EIN! I LOVE YOU! I LOVE YOU!
DOM!

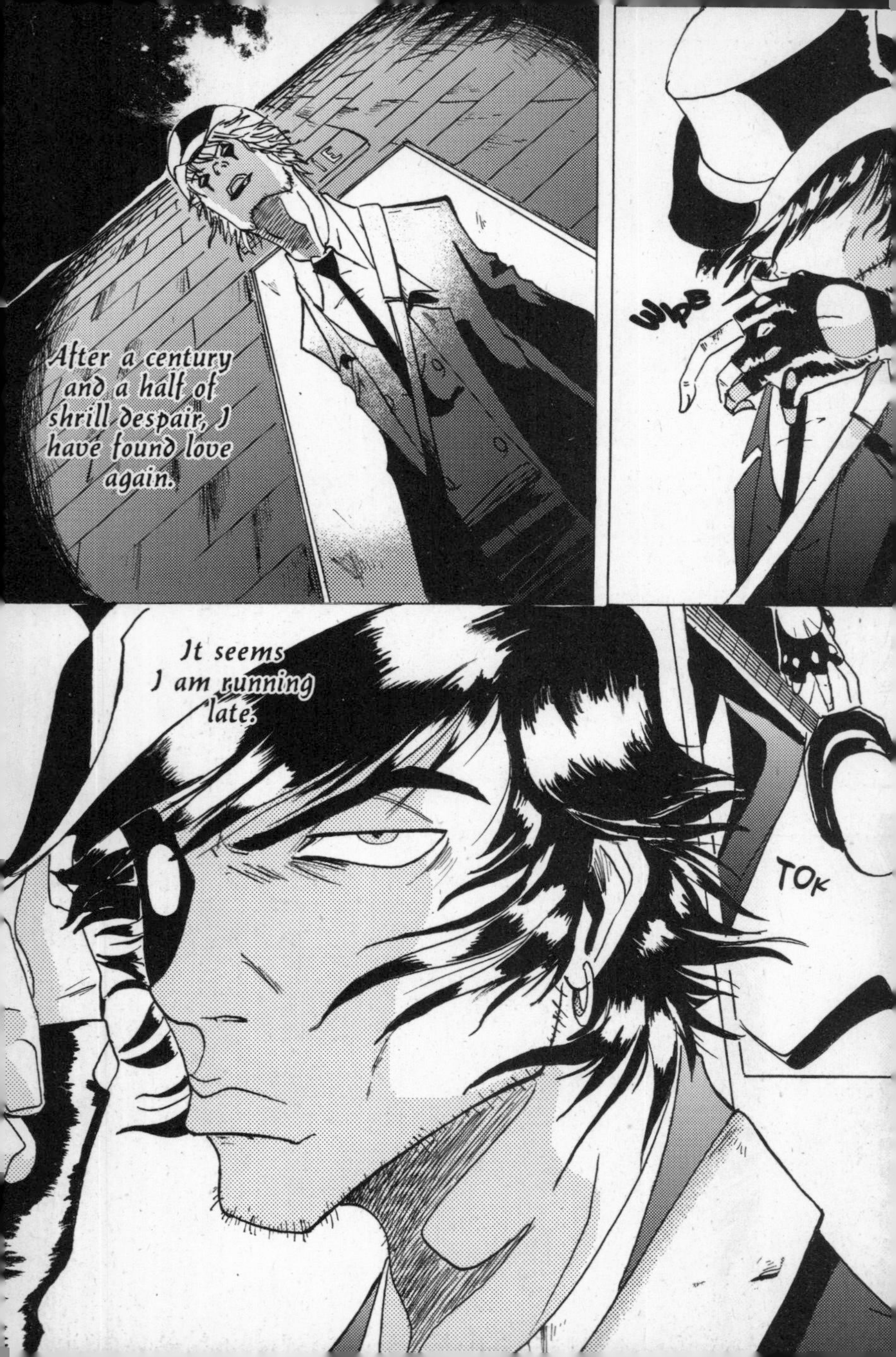
After a century and a half of shrill despair, I have found love again.
It seems I am running late.
TOK

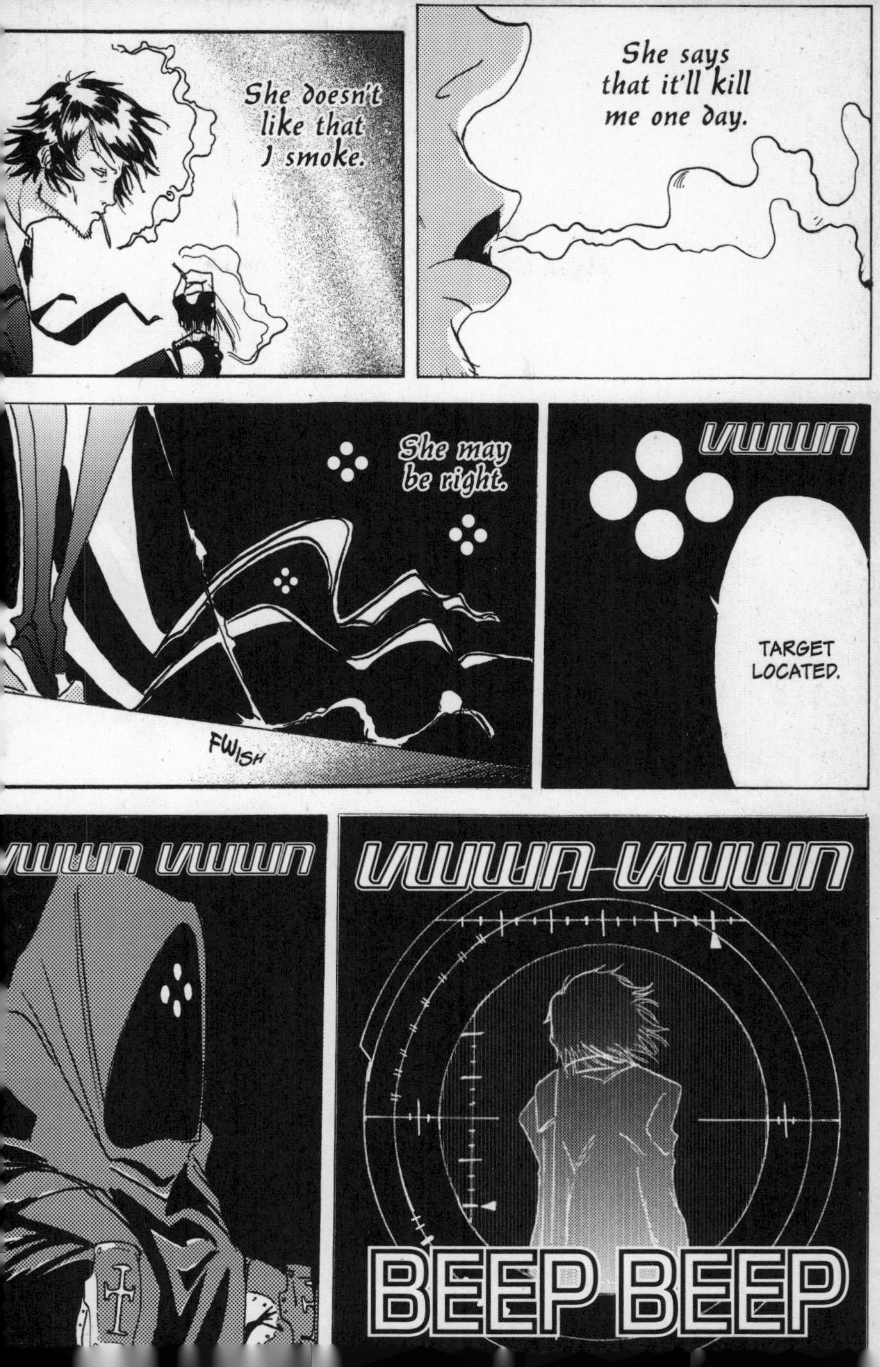
She doesn't like that I smoke.
She says that it'll kill me one day.
She may be right.
FWISH
VWWN
TARGET LOCATED.
VWWN VWWN
VWWN VWWN
BEEP BEEP

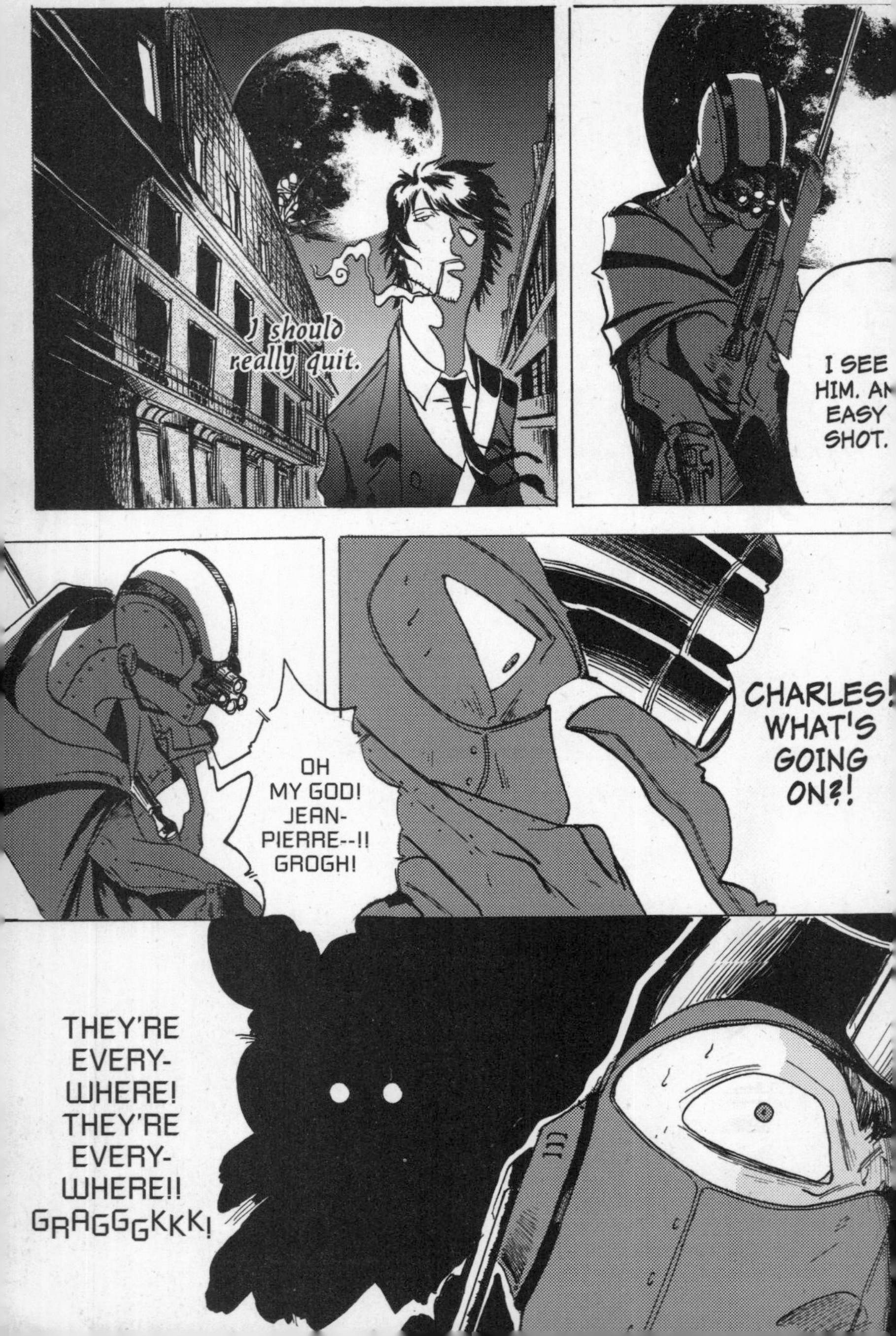
I should really quit.
I SEE HIM. AN EASY SHOT.
OH MY GOD! JEAN-PIERRE--!! GROGH!
CHARLES! WHAT'S GOING ON?!
THEY'RE EVERY-WHERE! THEY'RE EVERY-WHERE!! GRAGGGKKK!

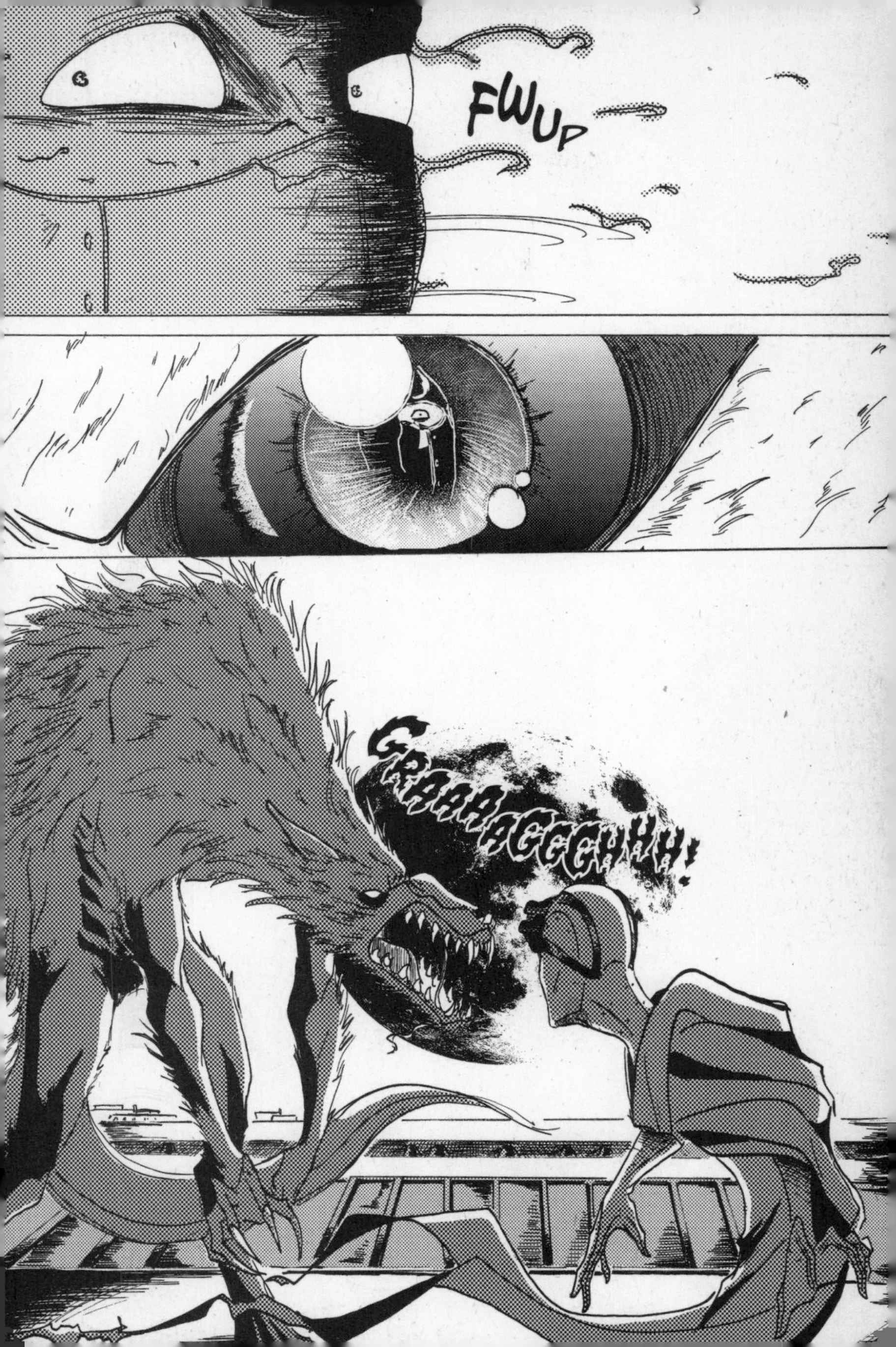
FWUP
GRAAAAGCCCHHH!

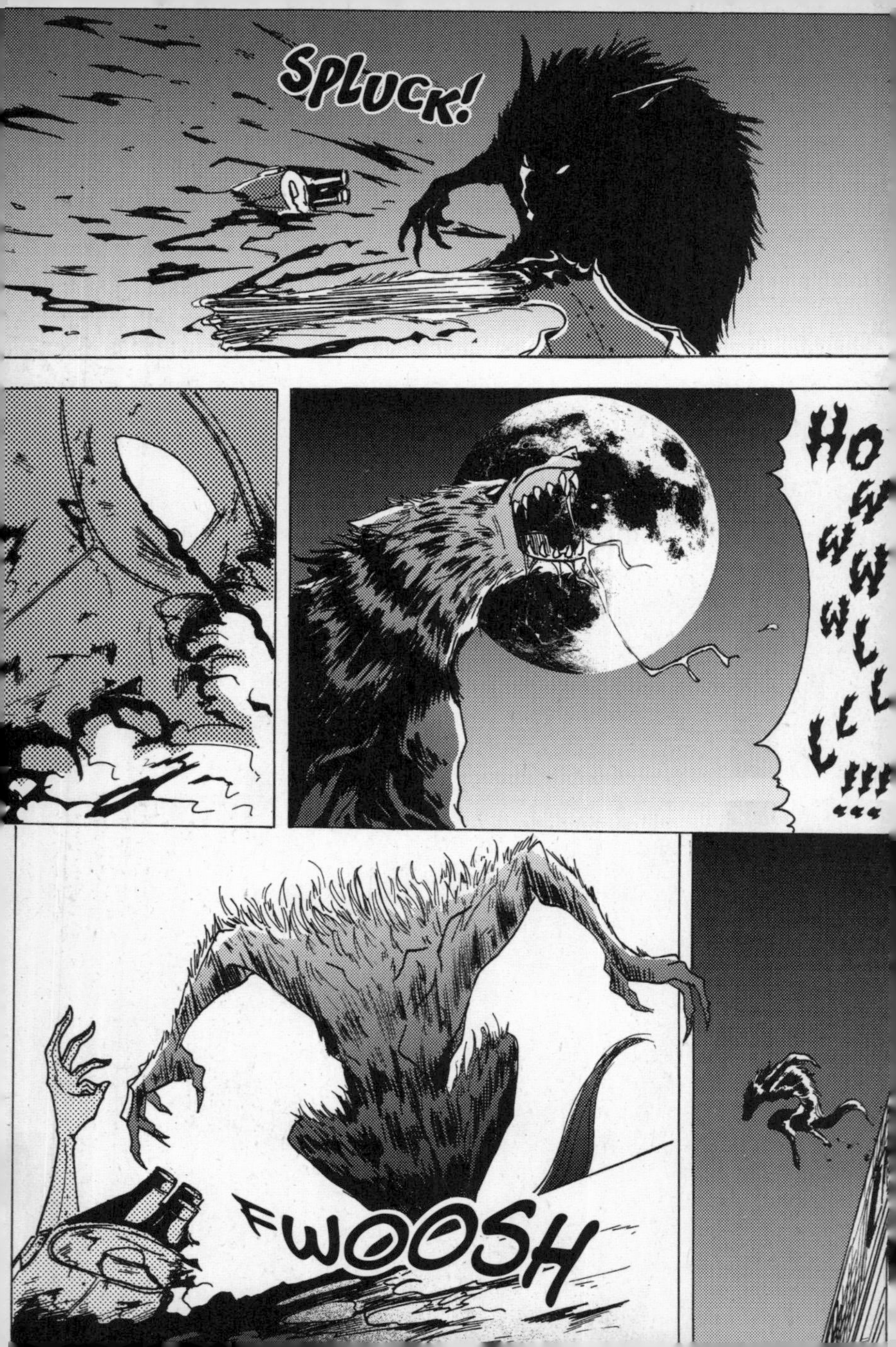
SPLUCK!
HOWWWWWLLLLLL!!!
FWOOSH

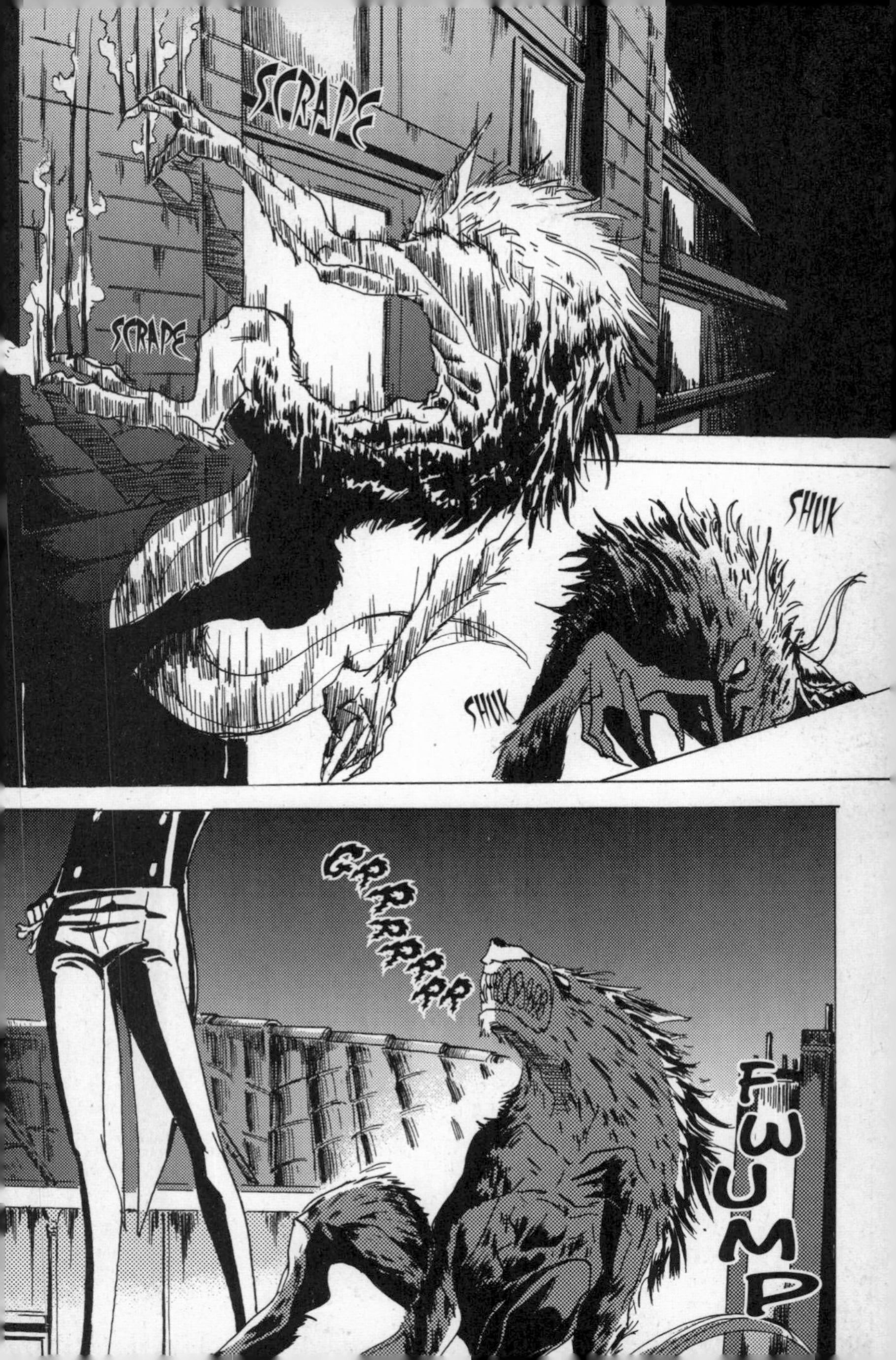
SCRAPE
SCRAPE
SHUK
SHUK
GRRRRRR
FWUMP

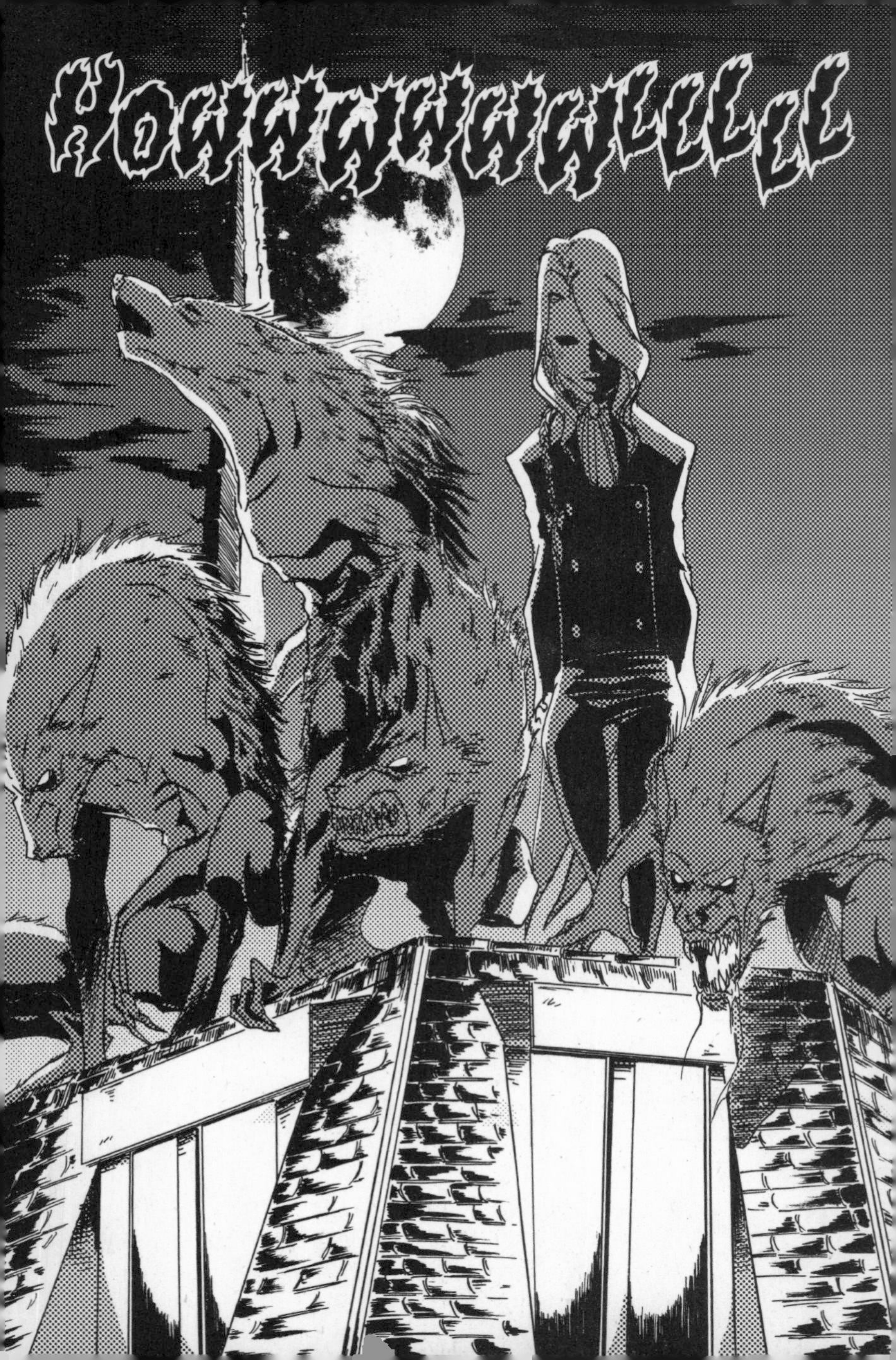
Howwwwwwllll

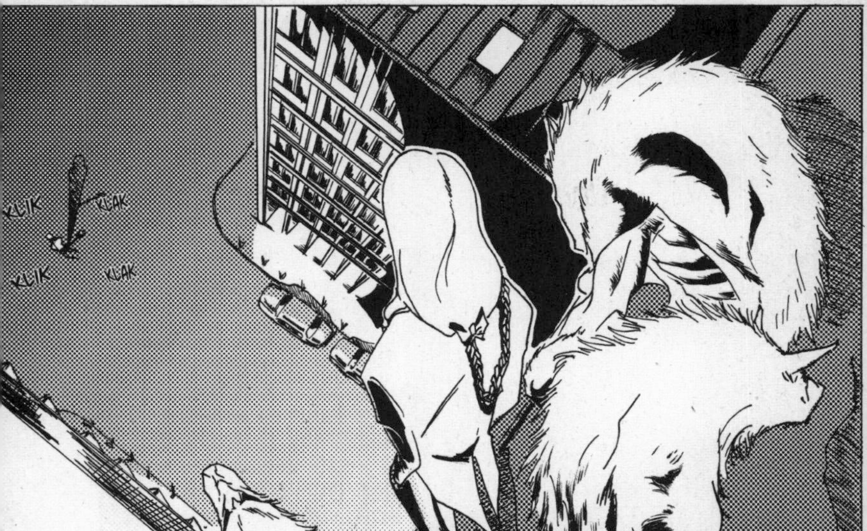
KLAK
KLIK
KLAK
KLIK

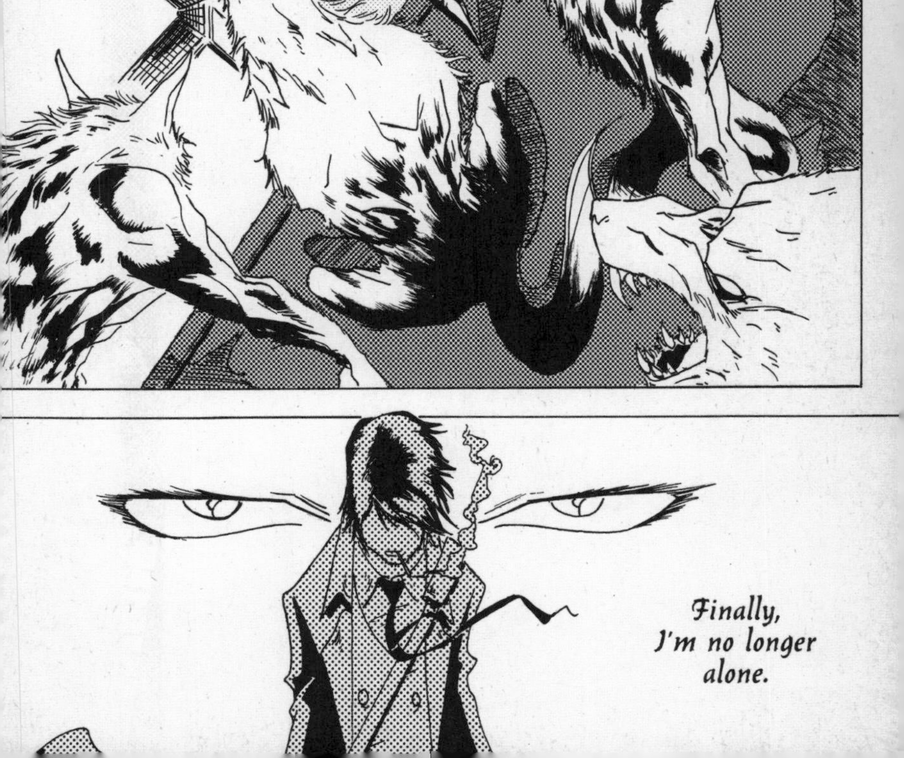
Finally,
I'm no longer
alone.

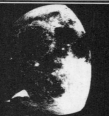

Vassy, France
1609

The remains of the
Church of Salvation

FOR NEARLY *FIFTY YEARS*, OUR KIND HAS STRUGGLED TO LIVE *PEACEFULLY* WITHIN A EUROPE THAT WOULD *DESPISE* US.

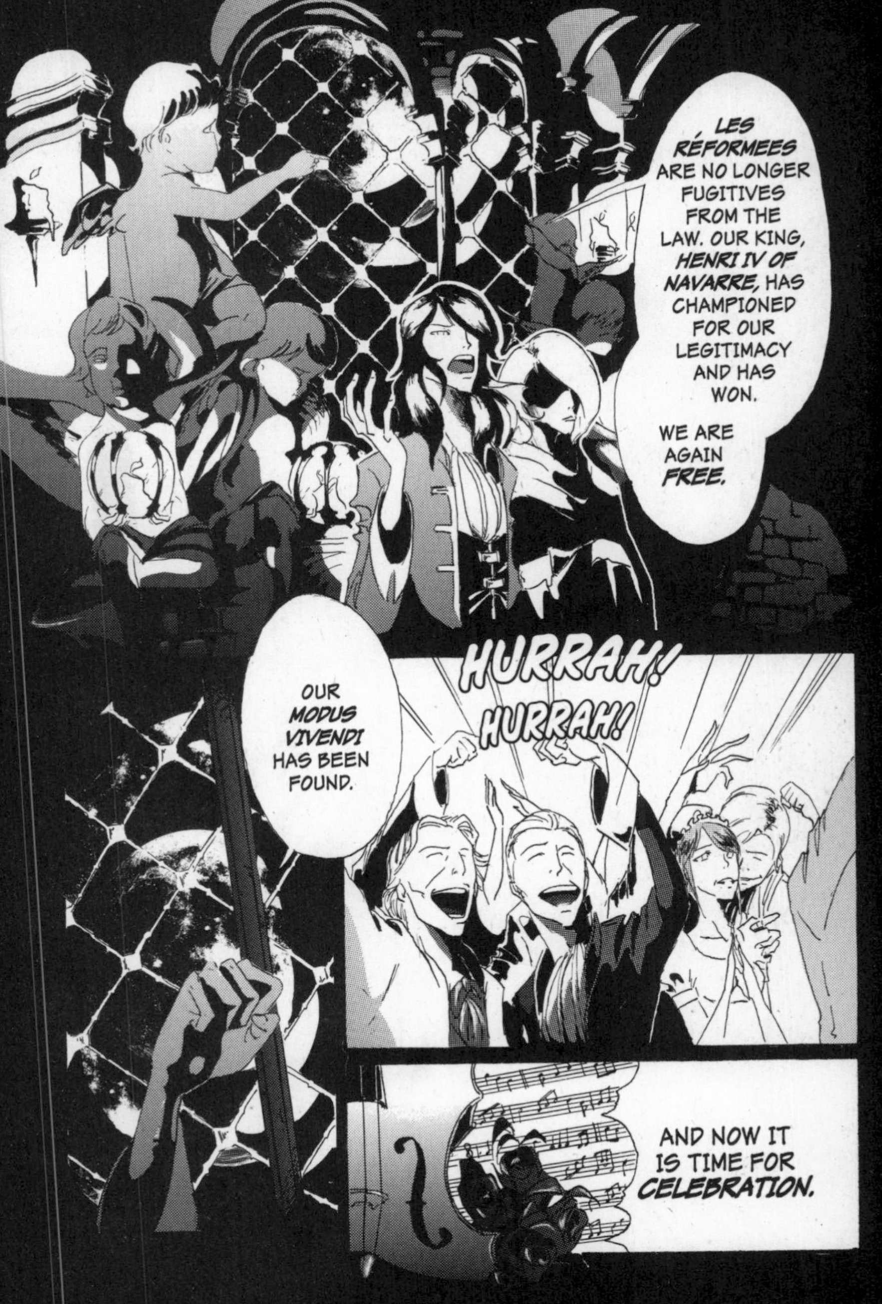
LES RÉFORMEES ARE NO LONGER FUGITIVES FROM THE LAW. OUR KING, HENRI IV OF NAVARRE, HAS CHAMPIONED FOR OUR LEGITIMACY AND HAS WON.
WE ARE AGAIN FREE.
OUR MODUS VIVENDI HAS BEEN FOUND.
HURRAH!
HURRAH!
AND NOW IT IS TIME FOR CELEBRATION.

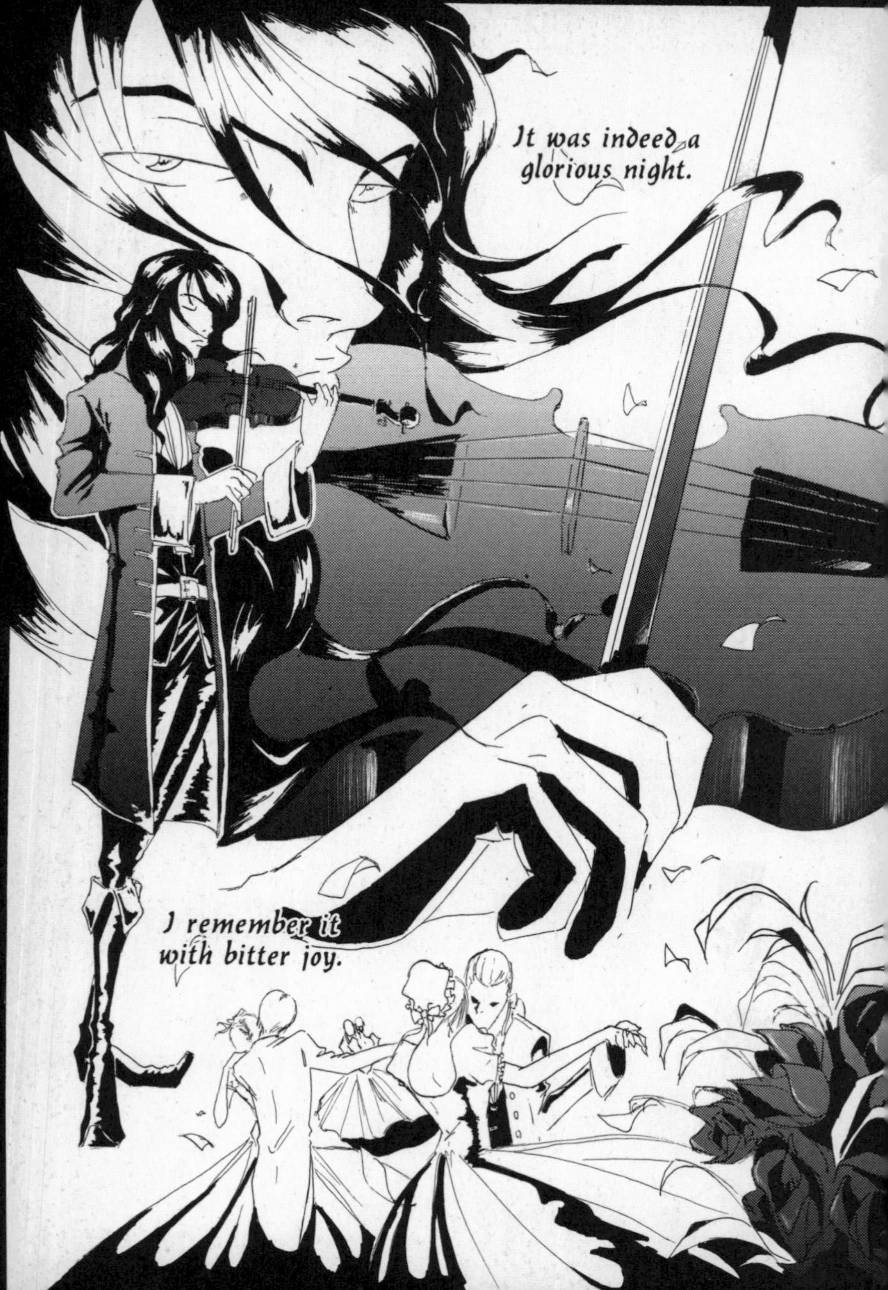
It was indeed a glorious night.
I remember it with bitter joy.

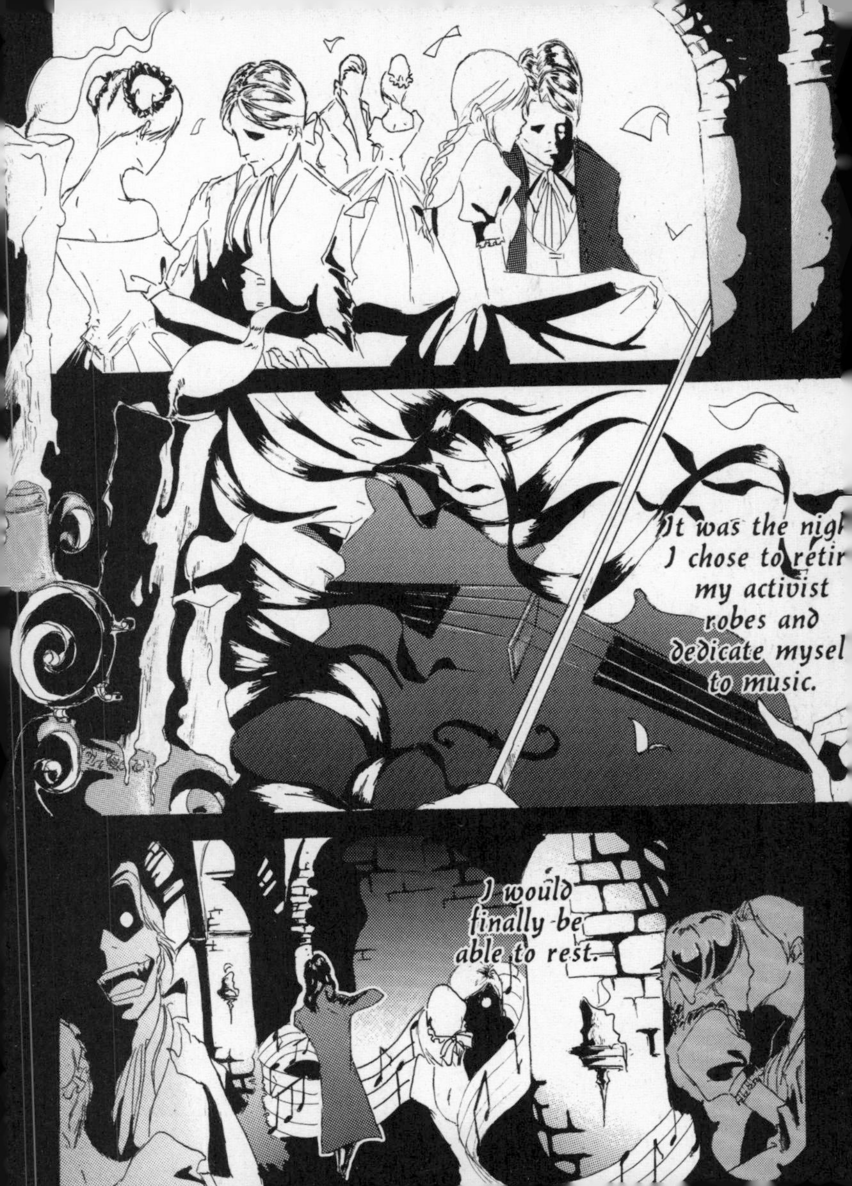
It was the nigh
I chose to retir
my activist
robes and
dedicate mysel
to music.
I would
finally be
able to rest.

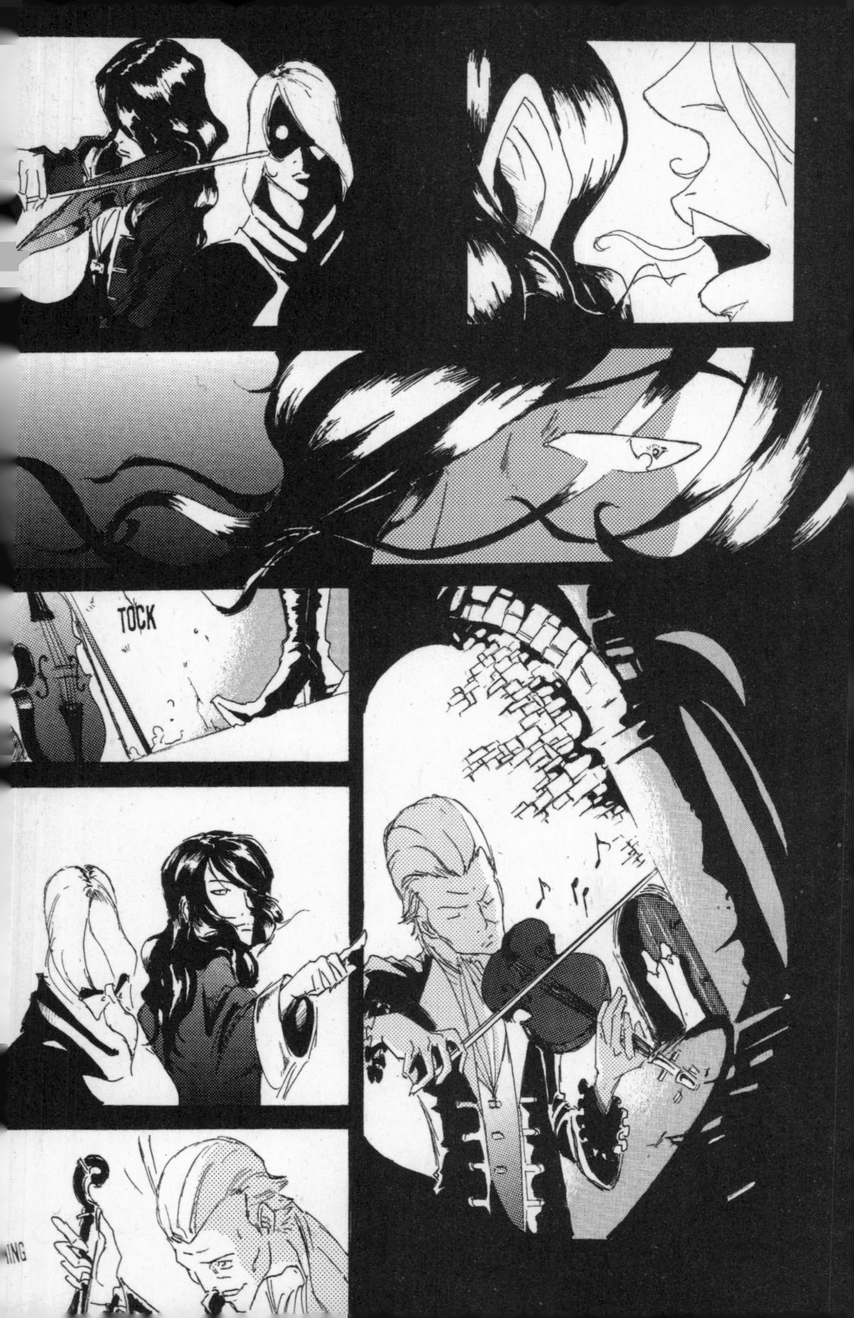
TOCK
...ING

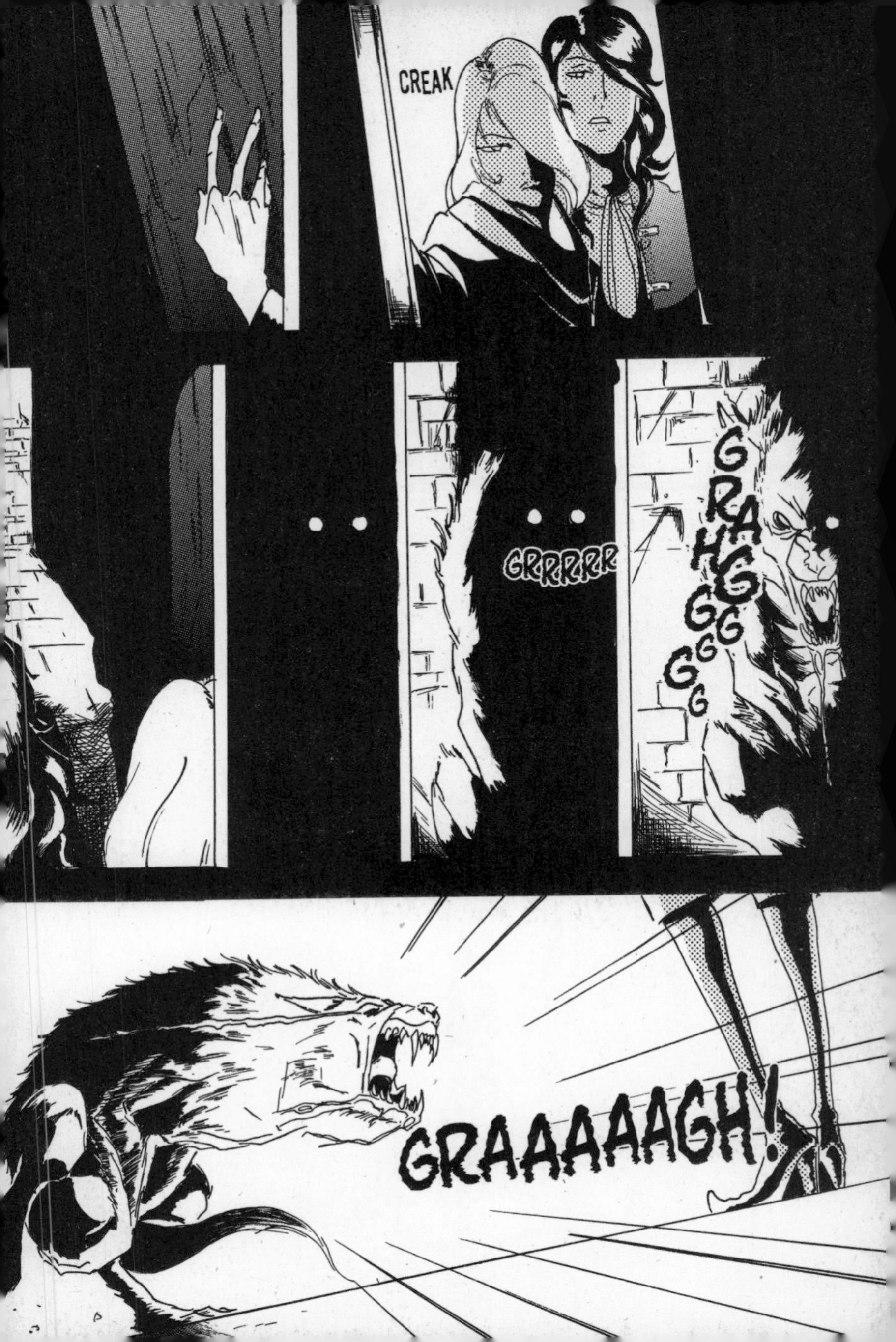
CREAK
GRAHGGGGGG
GRRRRR
GRAAAAAGH!

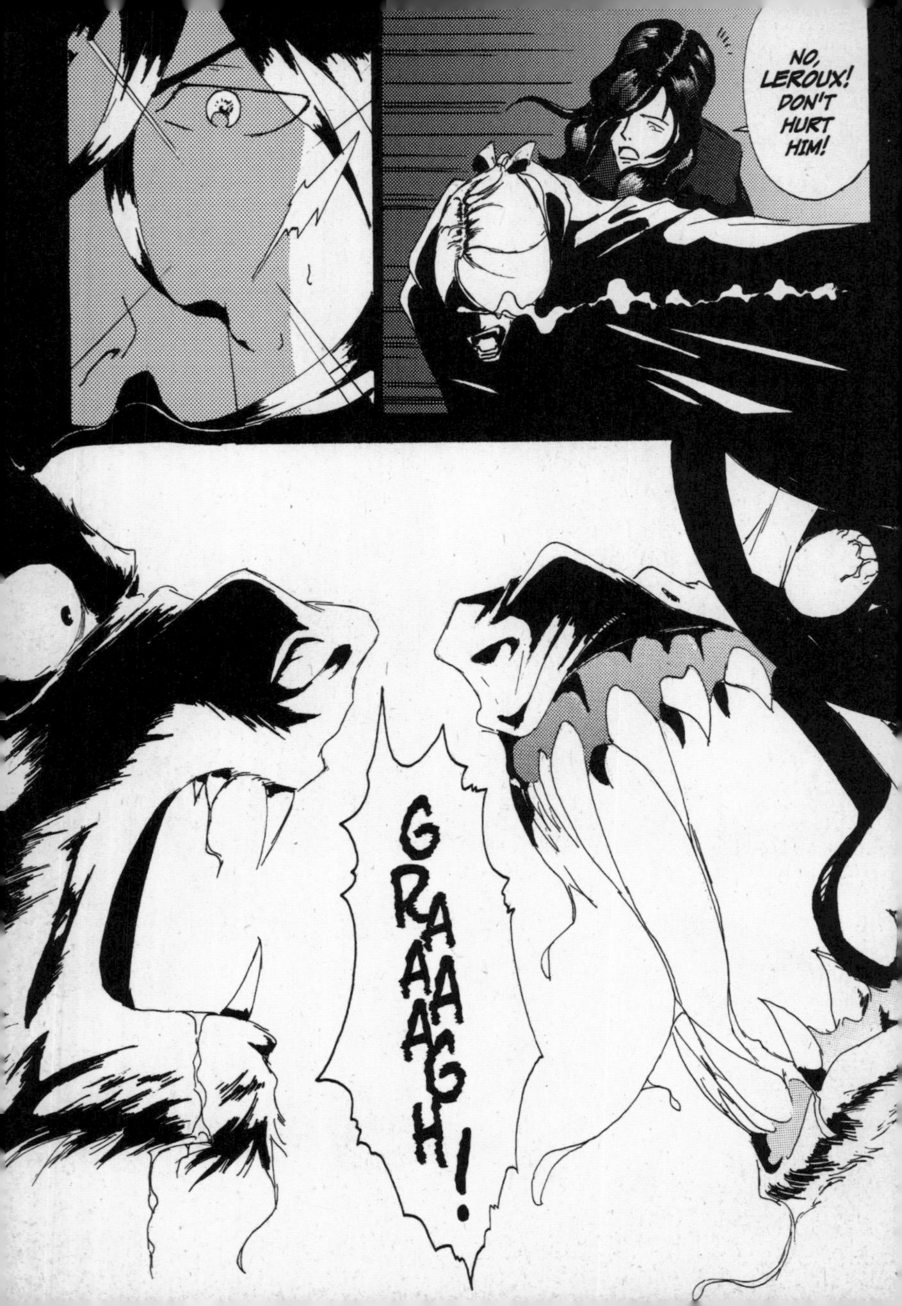
NO, LEROUX! DON'T HURT HIM!
GRAAAAGH!

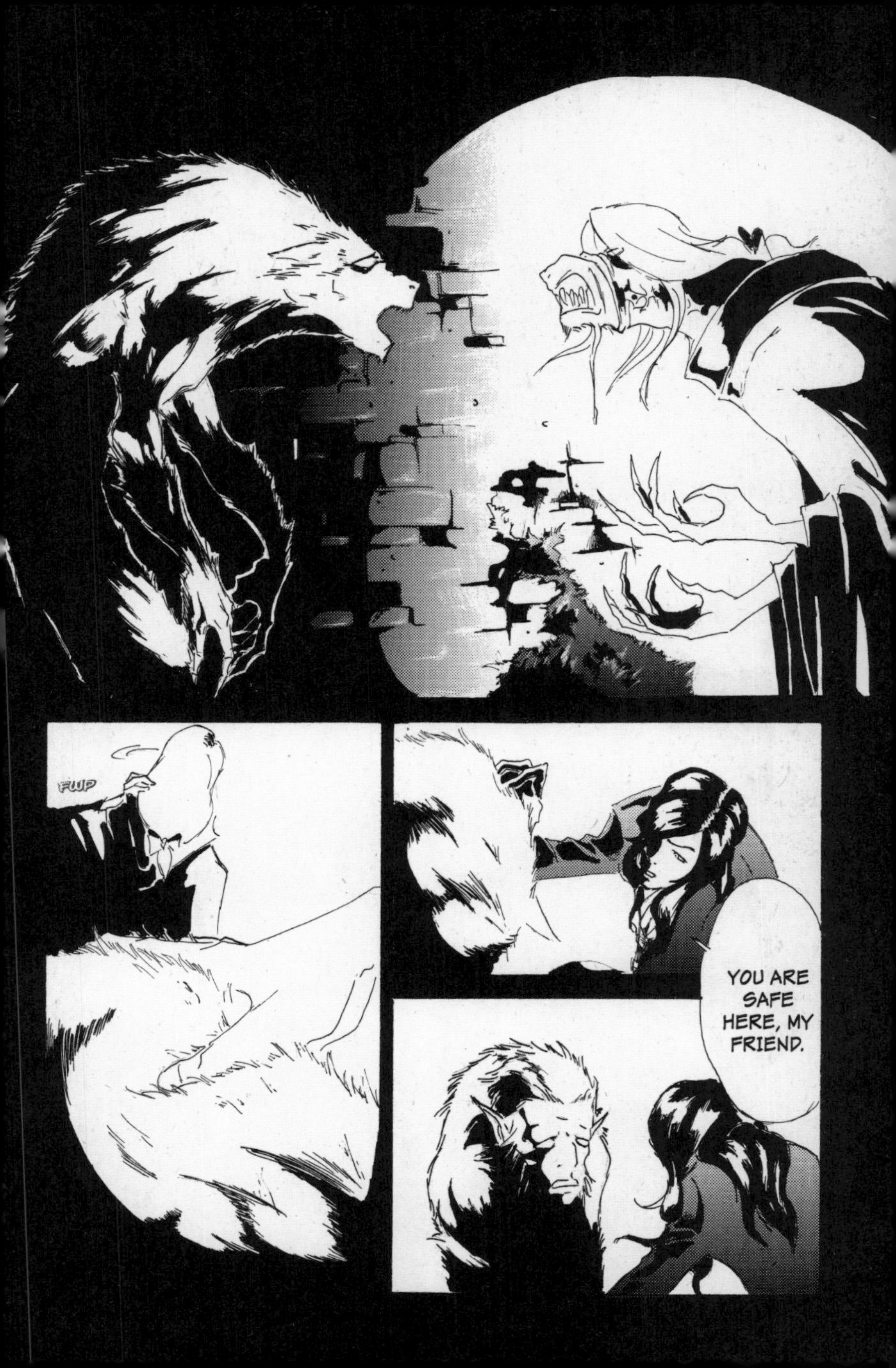
FWP
YOU ARE SAFE HERE, MY FRIEND.

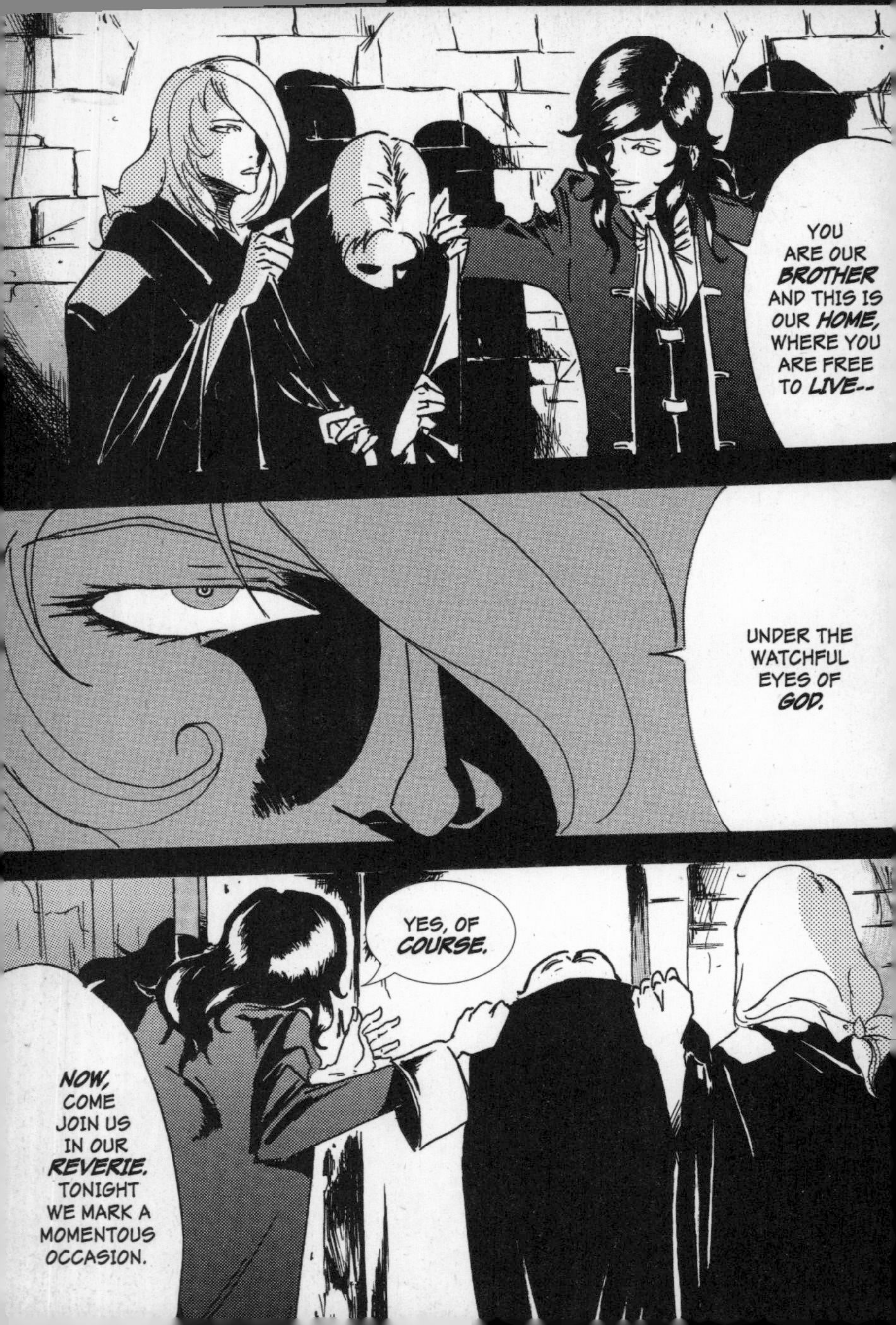
YOU ARE OUR BROTHER AND THIS IS OUR HOME, WHERE YOU ARE FREE TO LIVE--
UNDER THE WATCHFUL EYES OF GOD.
YES, OF COURSE.
NOW, COME JOIN US IN OUR REVERIE. TONIGHT WE MARK A MOMENTOUS OCCASION.

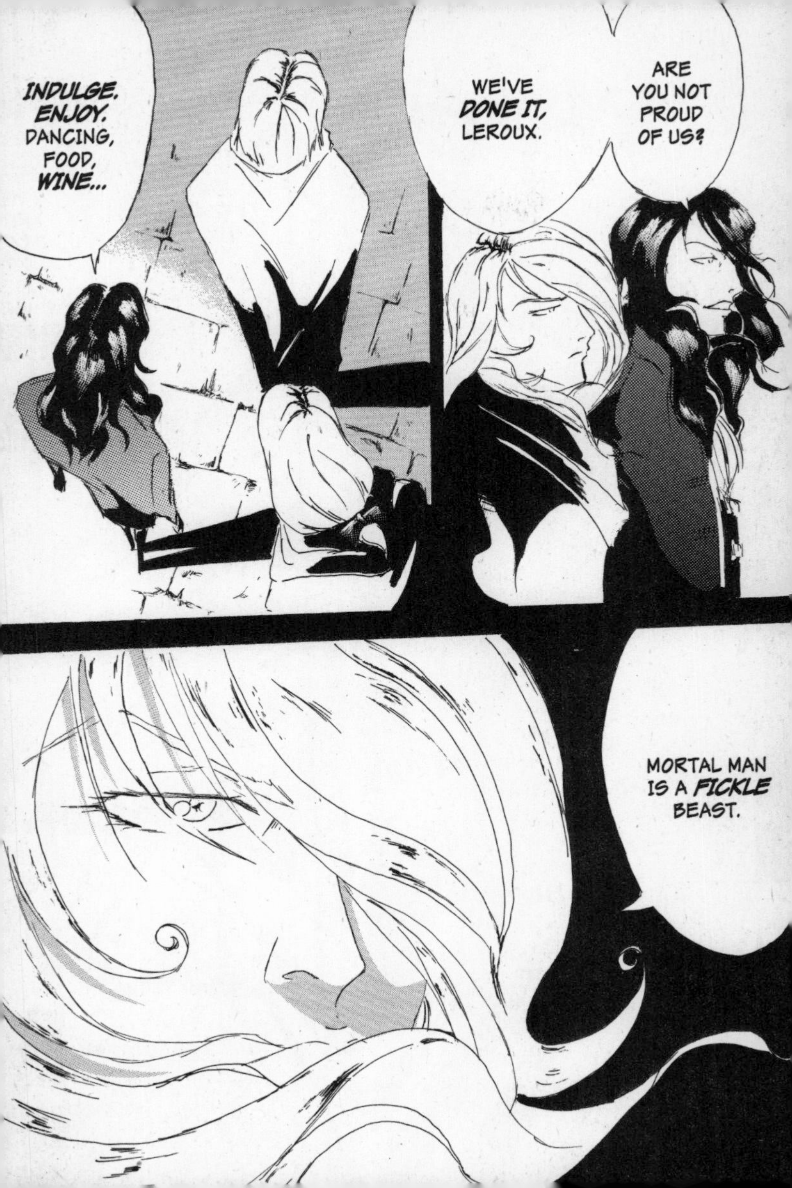
ARE YOU NOT PROUD OF US?
WE'VE DONE IT, LEROUX.
INDULGE. ENJOY. DANCING, FOOD, WINE...
MORTAL MAN IS A FICKLE BEAST.

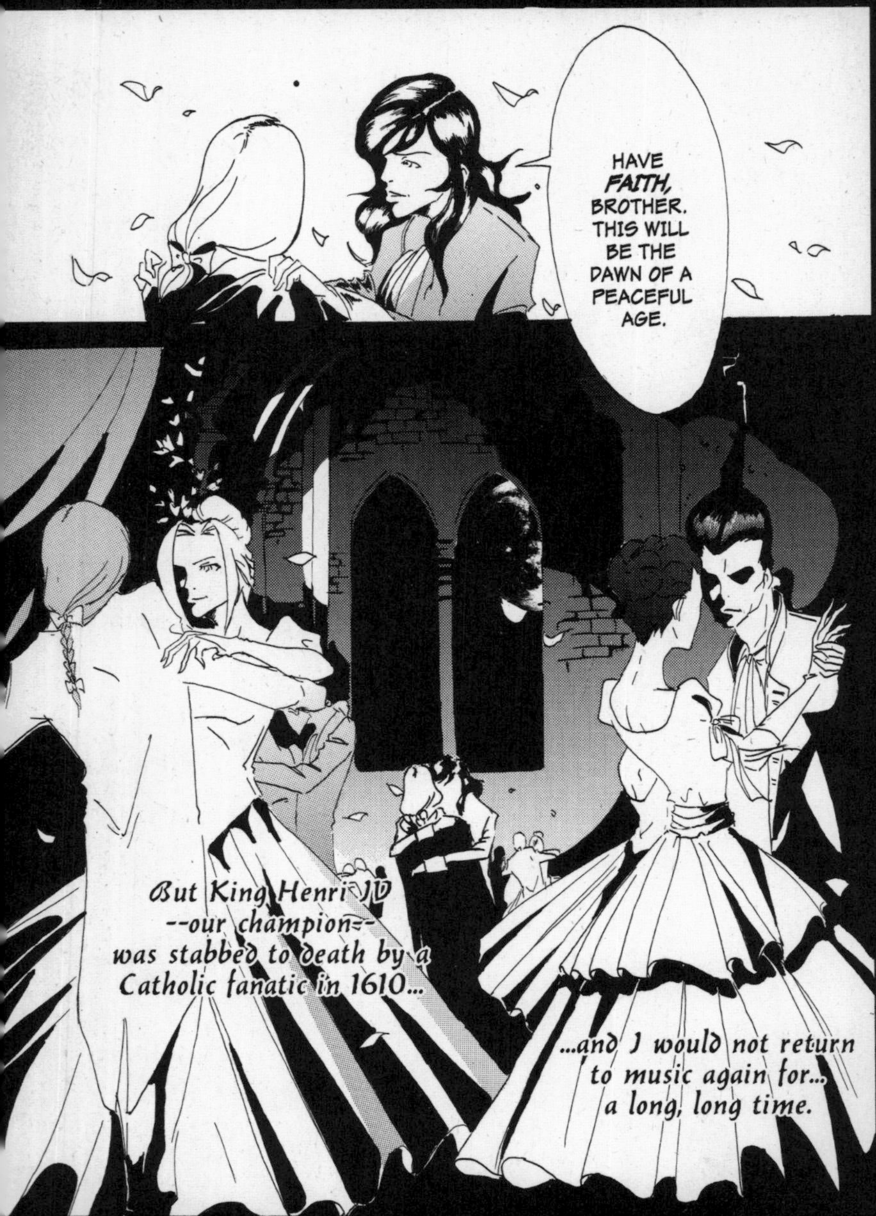
HAVE FAITH, BROTHER. THIS WILL BE THE DAWN OF A PEACEFUL AGE.
But King Henri IV --our champion-- was stabbed to death by a Catholic fanatic in 1610...
...and I would not return to music again for... a long, long time.

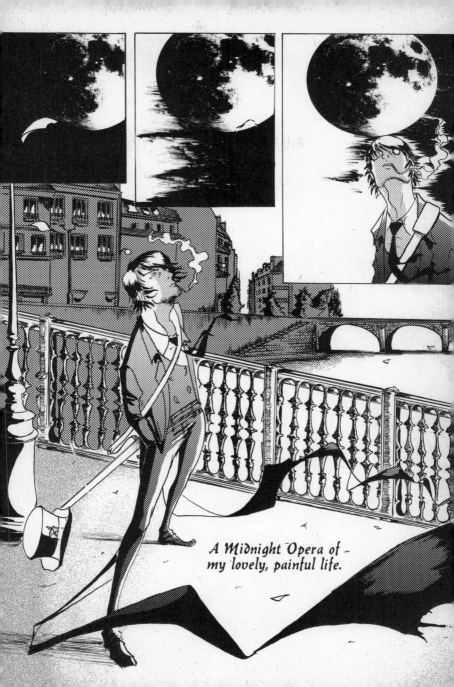

A Midnight Opera of
my lovely, painful life.

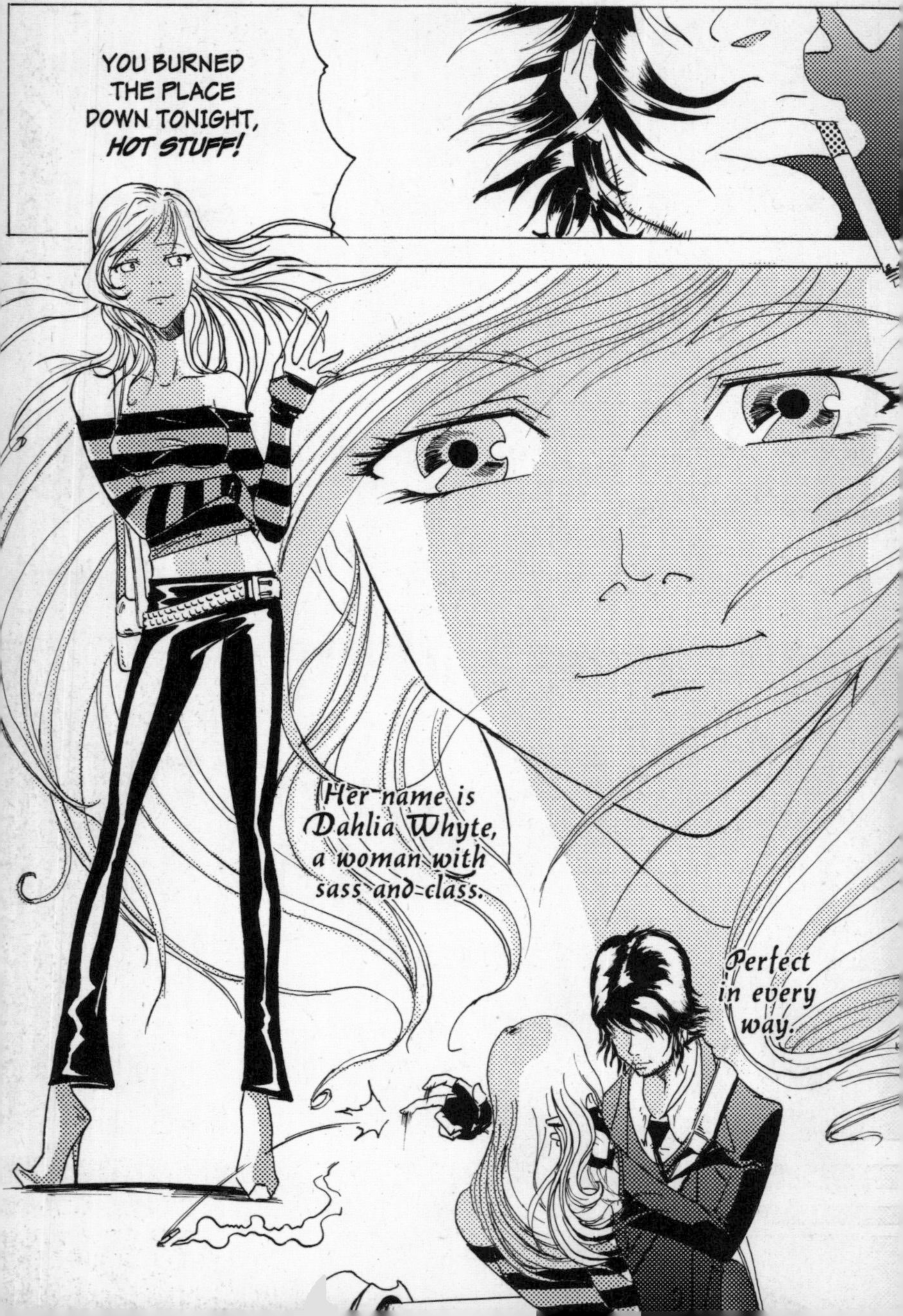
YOU BURNED THE PLACE DOWN TONIGHT, HOT STUFF!
Her name is Dahlia Whyte, a woman with sass and class.
Perfect in every way.

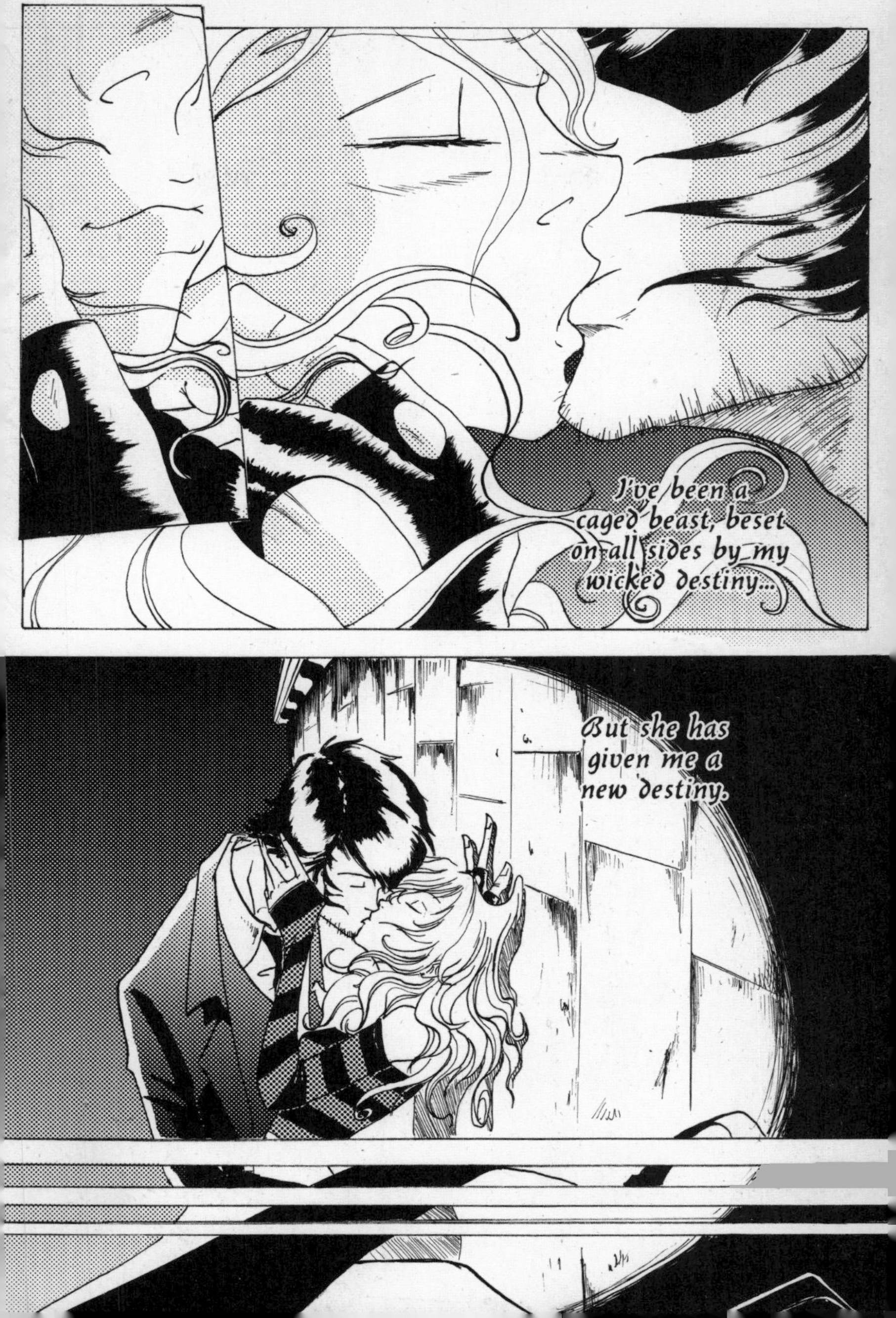
I've been a caged beast, beset on all sides by my wicked destiny...
But she has given me a new destiny.

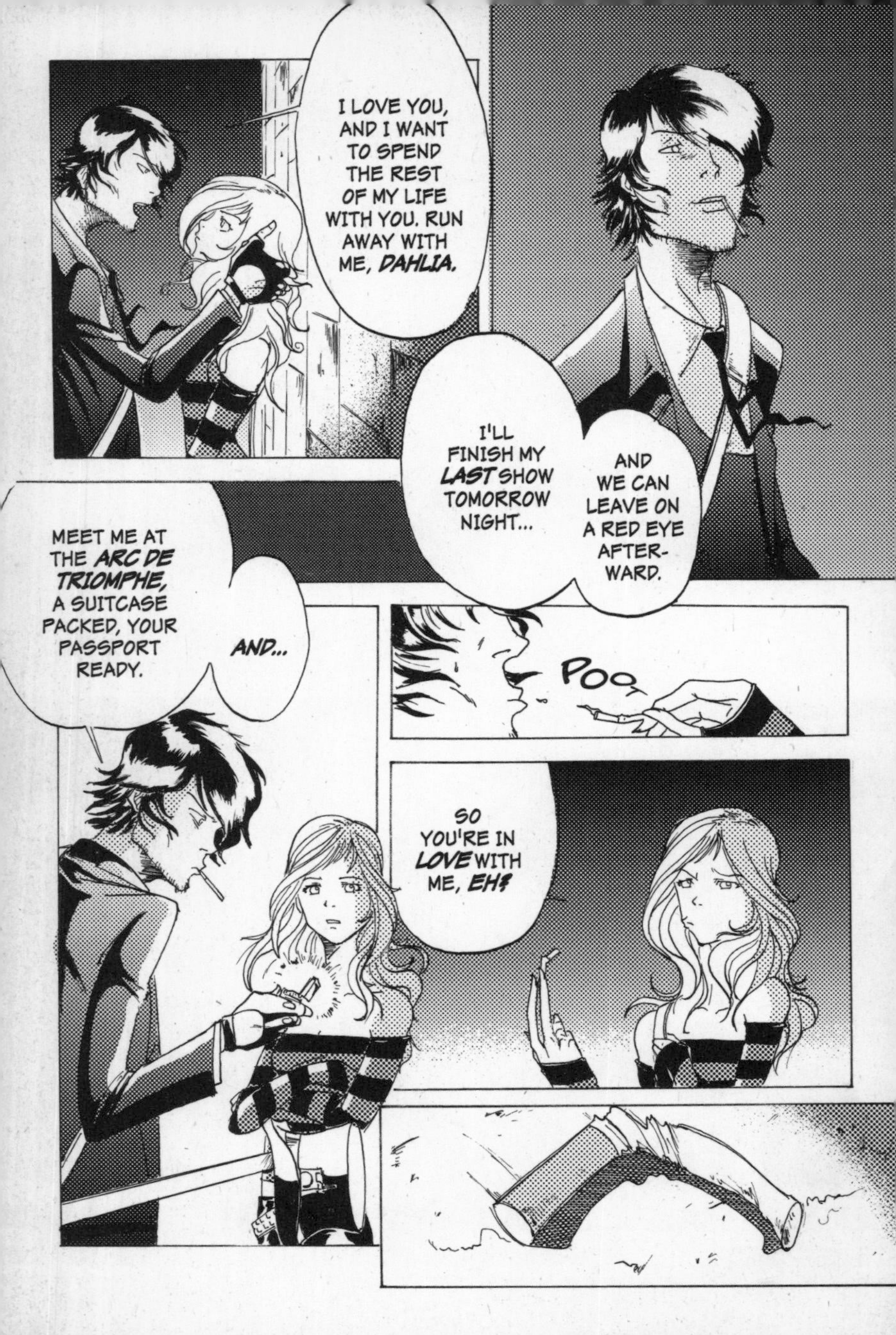
I LOVE YOU, AND I WANT TO SPEND THE REST OF MY LIFE WITH YOU. RUN AWAY WITH ME, DAHLIA.
I'LL FINISH MY LAST SHOW TOMORROW NIGHT...
AND WE CAN LEAVE ON A RED EYE AFTER-WARD.
MEET ME AT THE ARC DE TRIOMPHE, A SUITCASE PACKED, YOUR PASSPORT READY.
AND...
POOT
SO YOU'RE IN LOVE WITH ME, EH?

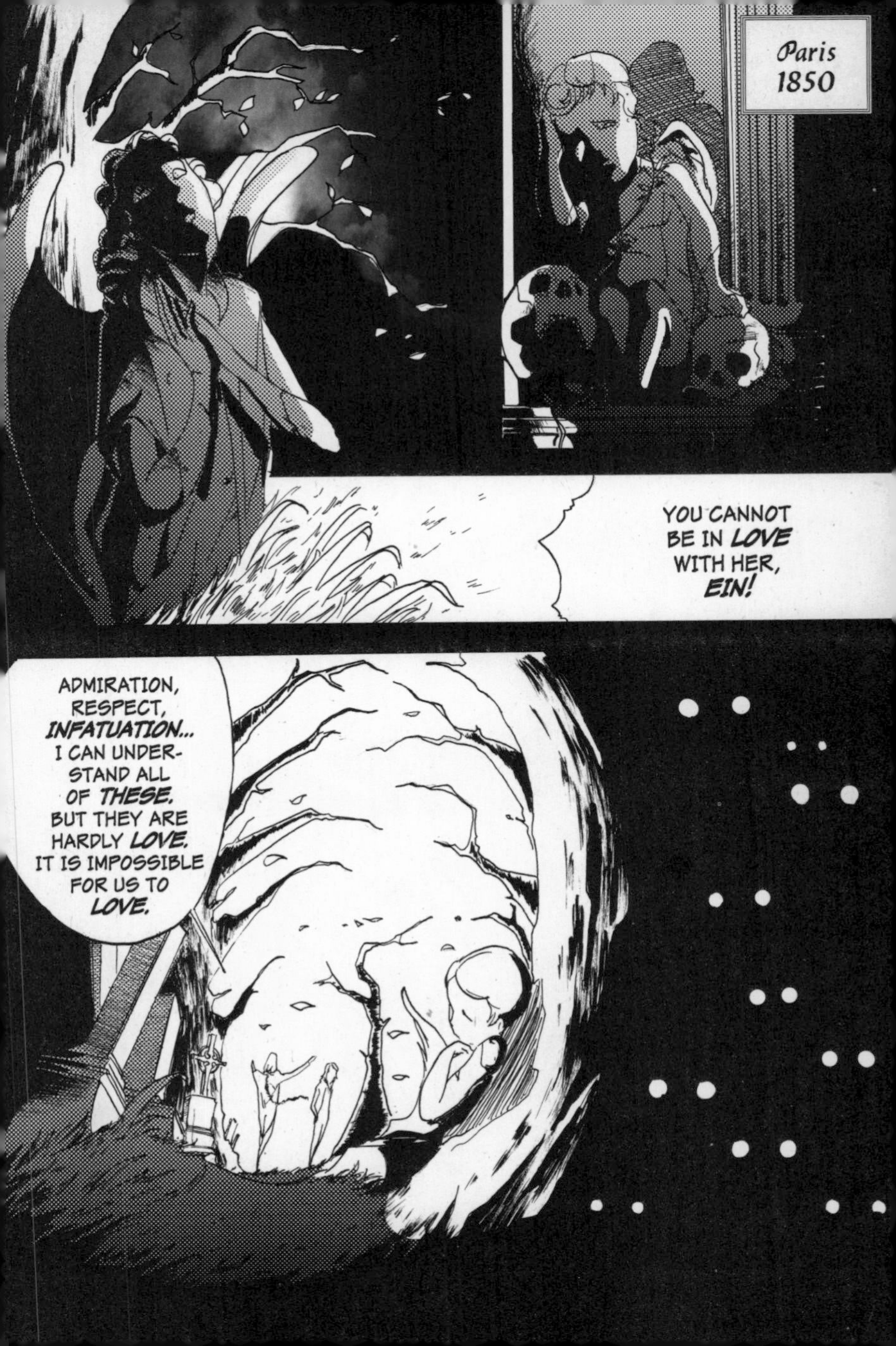
Paris 1850
YOU CANNOT BE IN LOVE WITH HER, EIN!
ADMIRATION, RESPECT, INFATUATION... I CAN UNDER-STAND ALL OF THESE. BUT THEY ARE HARDLY LOVE. IT IS IMPOSSIBLE FOR US TO LOVE.

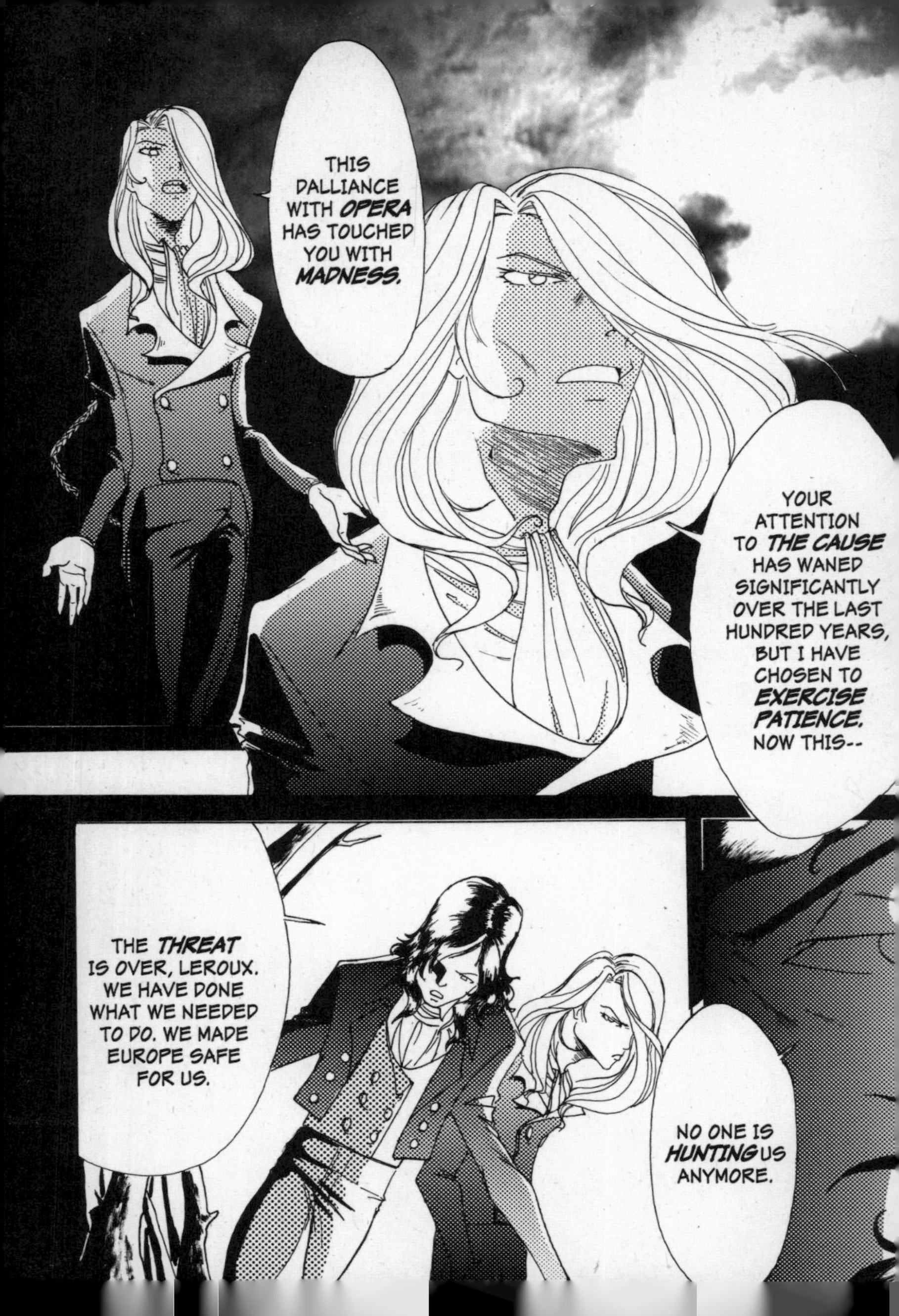
YOUR ATTENTION TO THE CAUSE HAS WANED SIGNIFICANTLY OVER THE LAST HUNDRED YEARS, BUT I HAVE CHOSEN TO EXERCISE PATIENCE. NOW THIS--
THIS DALLIANCE WITH OPERA HAS TOUCHED YOU WITH MADNESS.
NO ONE IS HUNTING US ANYMORE.
THE THREAT IS OVER, LEROUX. WE HAVE DONE WHAT WE NEEDED TO DO. WE MADE EUROPE SAFE FOR US.

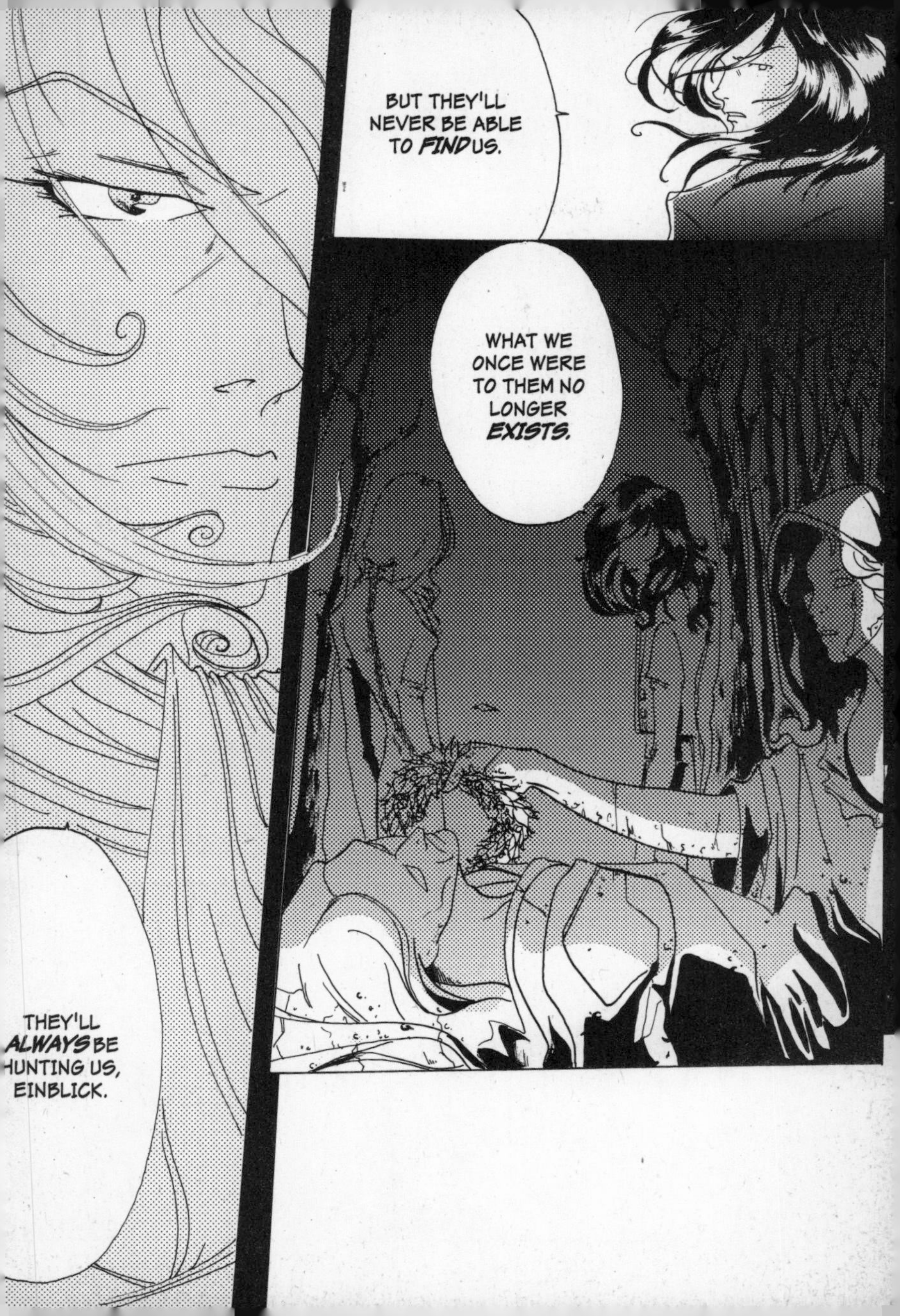
BUT THEY'LL NEVER BE ABLE TO FIND US.
WHAT WE ONCE WERE TO THEM NO LONGER EXISTS.
THEY'LL ALWAYS BE HUNTING US, EINBLICK.

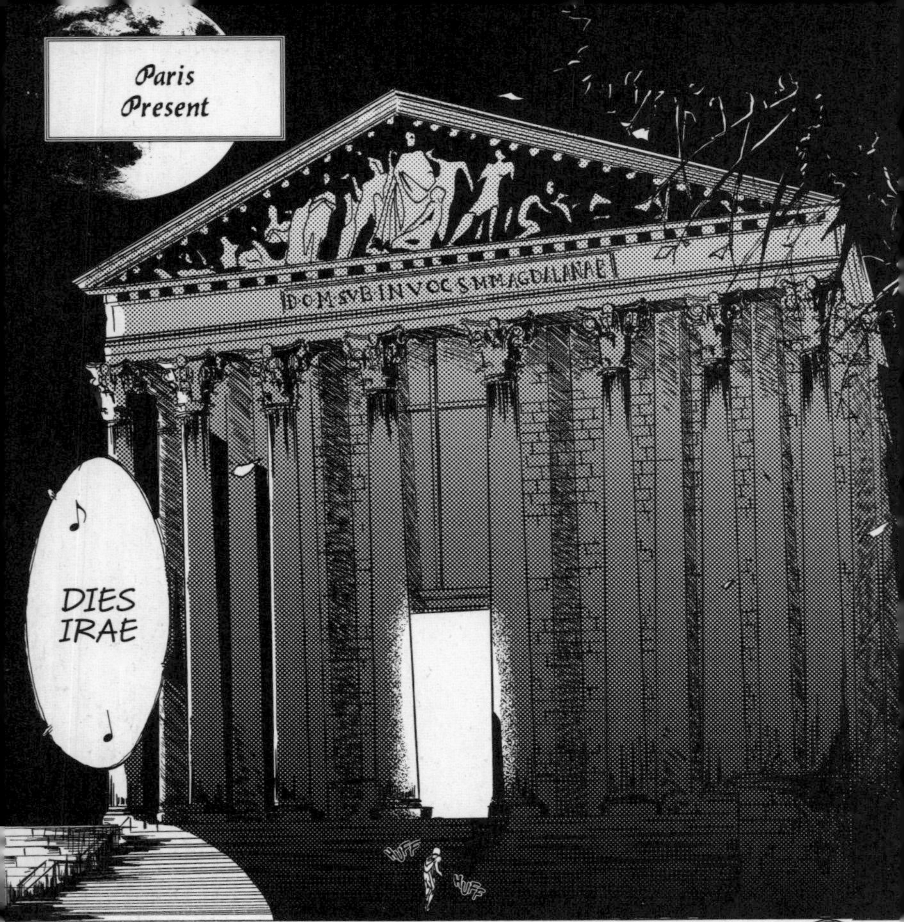
Paris
Present
DIES IRAE
HUFF
HUFF

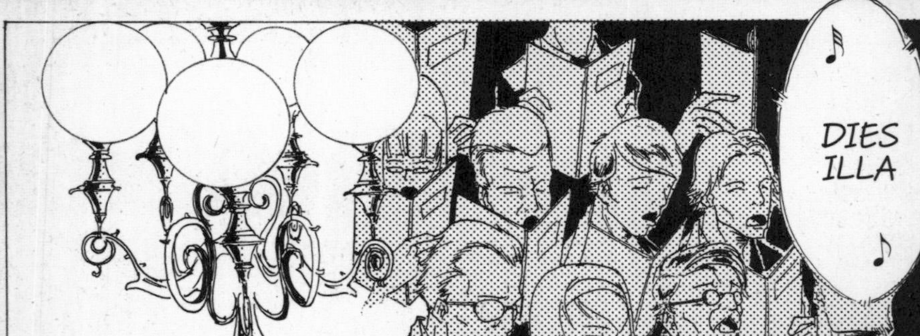
DIES ILLA

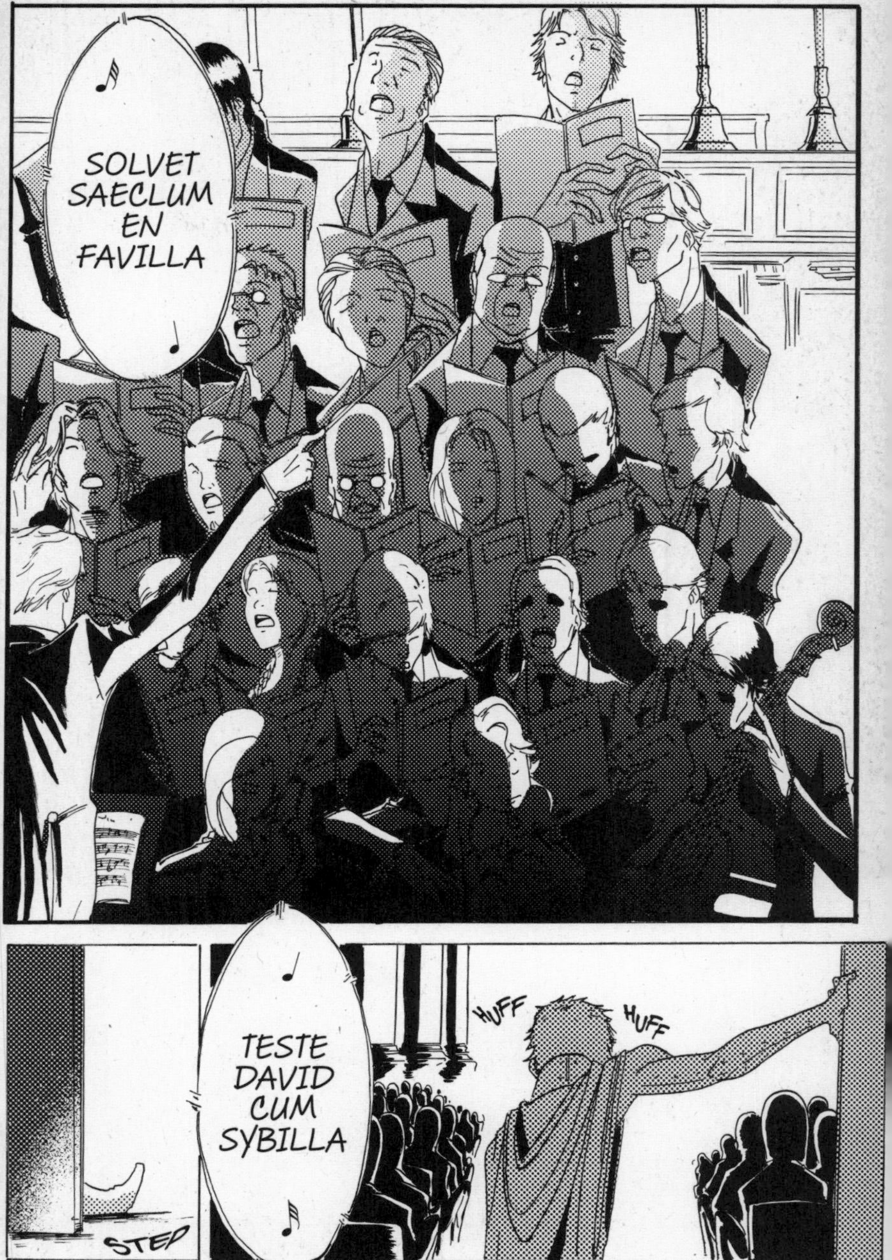
SOLVET SAECLUM EN FAVILLA
HUFF HUFF
TESTE DAVID CUM SYBILLA
STEP

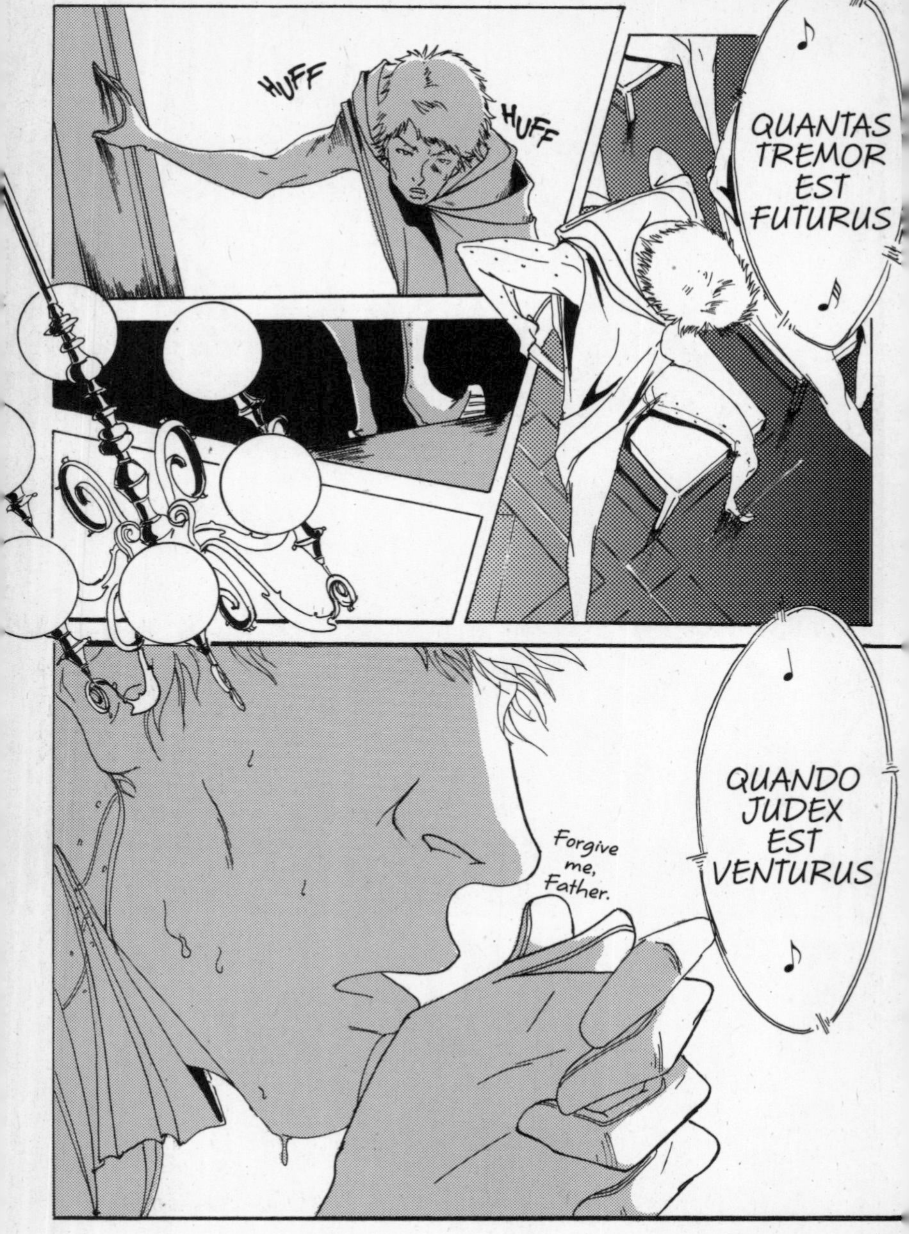
QUANTAS TREMOR EST FUTURUS
HUFF
HUFF
QUANDO JUDEX EST VENTURUS
Forgive me, Father.

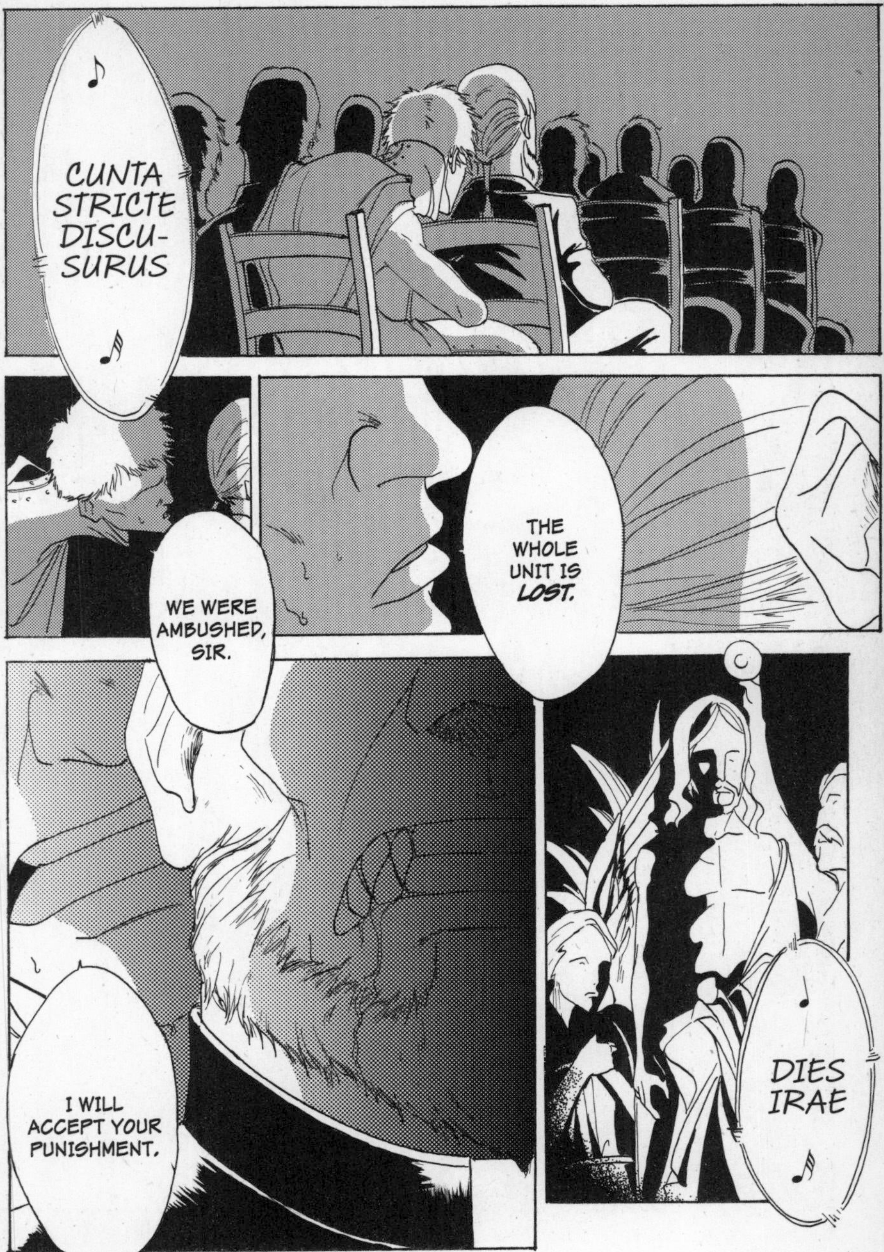
CUNTA STRICTE DISCU-SURUS
WE WERE AMBUSHED, SIR.
THE WHOLE UNIT IS *LOST.*
I WILL ACCEPT YOUR PUNISHMENT.
DIES IRAE

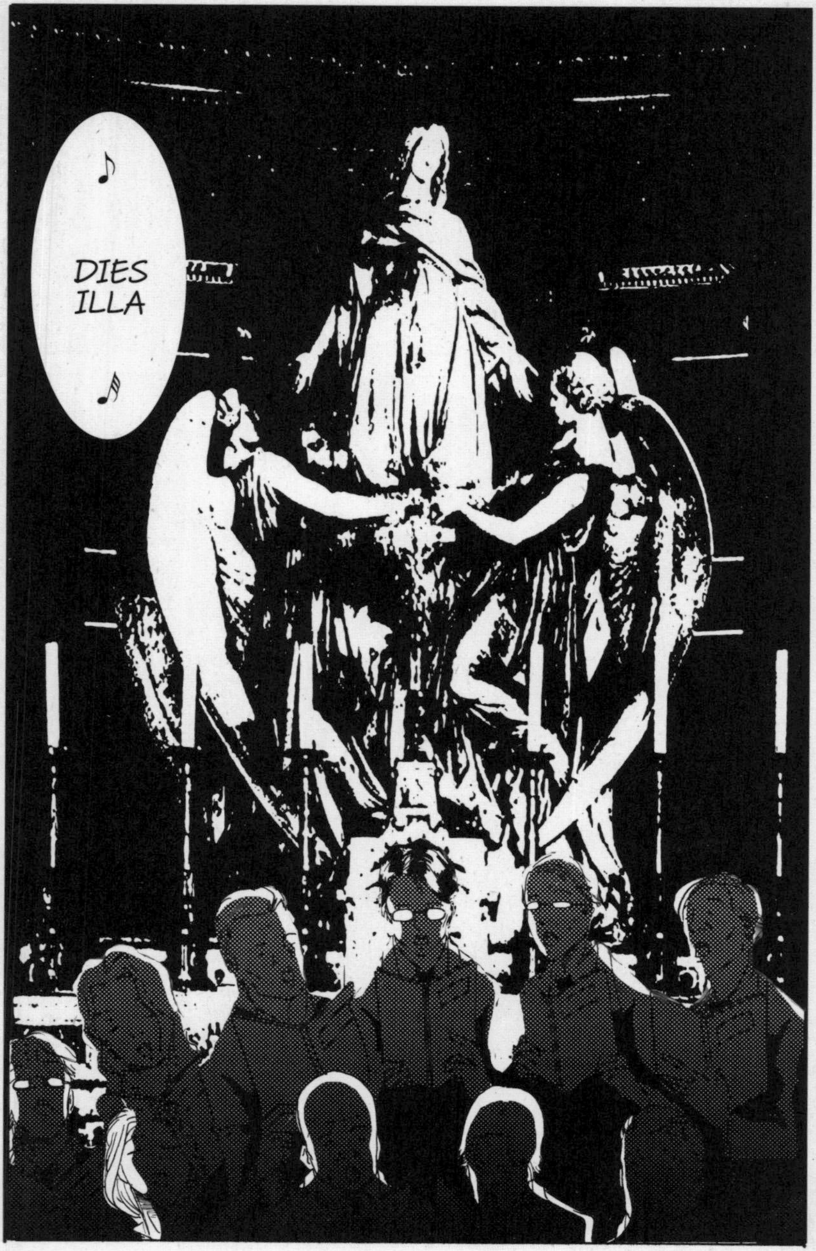
♪ DIES ILLA ♬

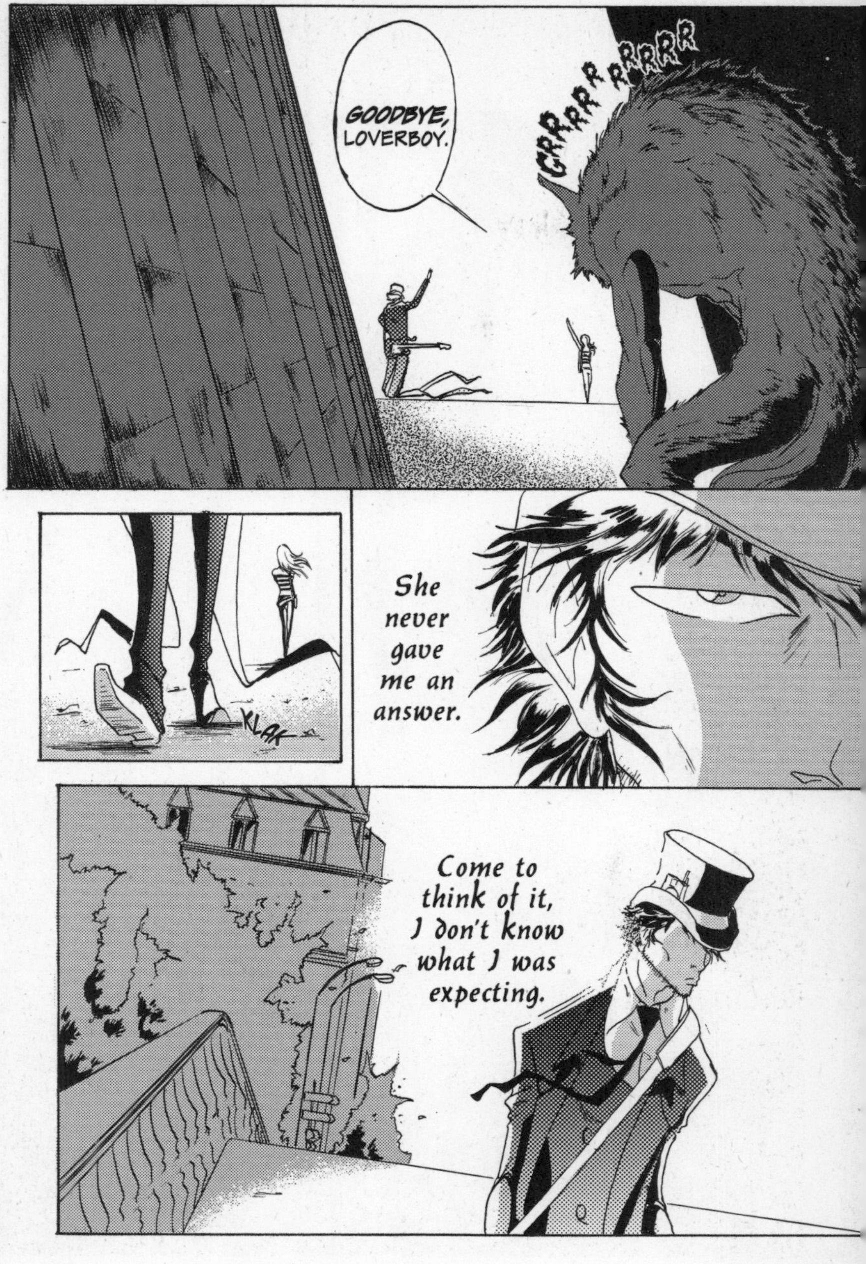
GRRRRRRRRRR
GOODBYE, LOVERBOY.
She never gave me an answer.
KLAK
Come to think of it, I don't know what I was expecting.

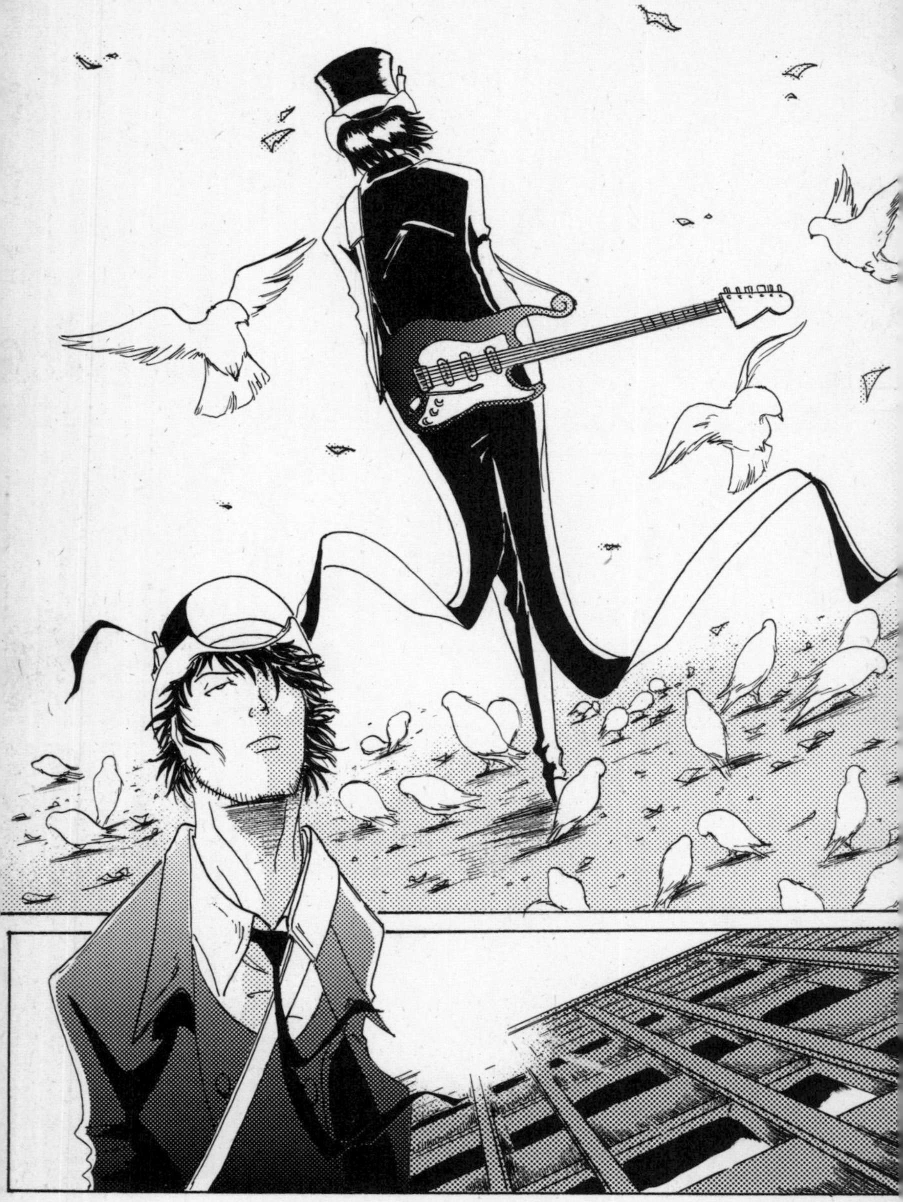

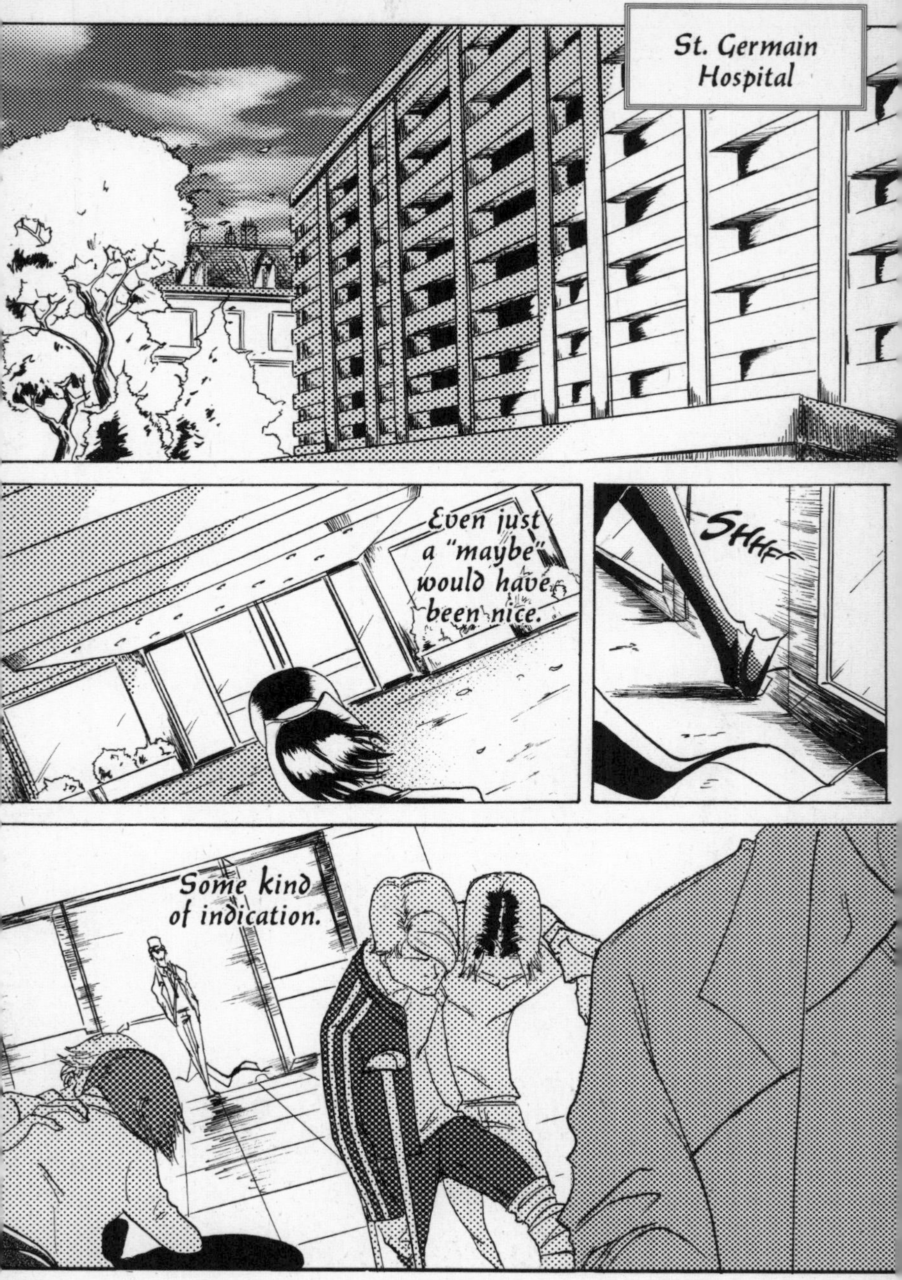
St. Germain Hospital
SHHFF
Even just a "maybe" would have been nice.
Some kind of indication.

She'll say yes.

She has to say yes.

GRAB

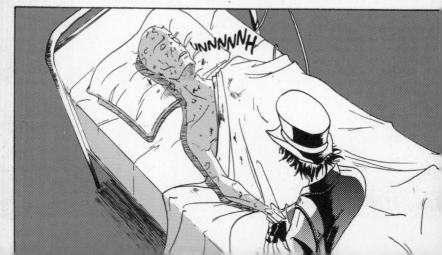

UNNNNNH

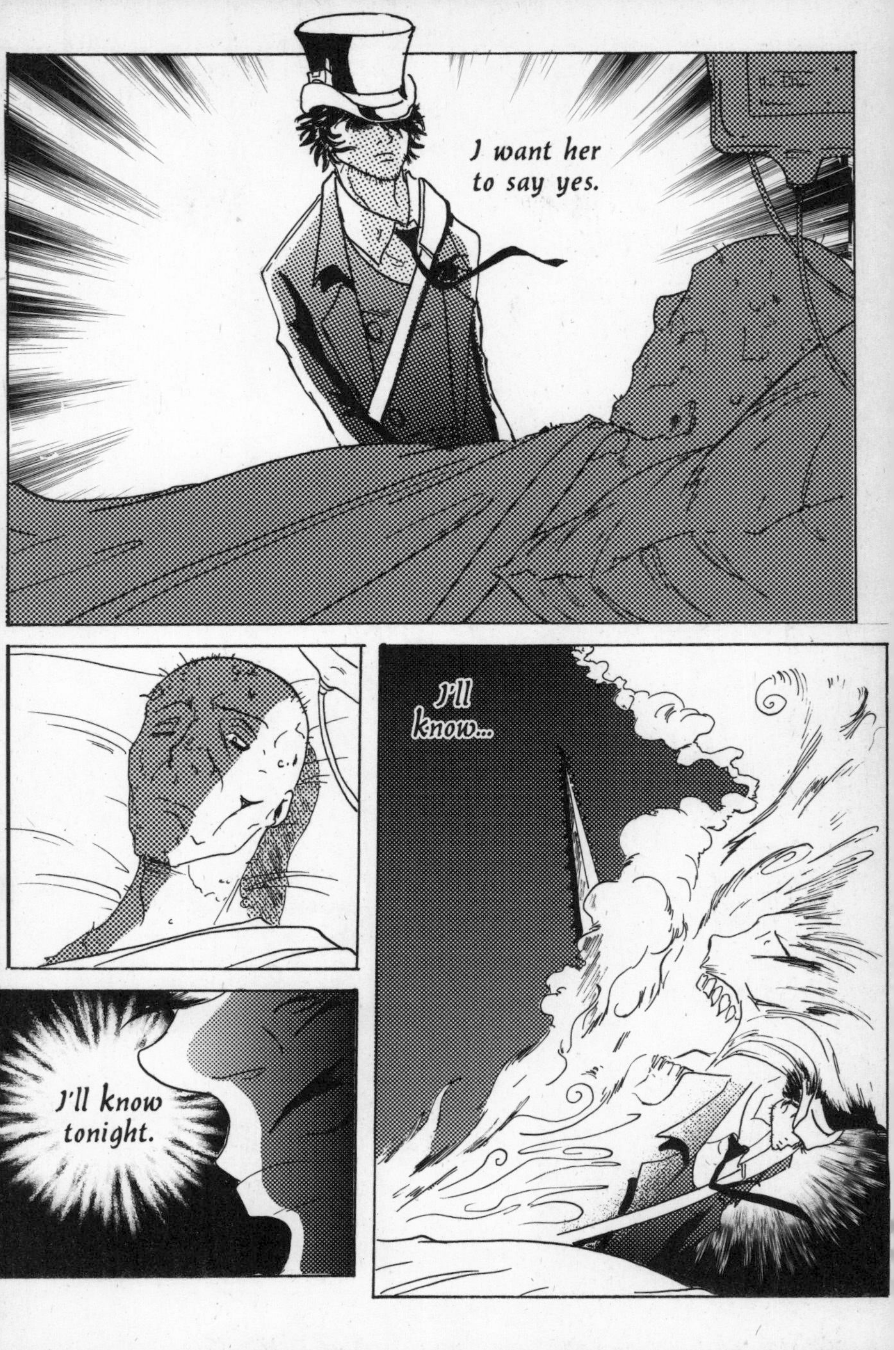
I want her to say yes.
I'll know...
I'll know tonight.

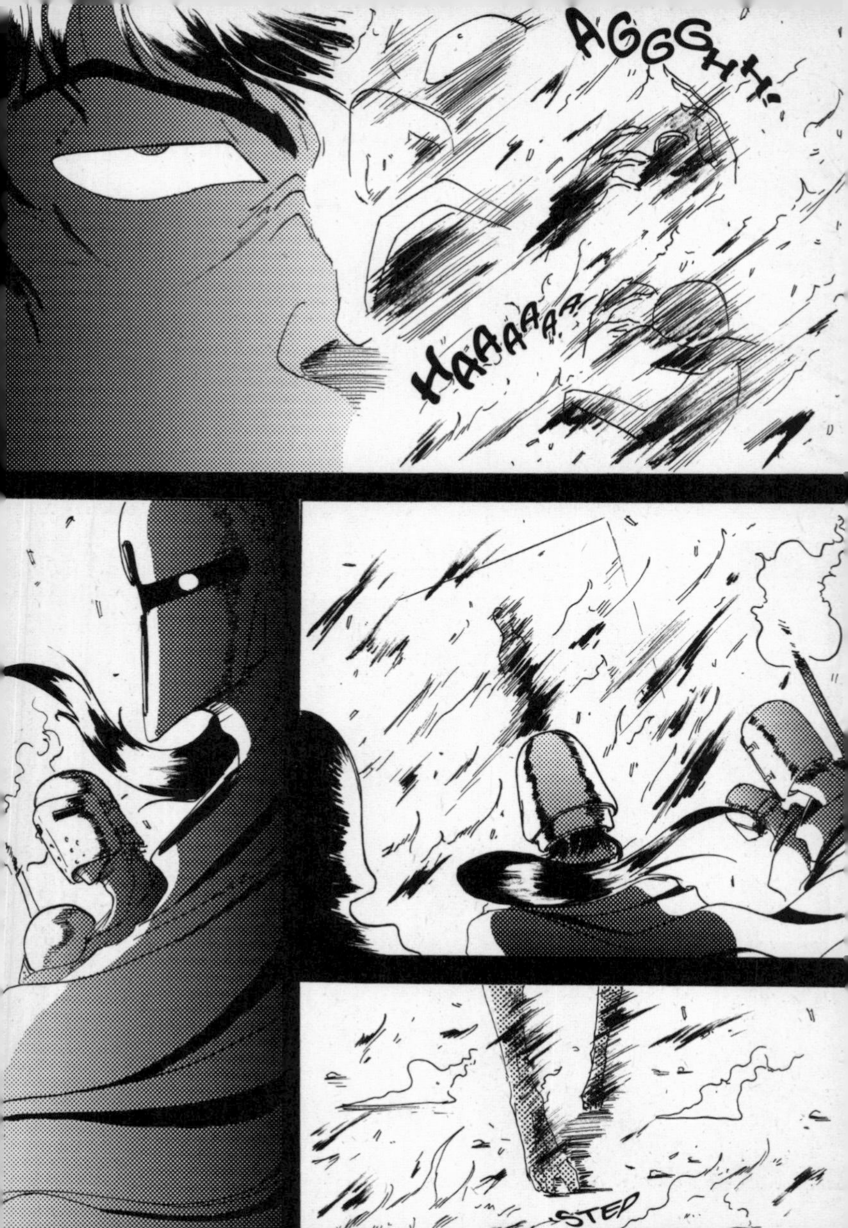
AGGGHH!
HAAAAAAA
STEP

Einblick....

UNNNNNH

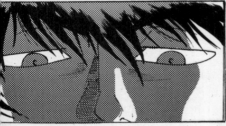

Don't let them keep me alive.

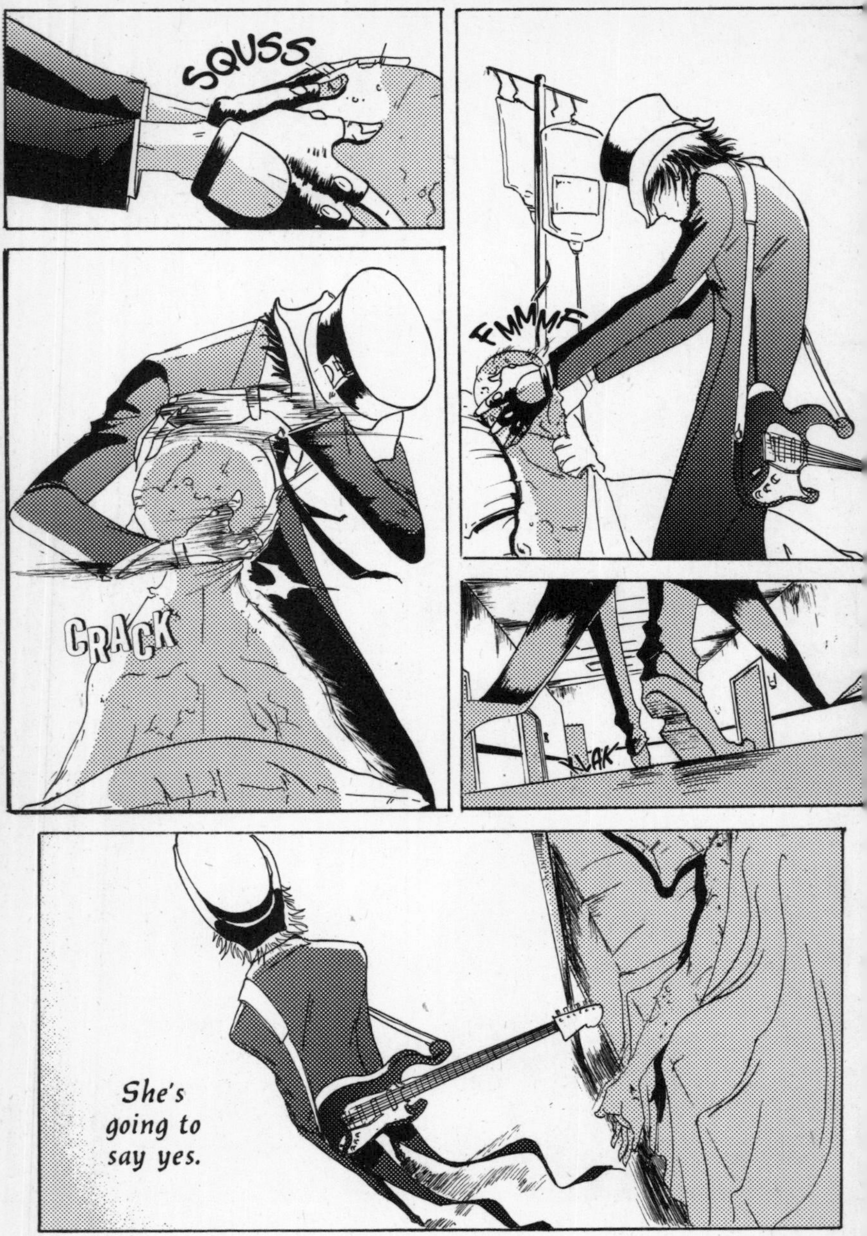
FMMMF
SQUSS
CRACK
She's going to say yes.

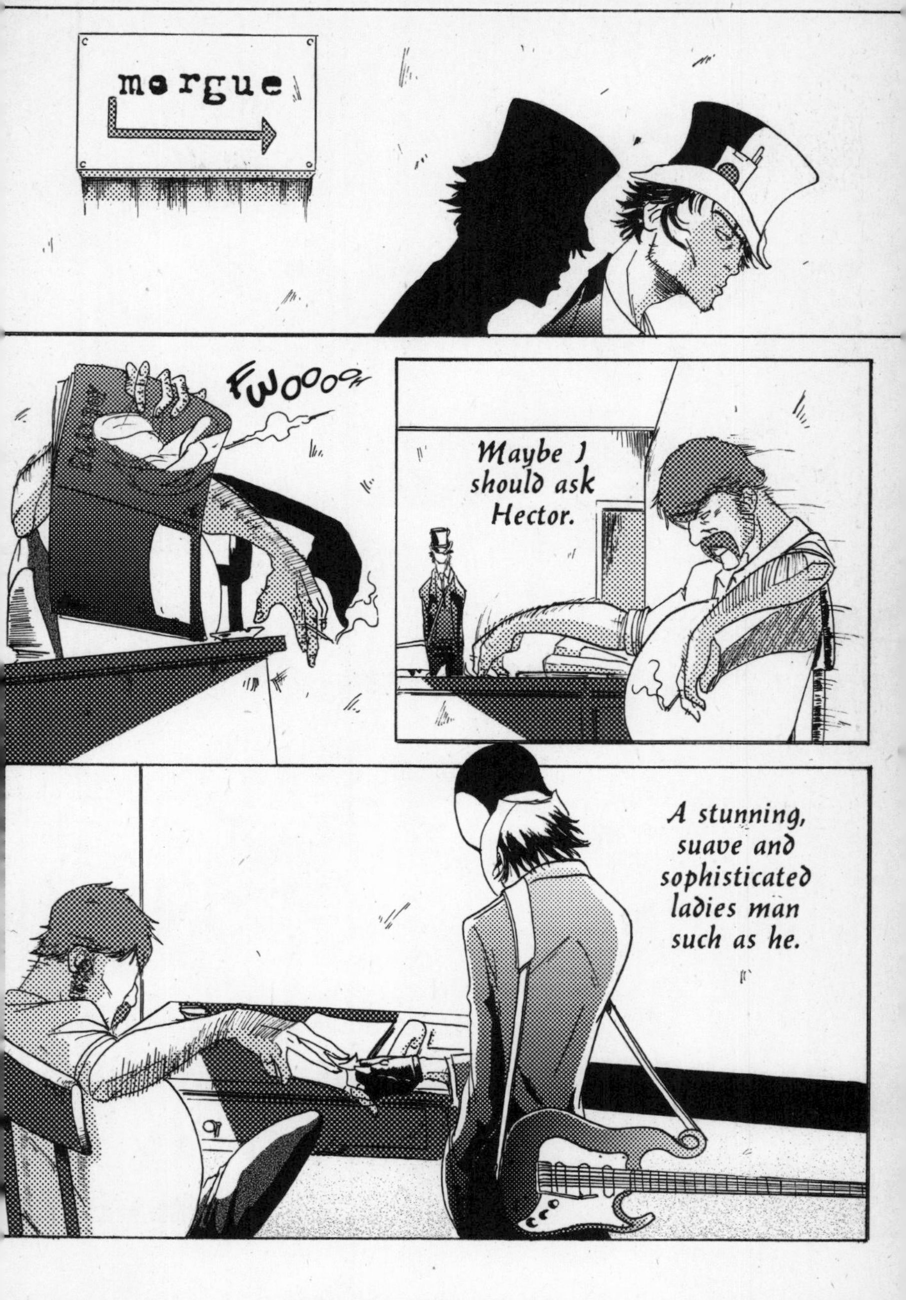
morgue
FWOOOOH
Maybe I should ask Hector.
A stunning, suave and sophisticated ladies man such as he.

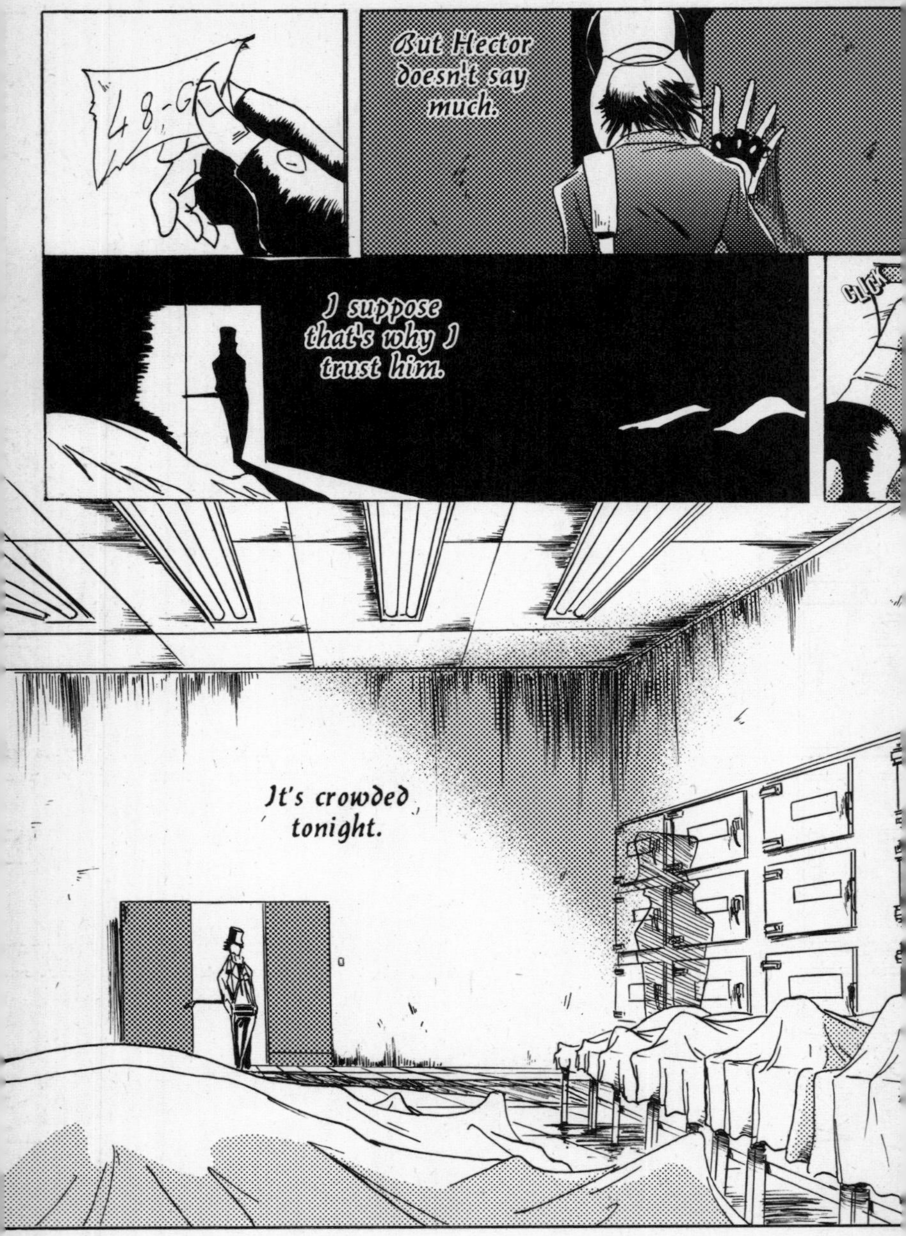

But Hector doesn't say much.
48-G
CLICK
I suppose that's why I trust him.
It's crowded tonight.

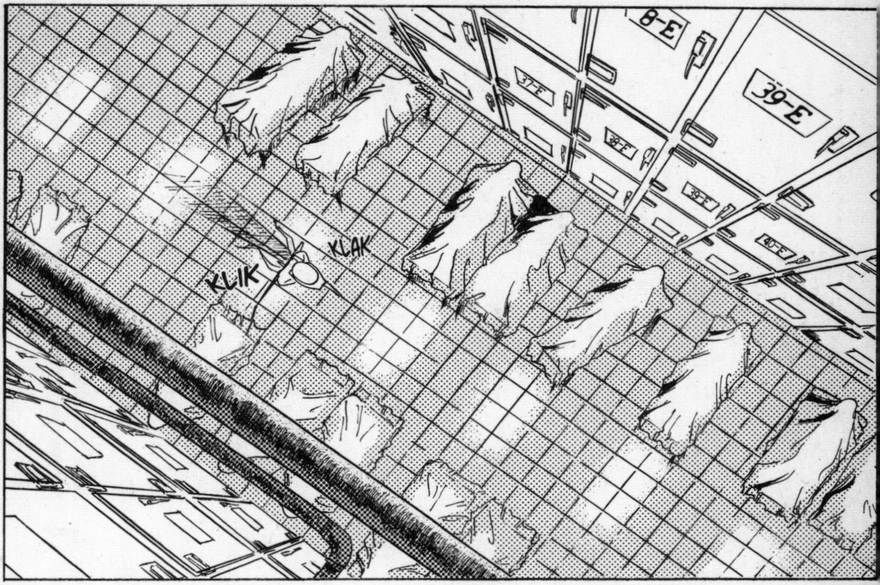
8-E
39-E
37-F
38-F
39-F
40-F
KLIK
KLAK

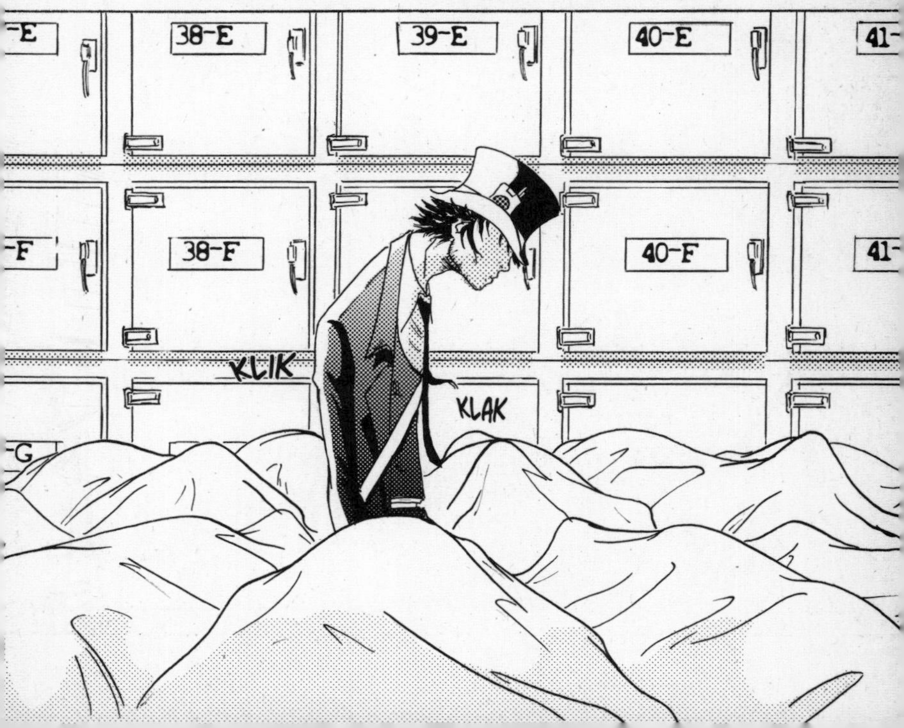
38-E
39-E
40-E
38-F
40-F
KLIK
KLAK

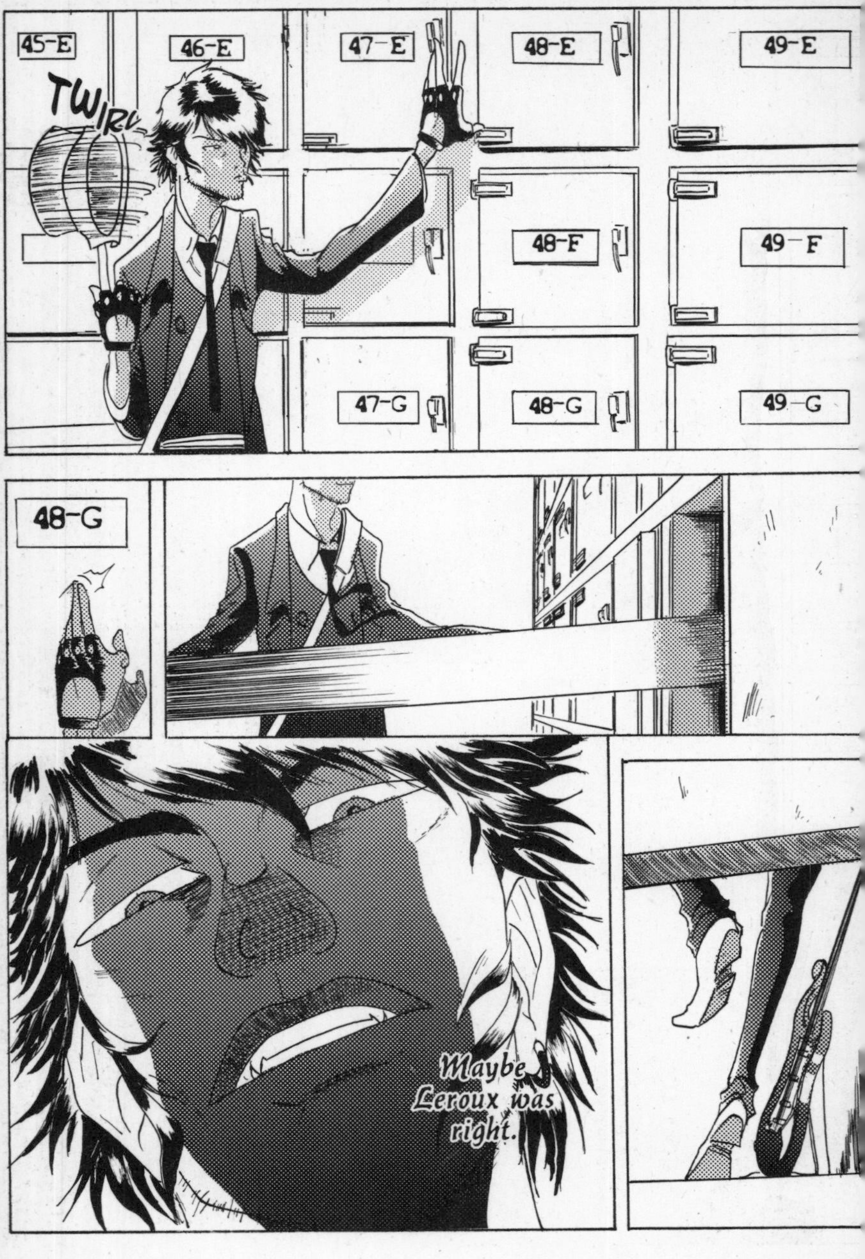
49-E
48-E
47-E
46-E
45-E
TWIRL
49-F
48-F
49-G
48-G
47-G
48-G
Maybe Leroux was right.

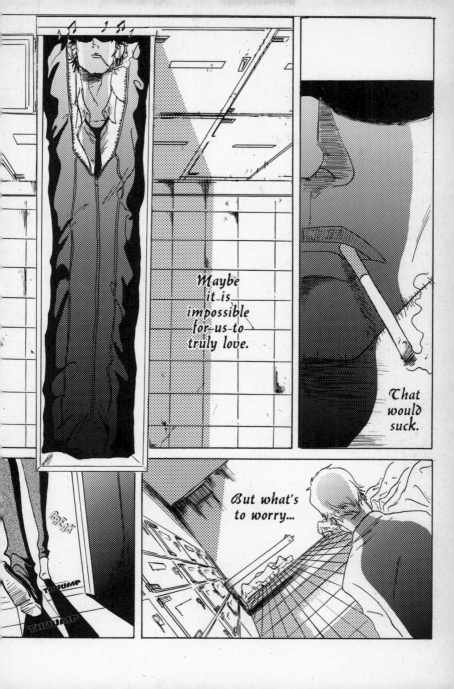

Maybe it is impossible for us to truly love.

That would suck.

But what's to worry...

BREAK

THUMP

THUMP

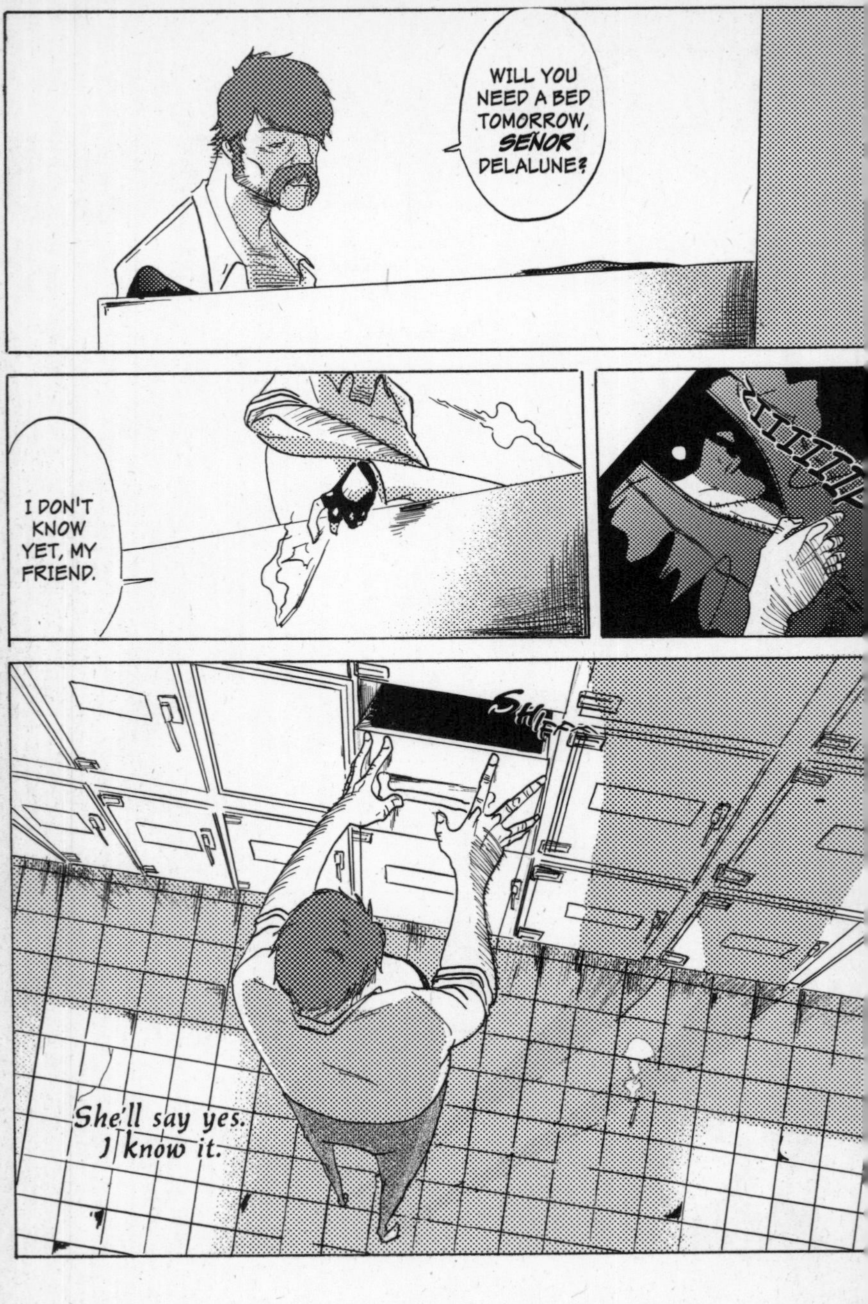
WILL YOU NEED A BED TOMORROW, *SEÑOR* DELALUNE?
I DON'T KNOW YET, MY FRIEND.
She'll say yes. I know it.

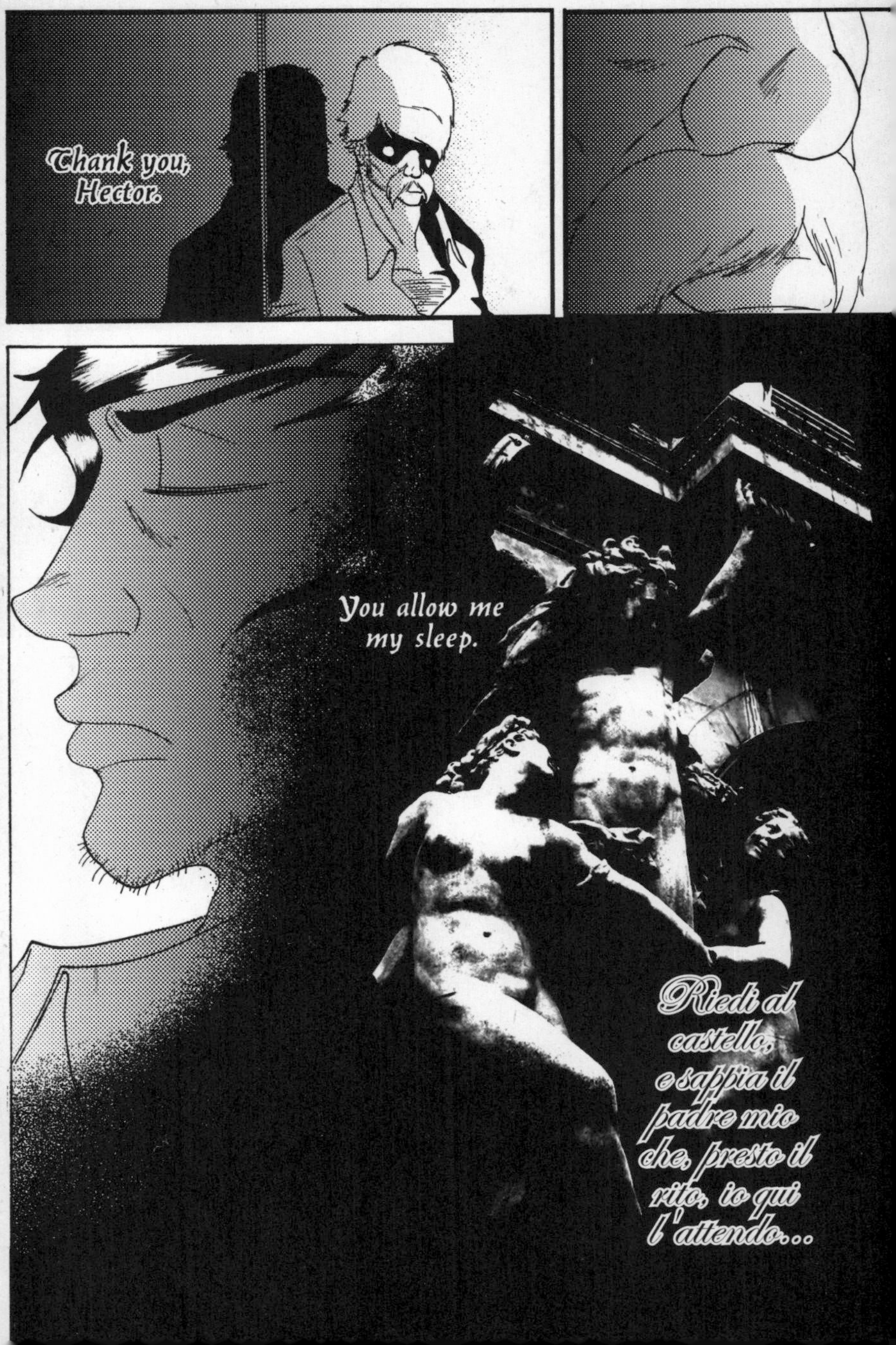
Thank you, Hector.
You allow me my sleep.
Riedi al castello, e sappia il padre mio che, presto il rito, io qui l'attendo...

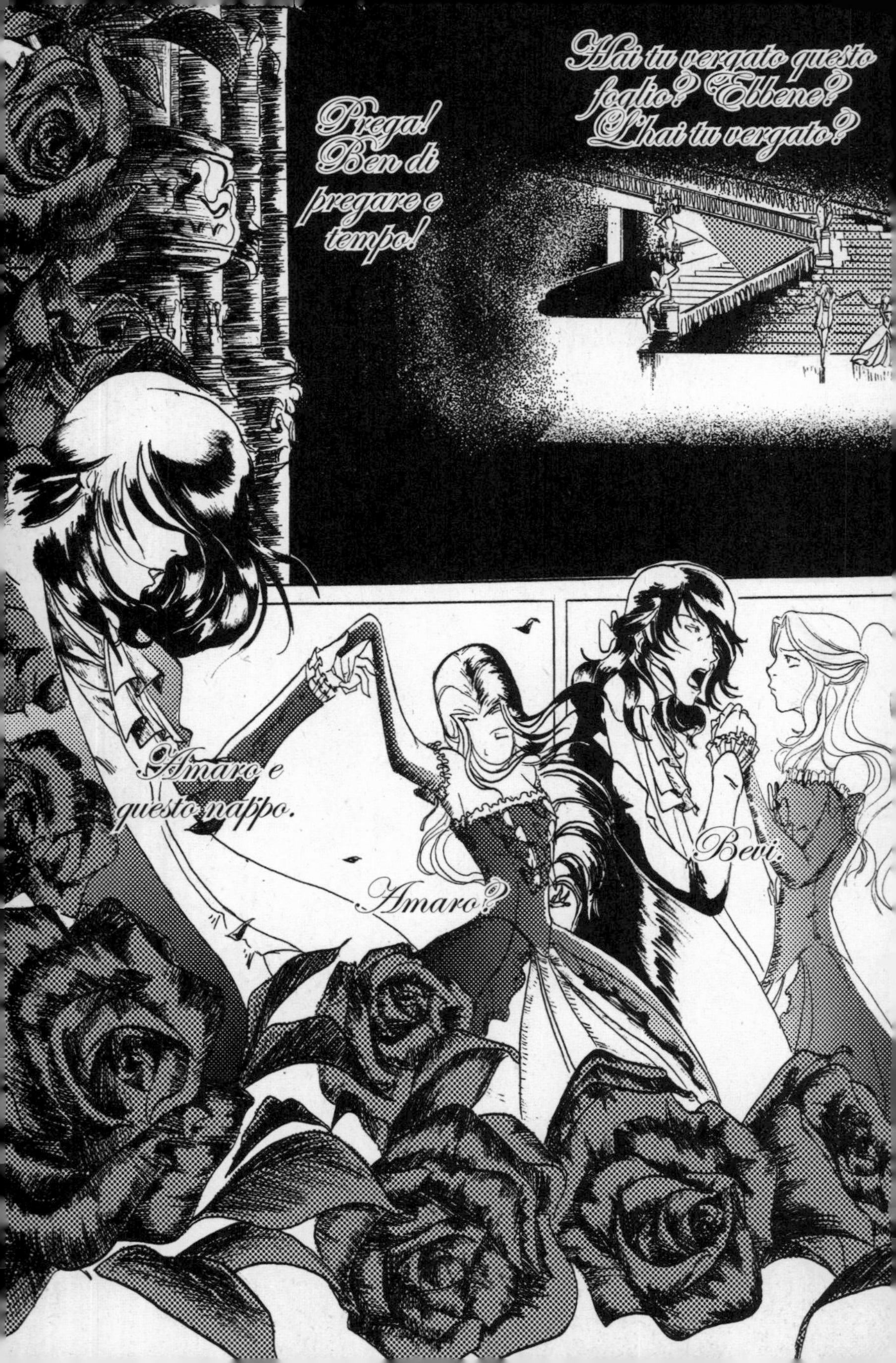
Hai tu vergato questo foglio? Ebbene? L'hai tu vergato?
Prega! Ben di pregare e tempo!
Bevi.
Amaro?
Amaro e questo nappo.

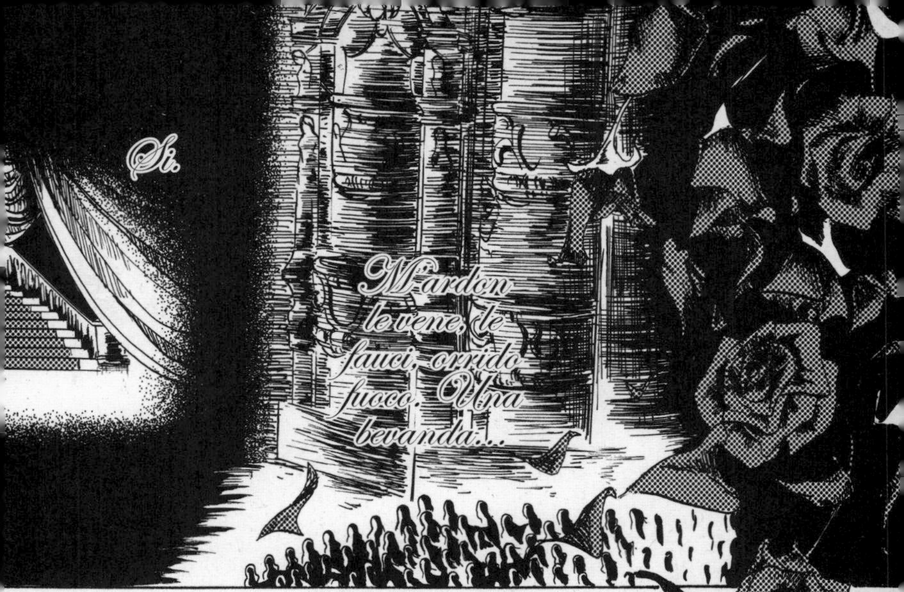
Sì.
M'ardon le vene, le fauci, orrido fuoco. Una bevanda...

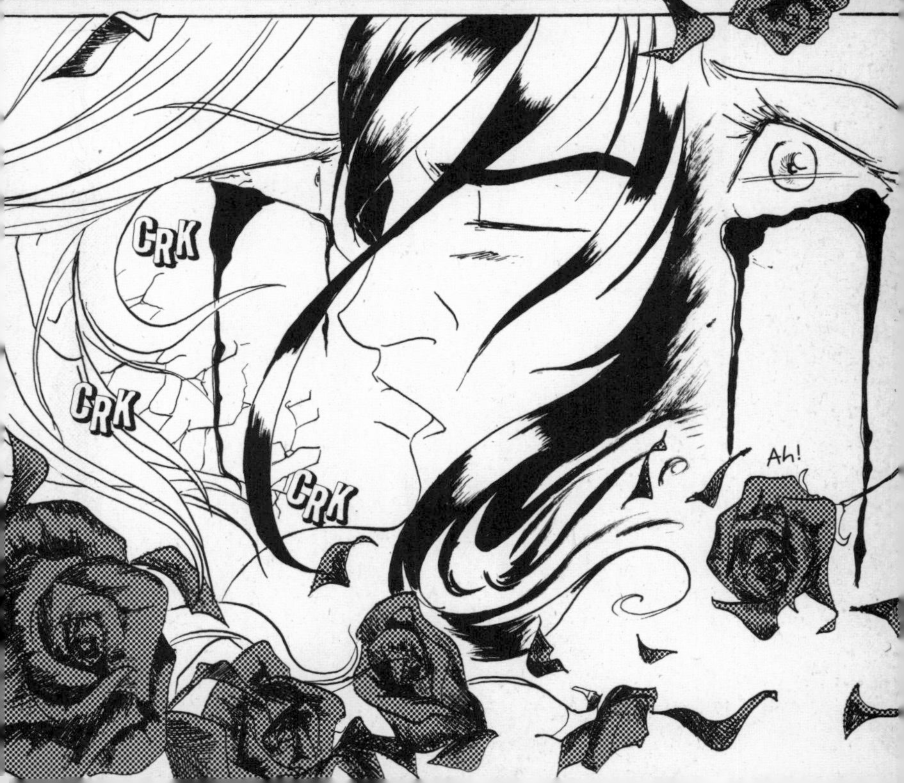
CRK
CRK
CRK
Ah!

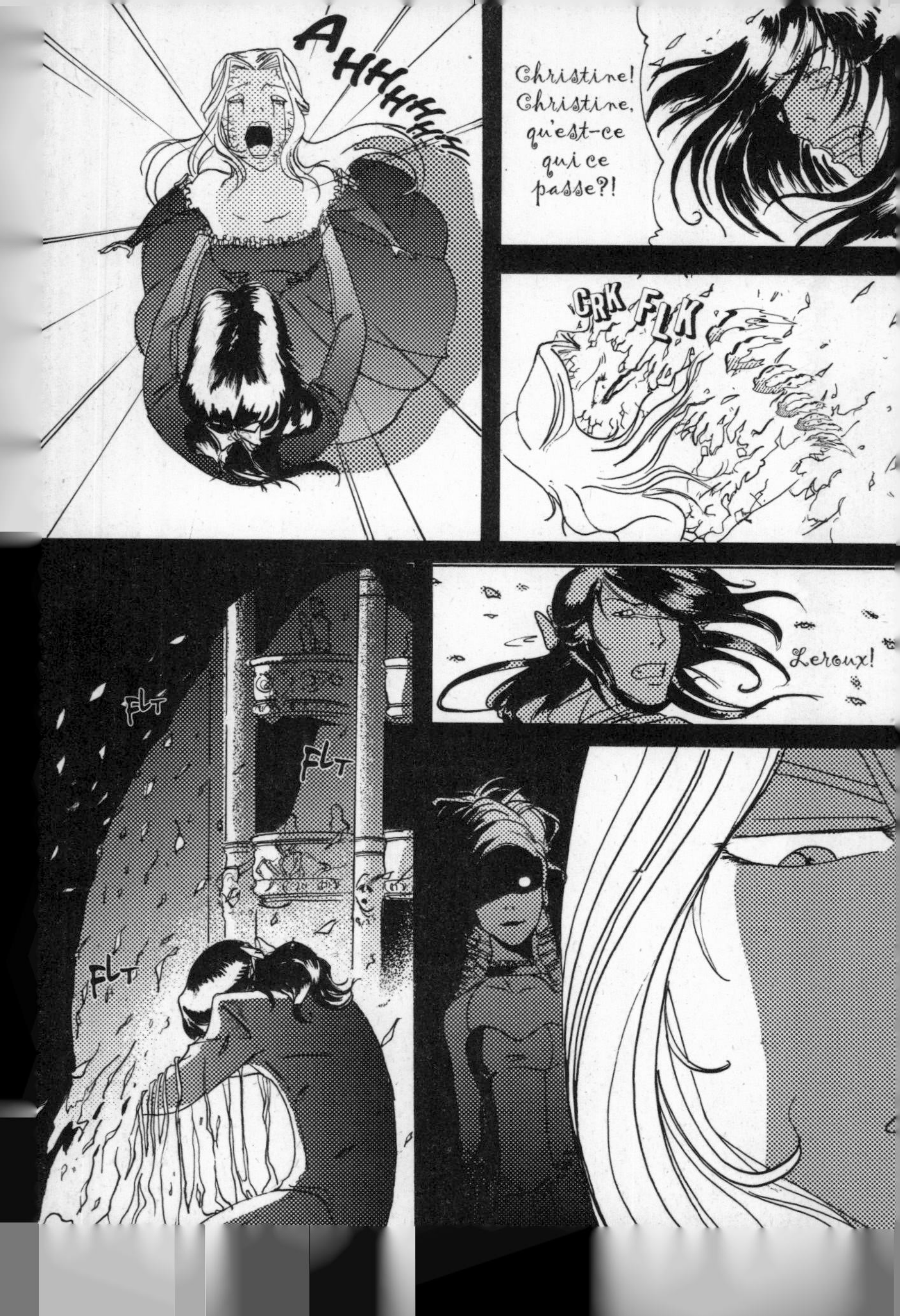
Christine! Christine, qu'est-ce qui ce passe?!
CRK FLK
AHHHHHH!!
Leroux!
FLT
FLT
FLT

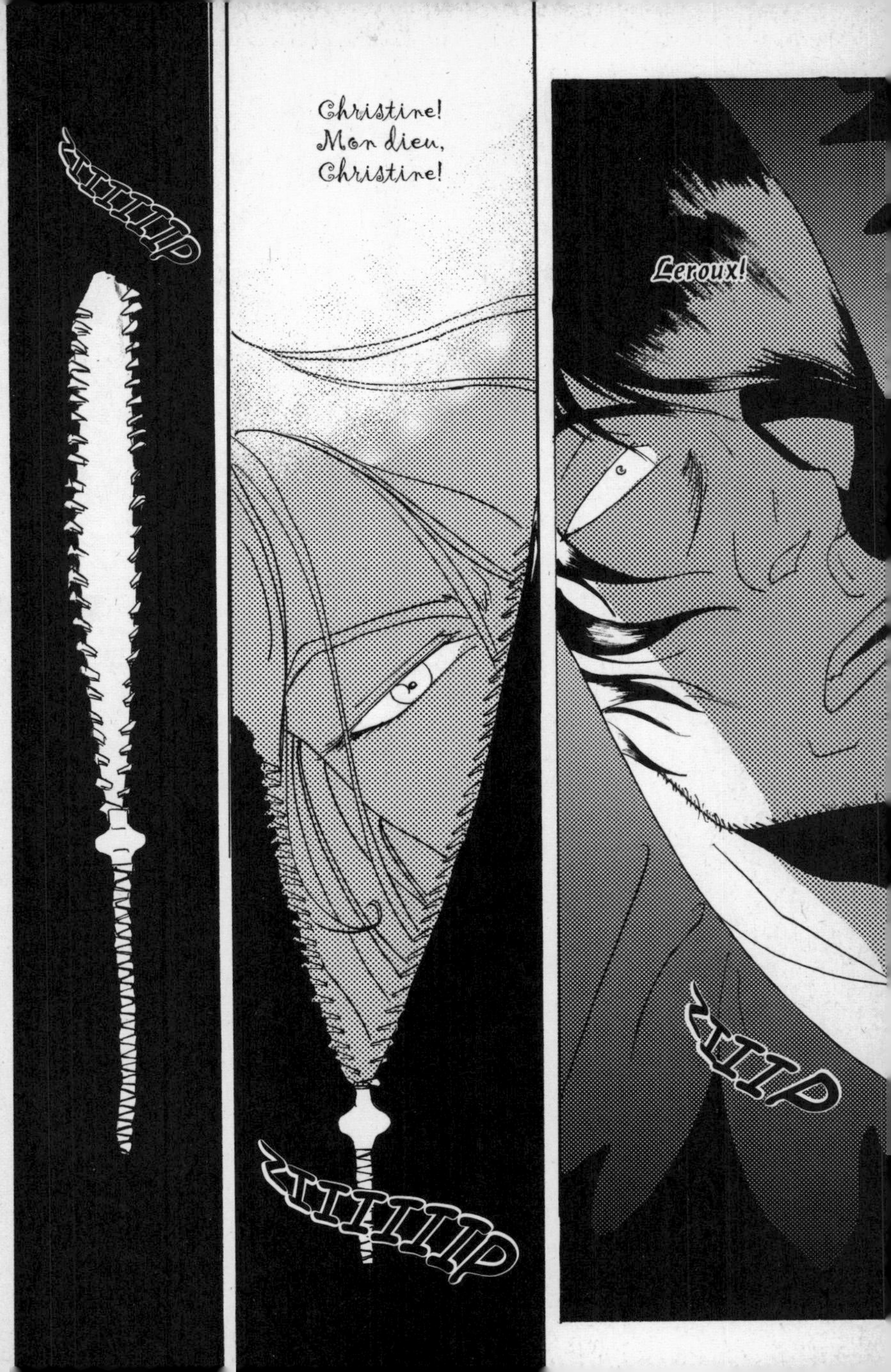
ZIIIIIP
Christine! Mon dieu, Christine!
ZIIIIIIP
Leroux!
ZIIIP

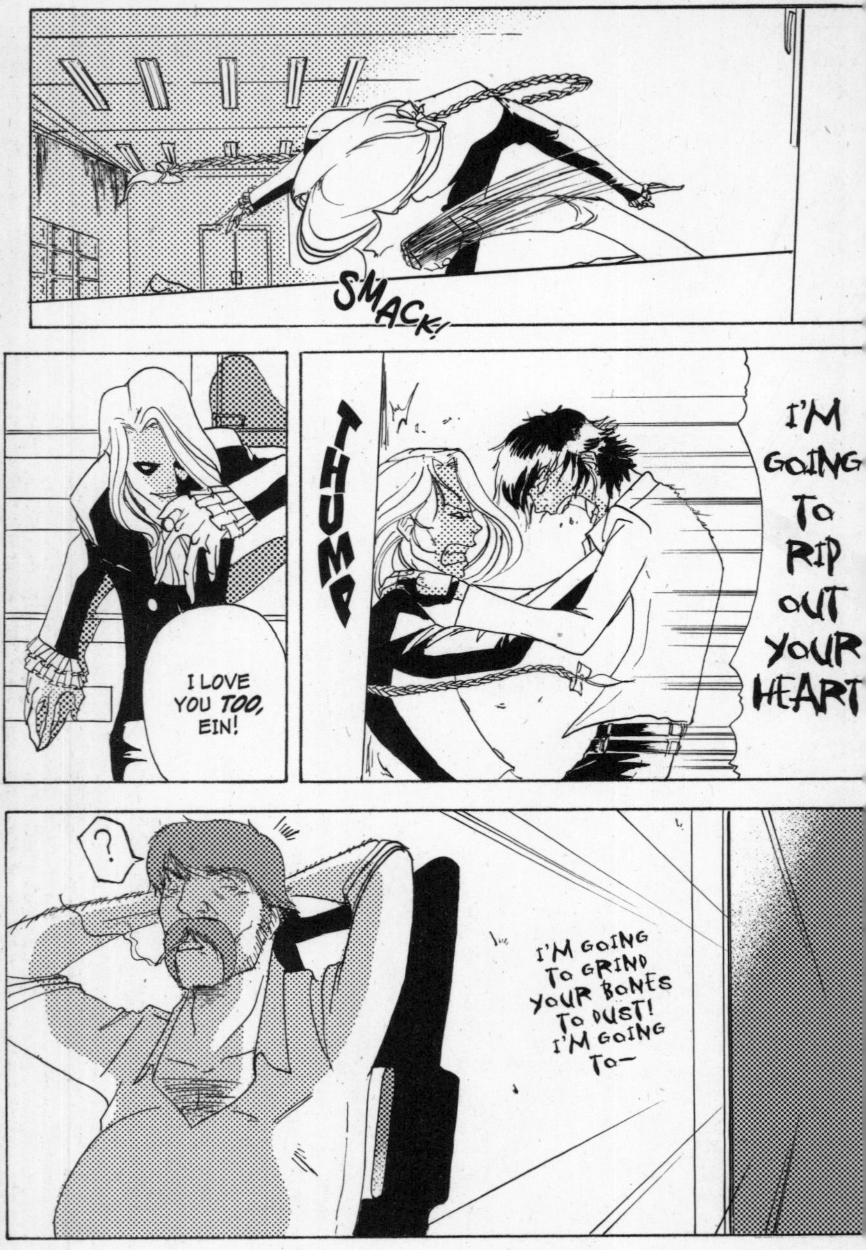
SMACK!
THUMP
I'M GOING TO RIP OUT YOUR HEART
I LOVE YOU *TOO,* EIN!
?
I'M GOING TO GRIND YOUR BONES TO DUST! I'M GOING TO—

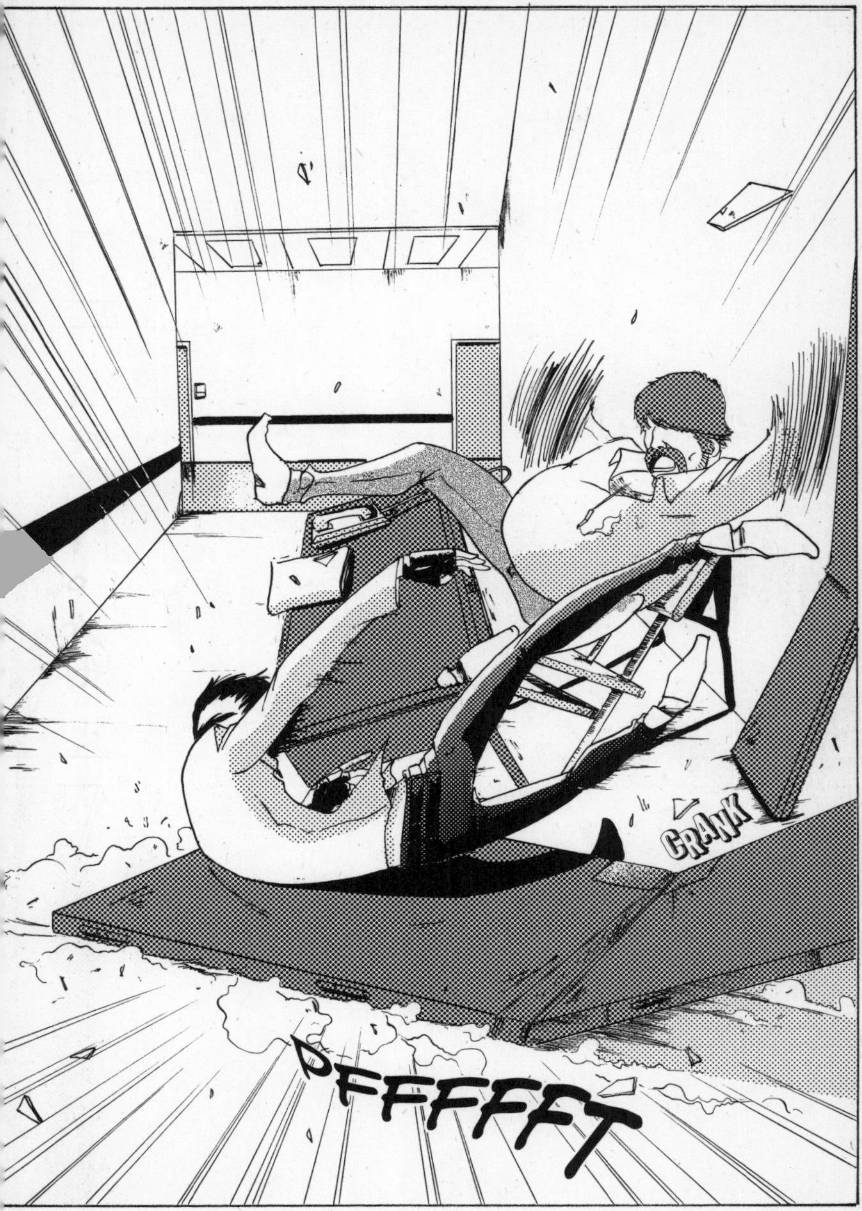
CRANK
PFFFFFT

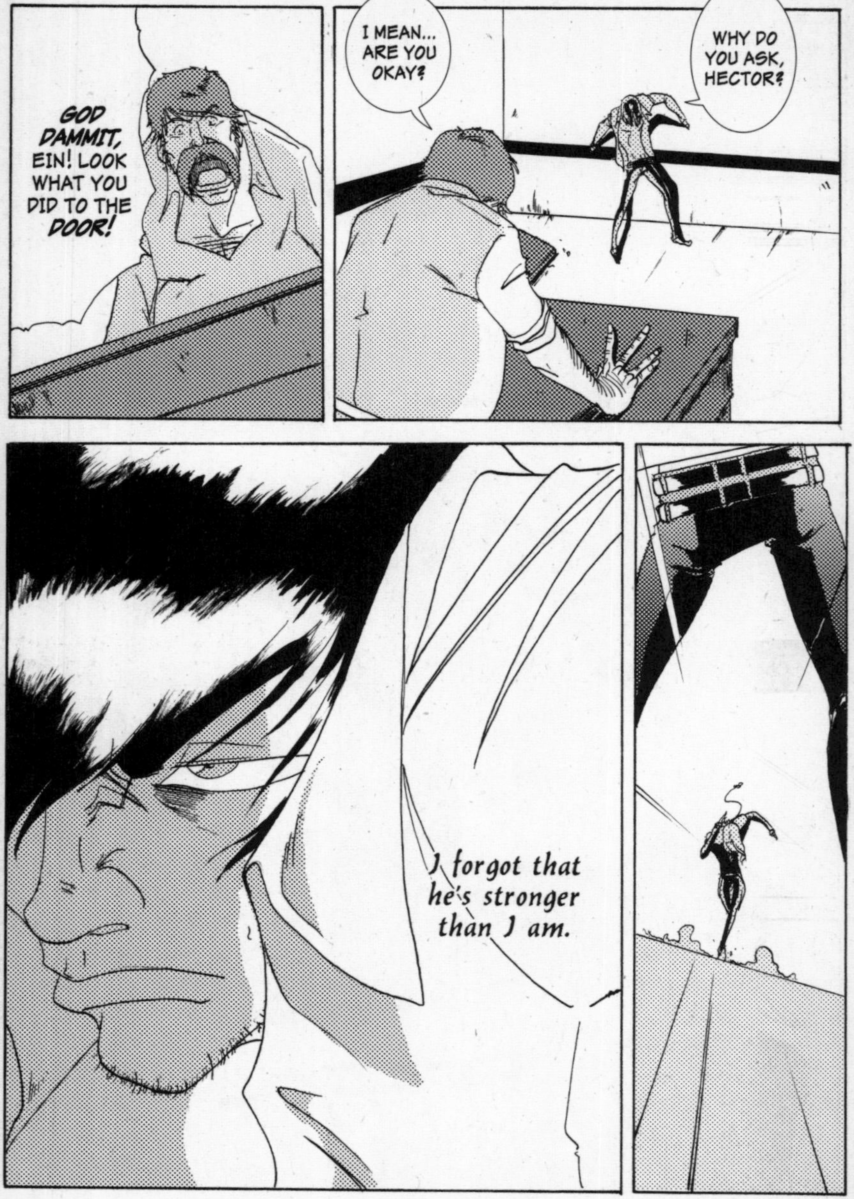
GOD DAMMIT, EIN! LOOK WHAT YOU DID TO THE DOOR!
I MEAN... ARE YOU OKAY?
WHY DO YOU ASK, HECTOR?
I forgot that he's stronger than I am.

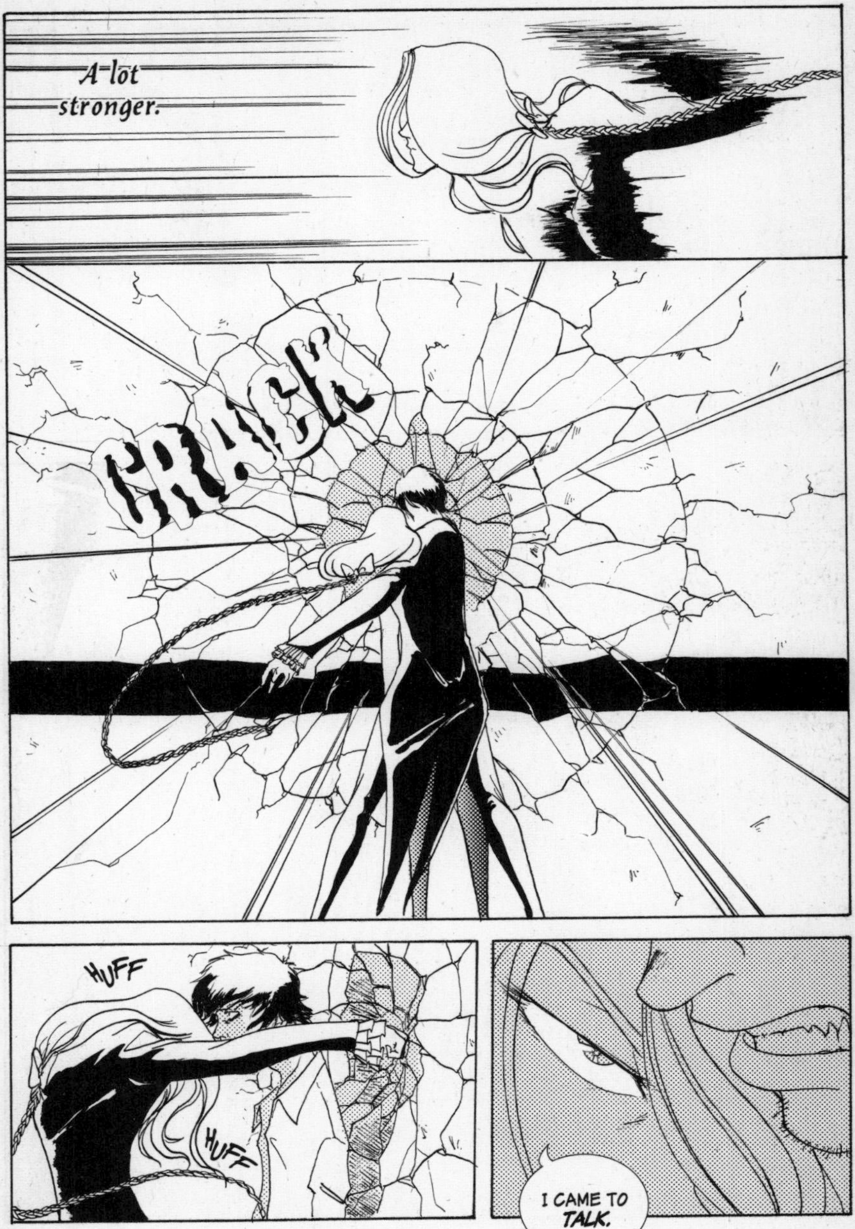
A lot stronger.
CRACK
I CAME TO TALK.
HUFF
HUFF

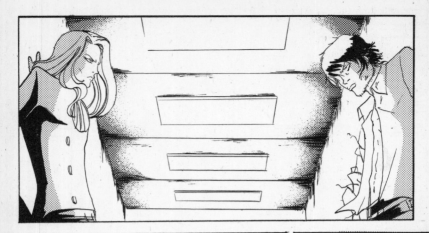

AGGGGHHHHH!

OH, EIN.

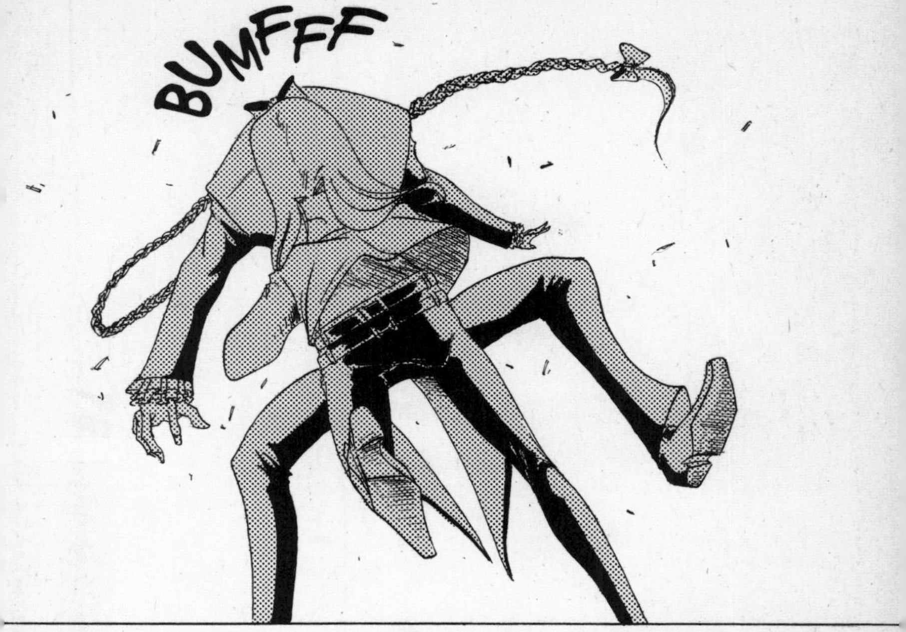
BUMFFF
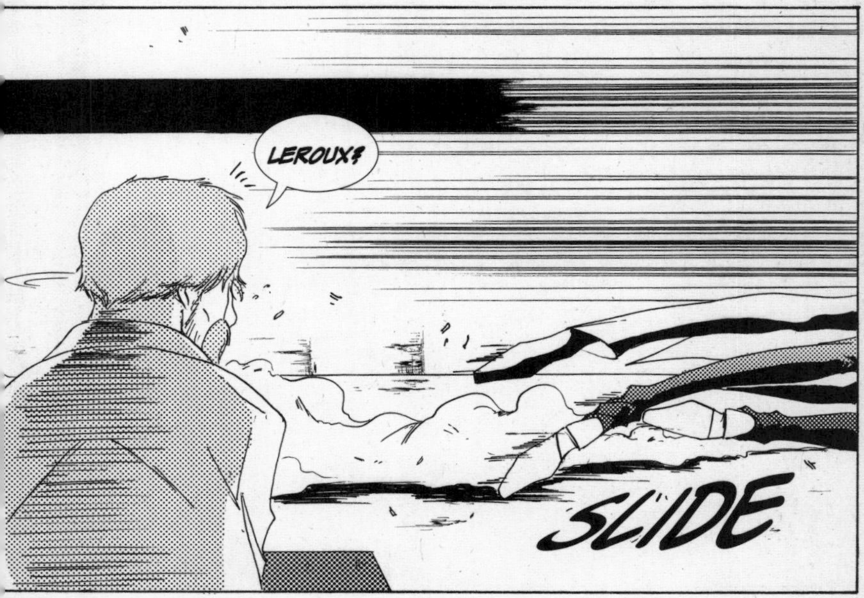
LEROUX!
SLIDE

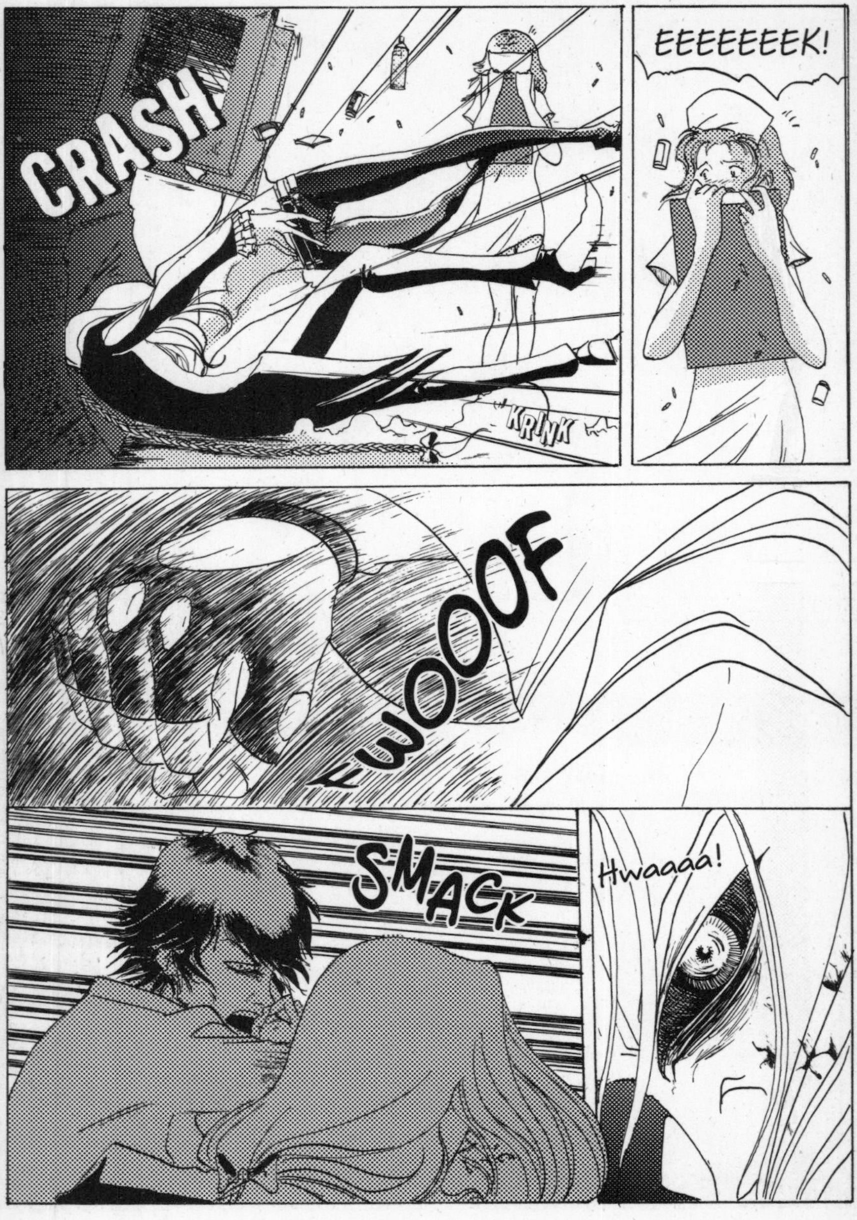
EEEEEEEK!
CRASH
KRINK
FWOOOF
Hwaaaa!
SMACK

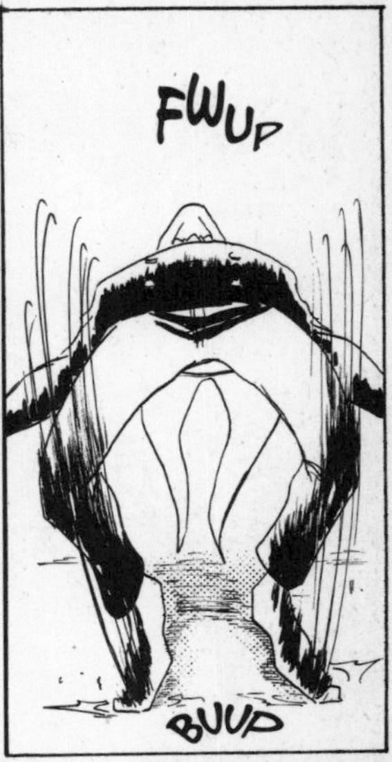
FWUP
BUUP
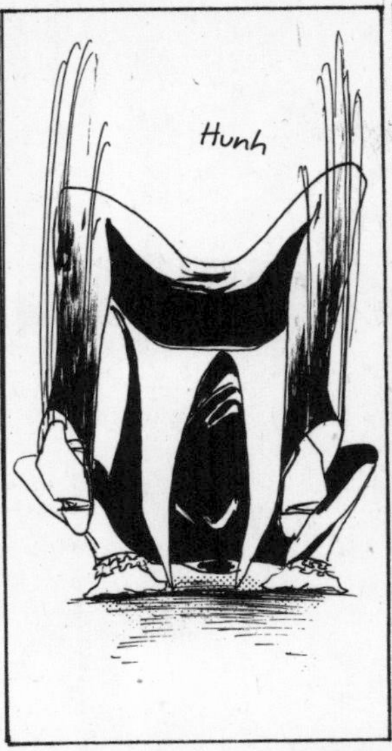
Hunh
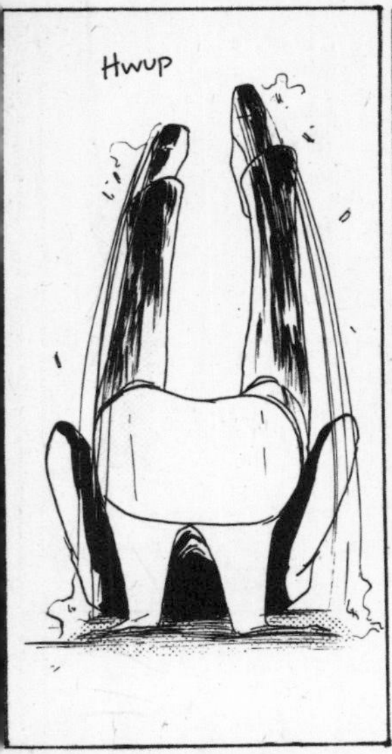
Hwup
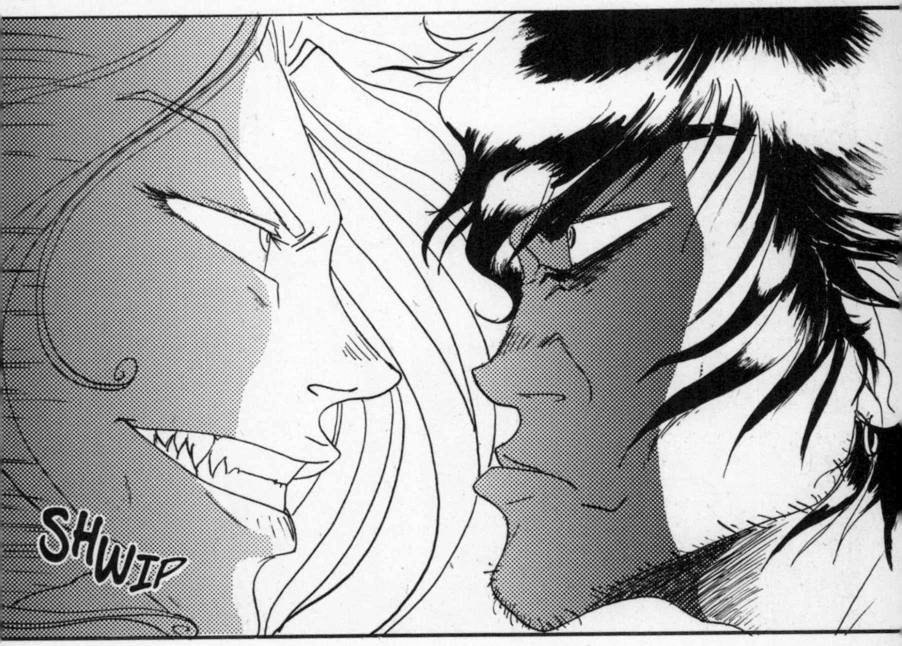
SHWIP

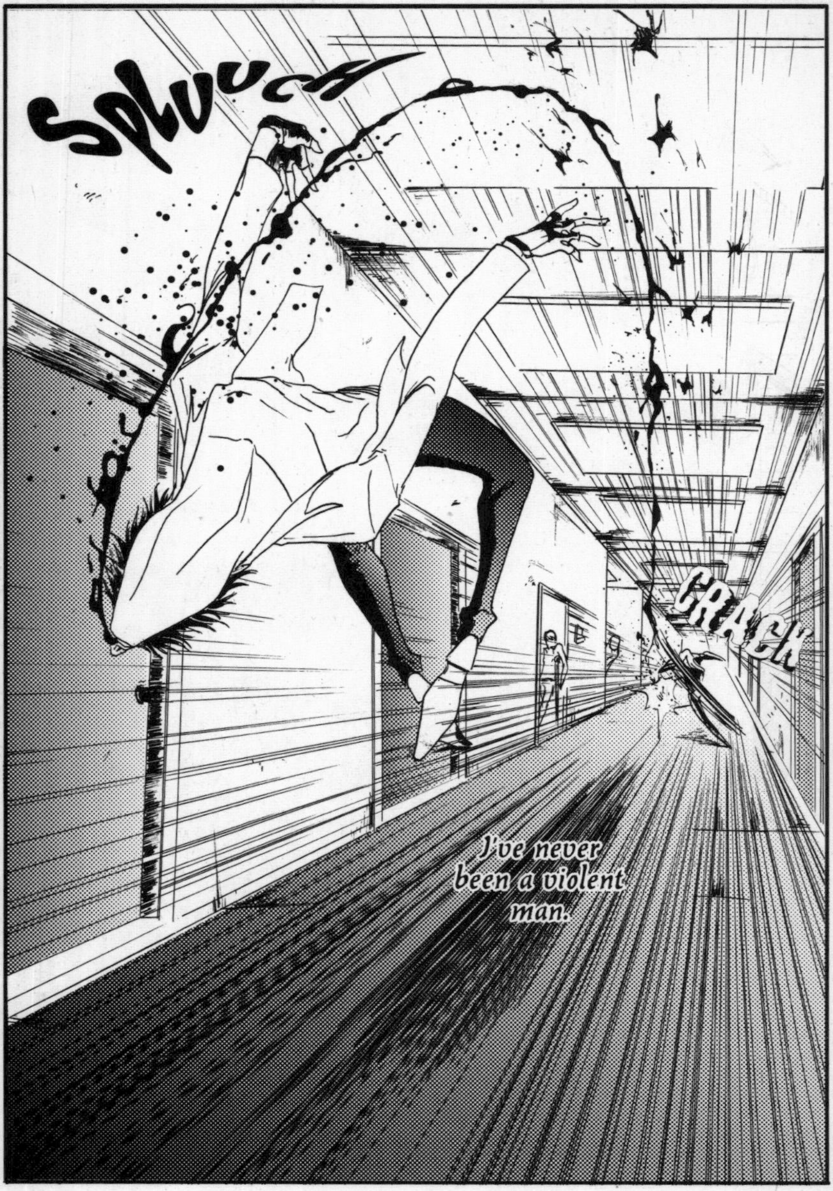
SPLUUCH
CRACK
I've never been a violent man.

BZZZTZZZZ!

ANOTHER SPONGE, NURSE. AH, THERE. YOU HAVE *AMAZING* FINGERS, AMANDINE.

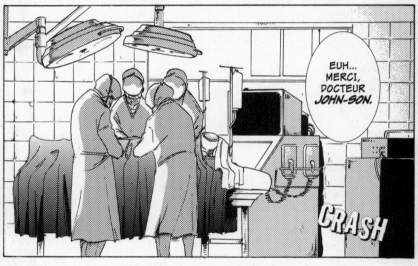

EUH... MERCI, DOCTEUR *JOHN-SON.*

CRASH

Huh?

Uh?

Euh?

*PUBLIC MEDICINE.* LETS IN ALL THE *RIFF-RAFF.*

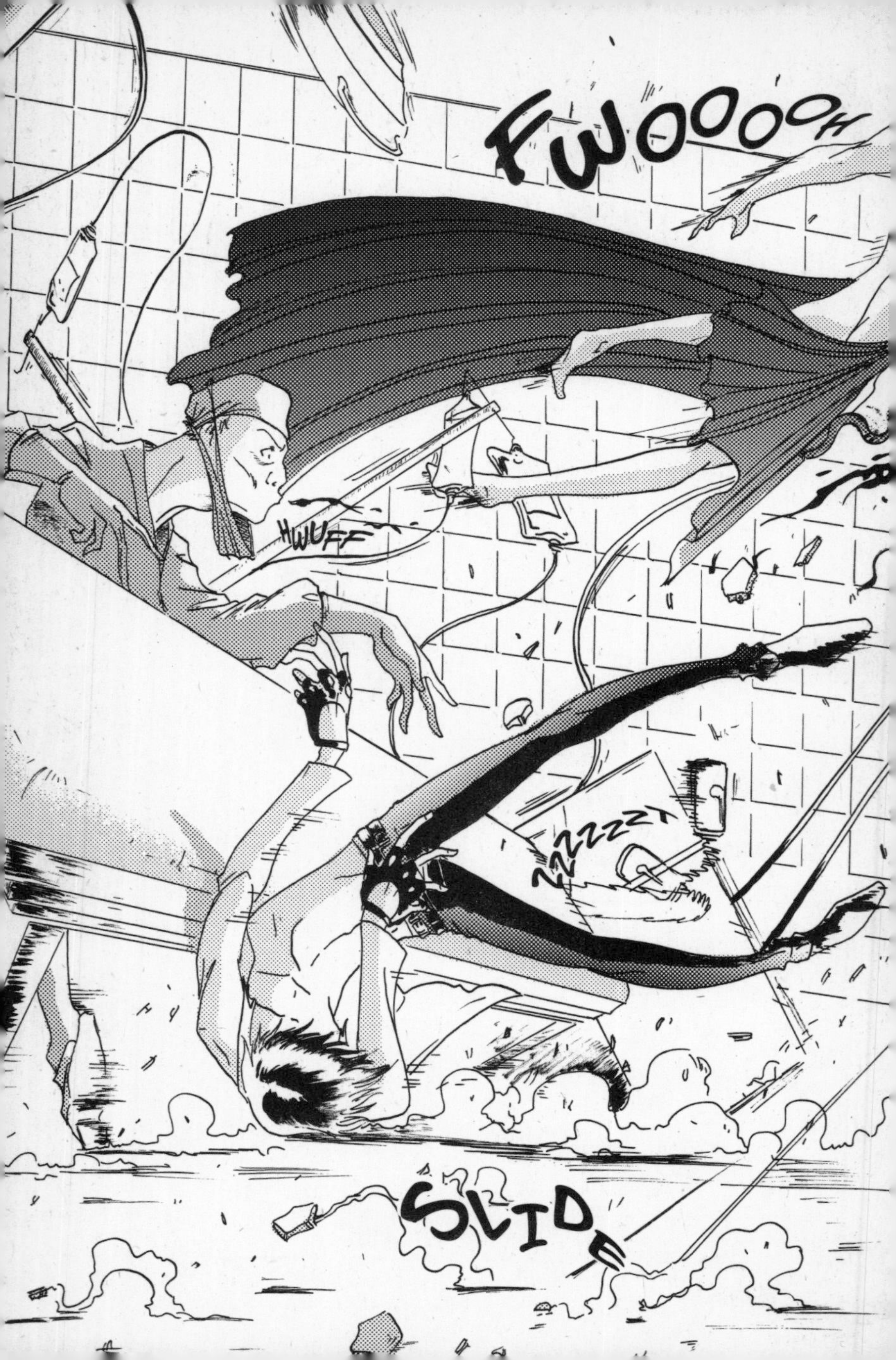
FWOOOOH
HWUFF
ZZZZZZZT
SLIDE

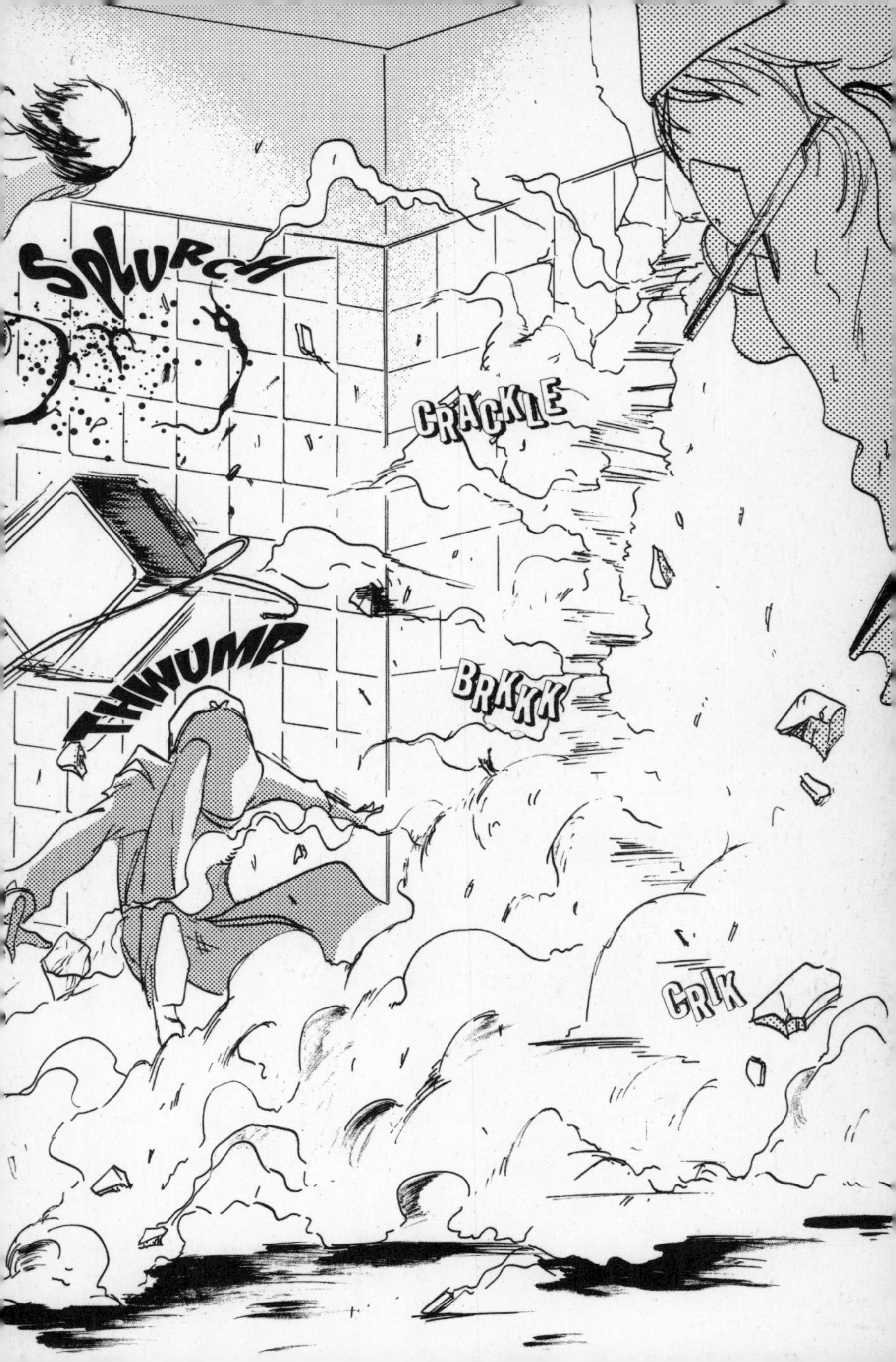
SPLURCH
CRACKLE
BRKKK
THWUMP
CRIK

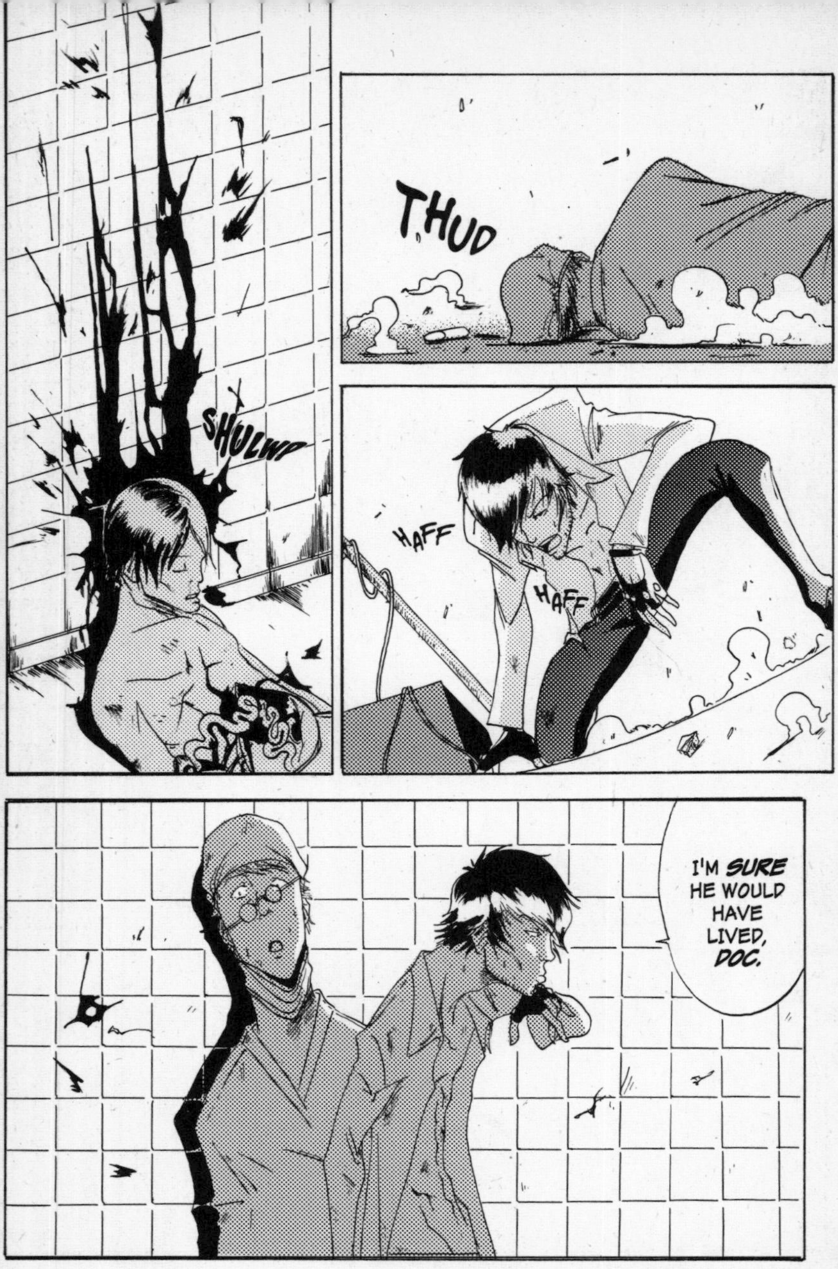
THUD
HAFF
HAFF
SHULWP
I'M SURE HE WOULD HAVE LIVED, DOC.

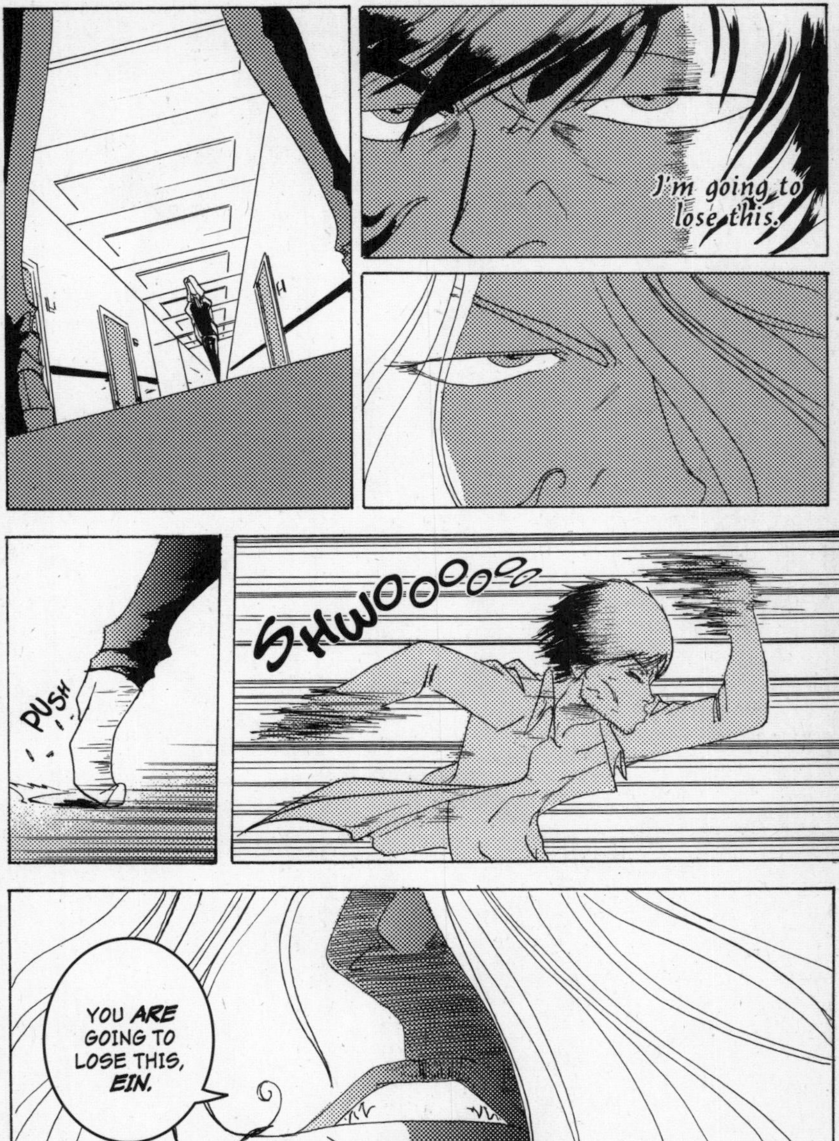
I'm going to lose this.
SHWOOOOOO
PUSH
YOU ARE GOING TO LOSE THIS, EIN.

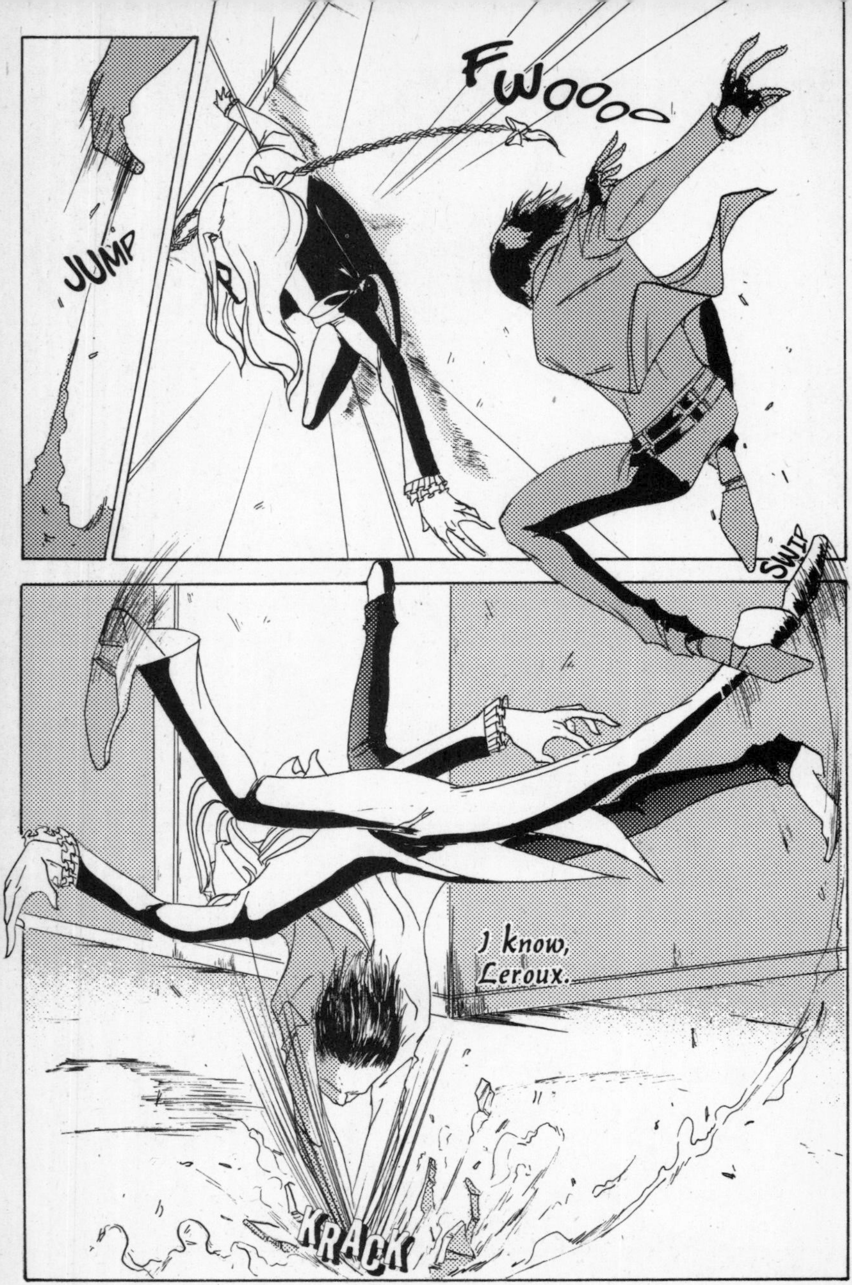
FWOOOO
JUMP
SWIP
I know, Leroux.
KRACK

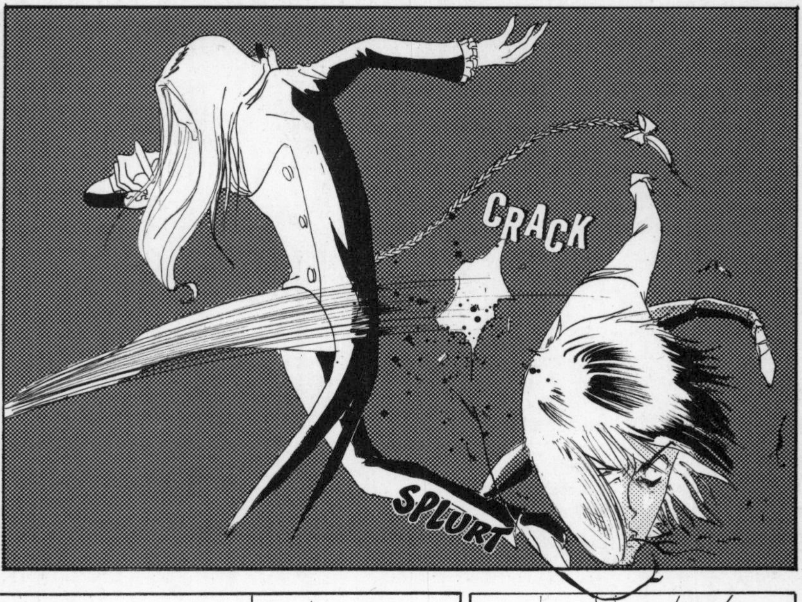
CRACK
SPLURT
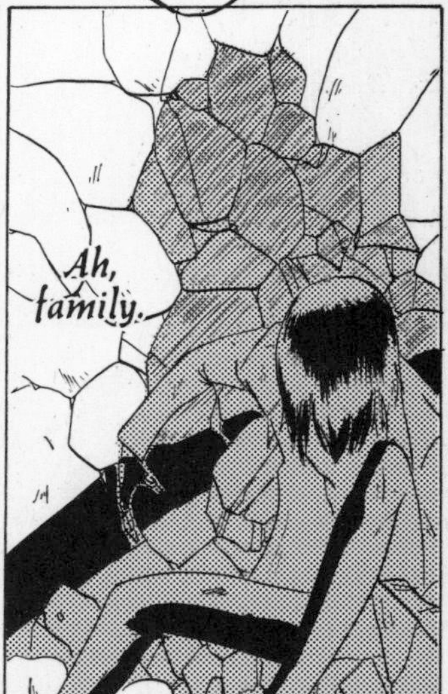
Ah, family.
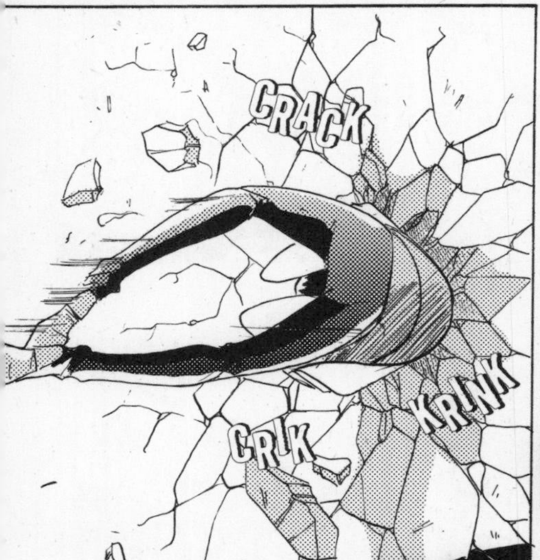
CRACK
KRINK
CRIK

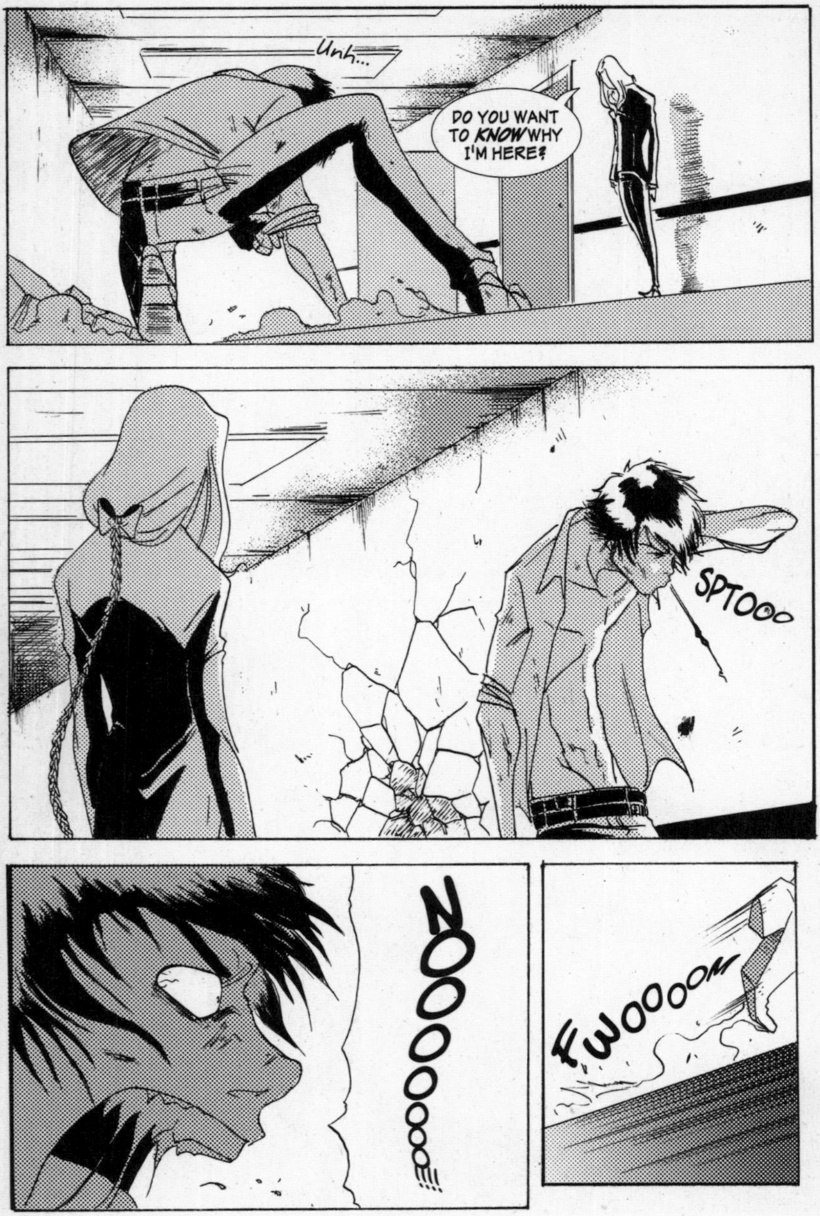
Unh...
DO YOU WANT TO KNOW WHY I'M HERE?
SPTOOO
FWOOOOM
NOOOOOOOOO!!!

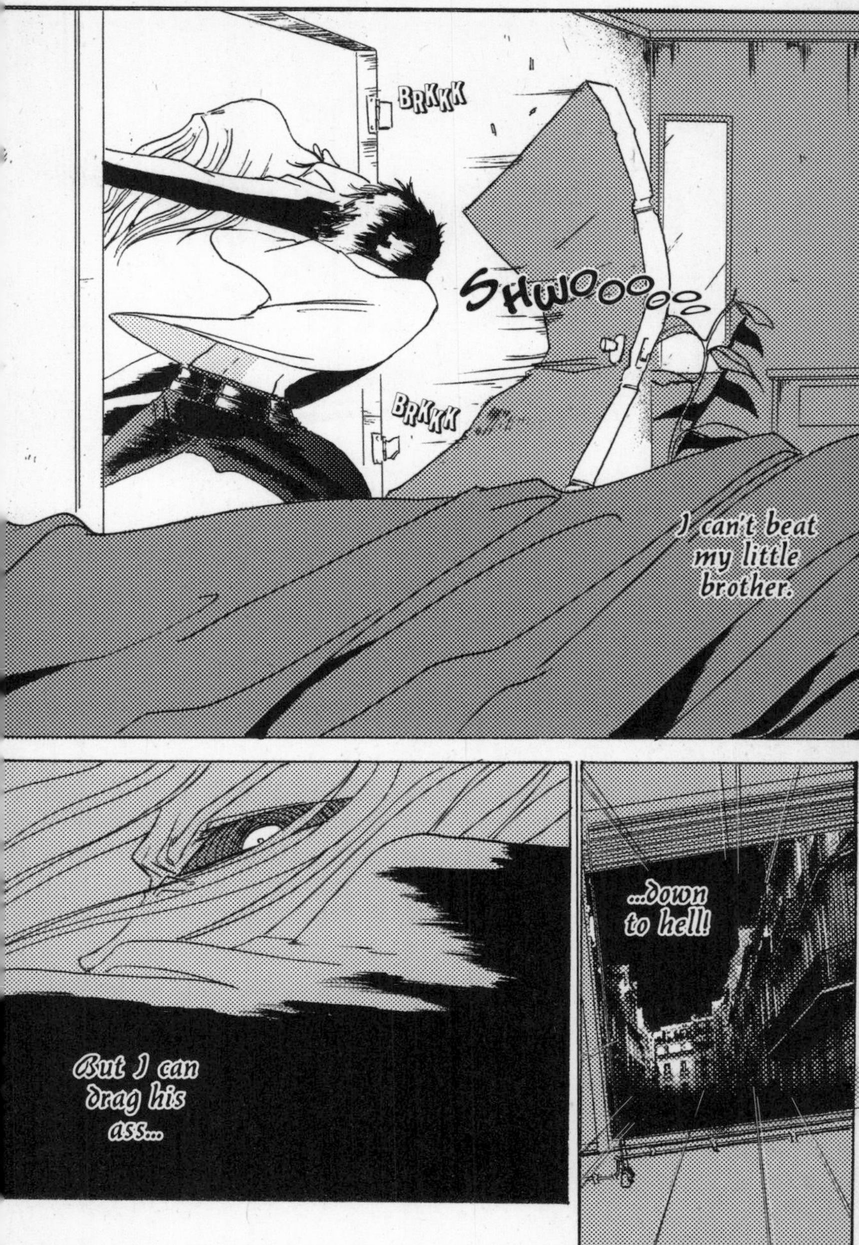
BRKKK
SHWOOOOOOO
BRKKK
I can't beat my little brother.
But I can drag his ass...
...down to hell!

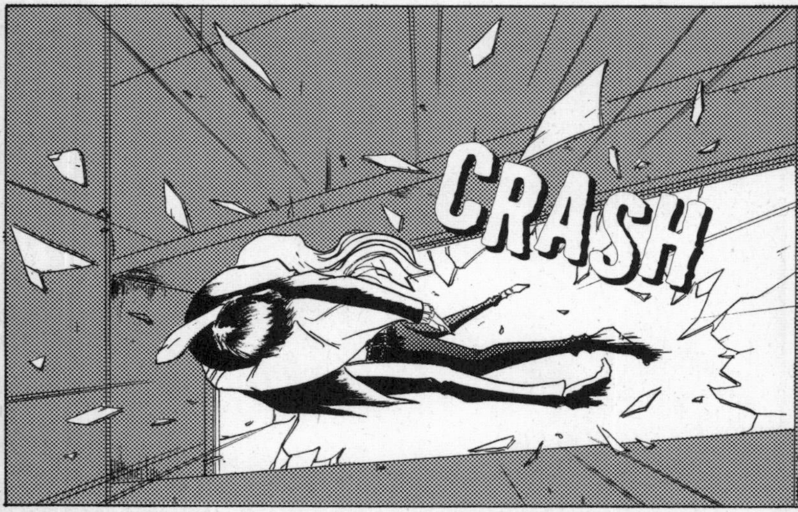
CRASH

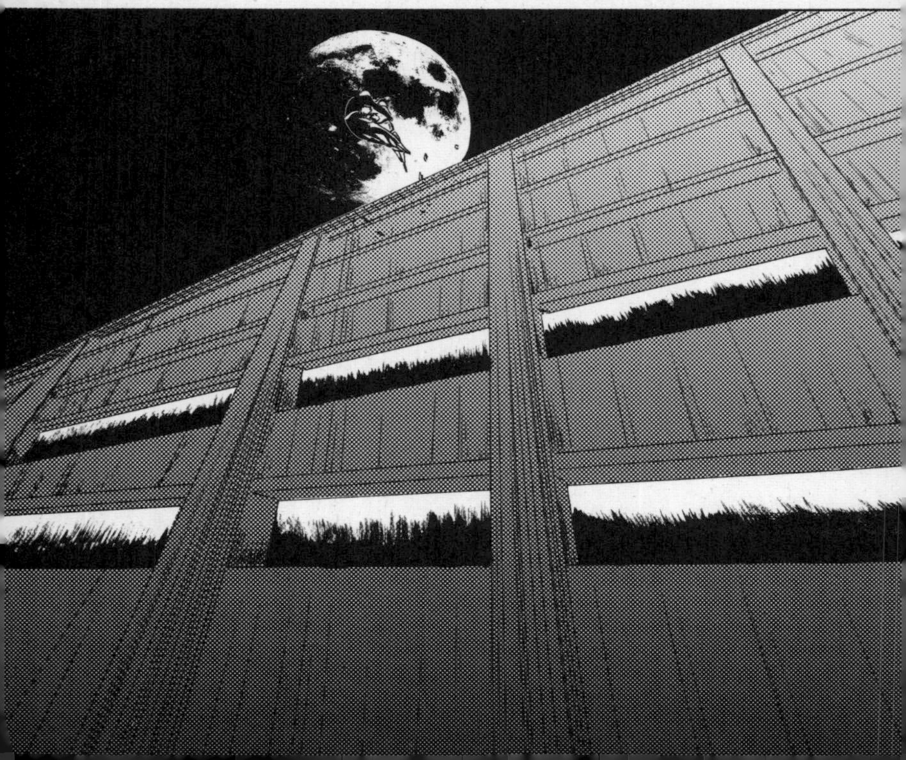

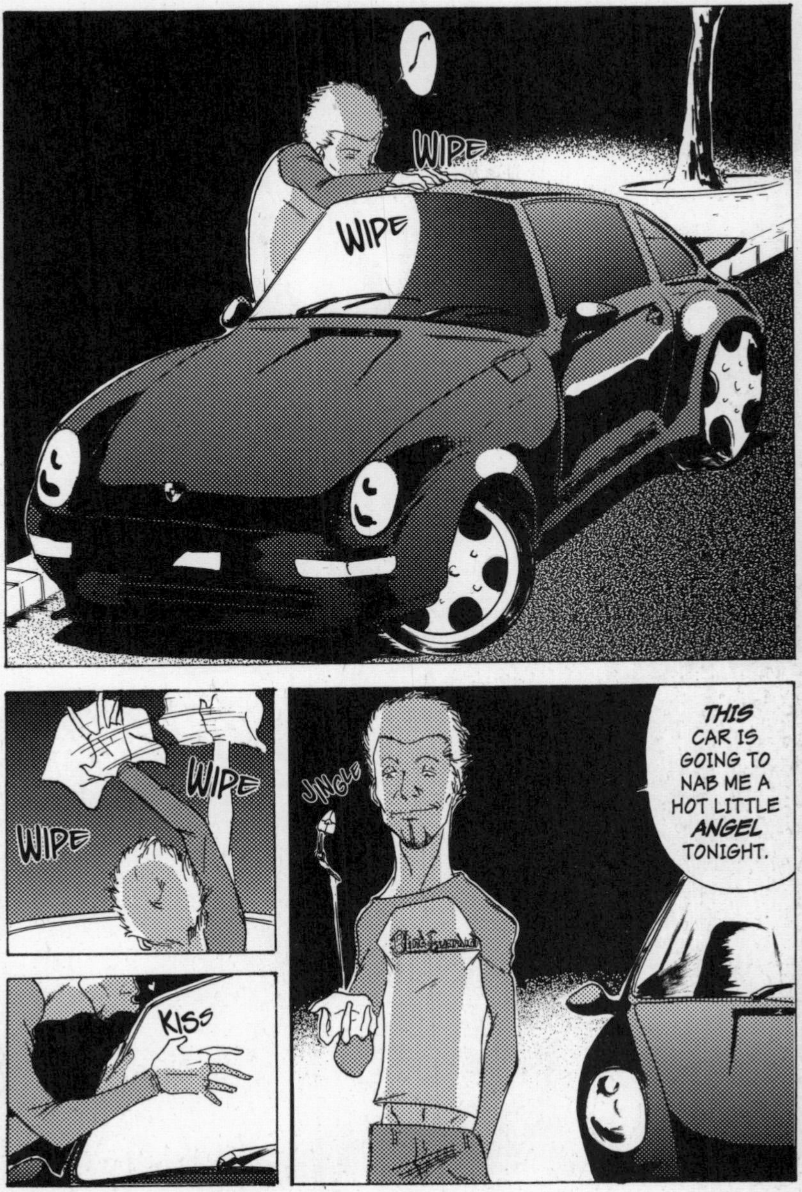
WIPE
WIPE
WIPE
WIPE
KISS
JINGLE
THIS CAR IS GOING TO NAB ME A HOT LITTLE ANGEL TONIGHT.

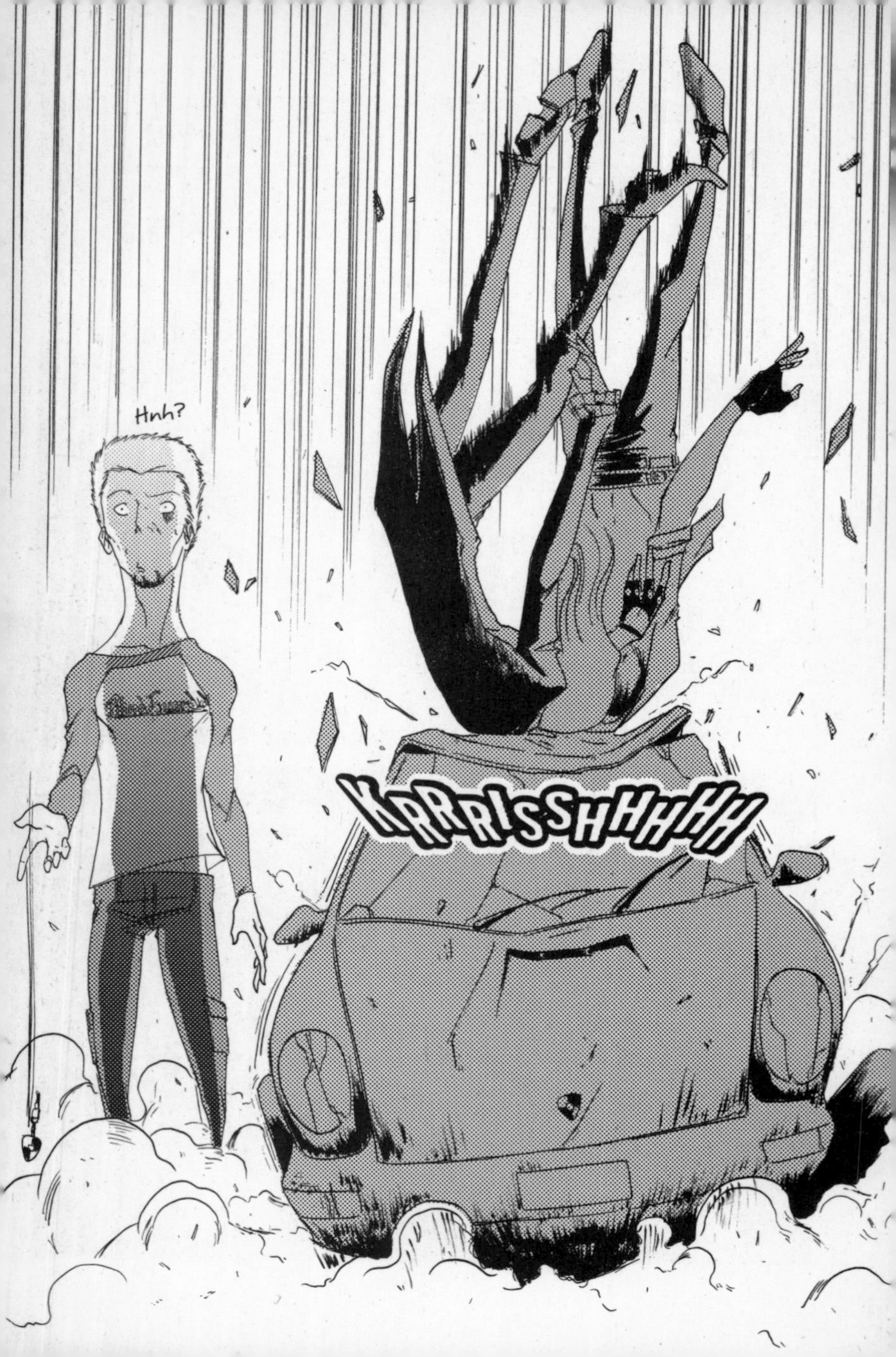
KRRRISSHHHHH
Hnh?

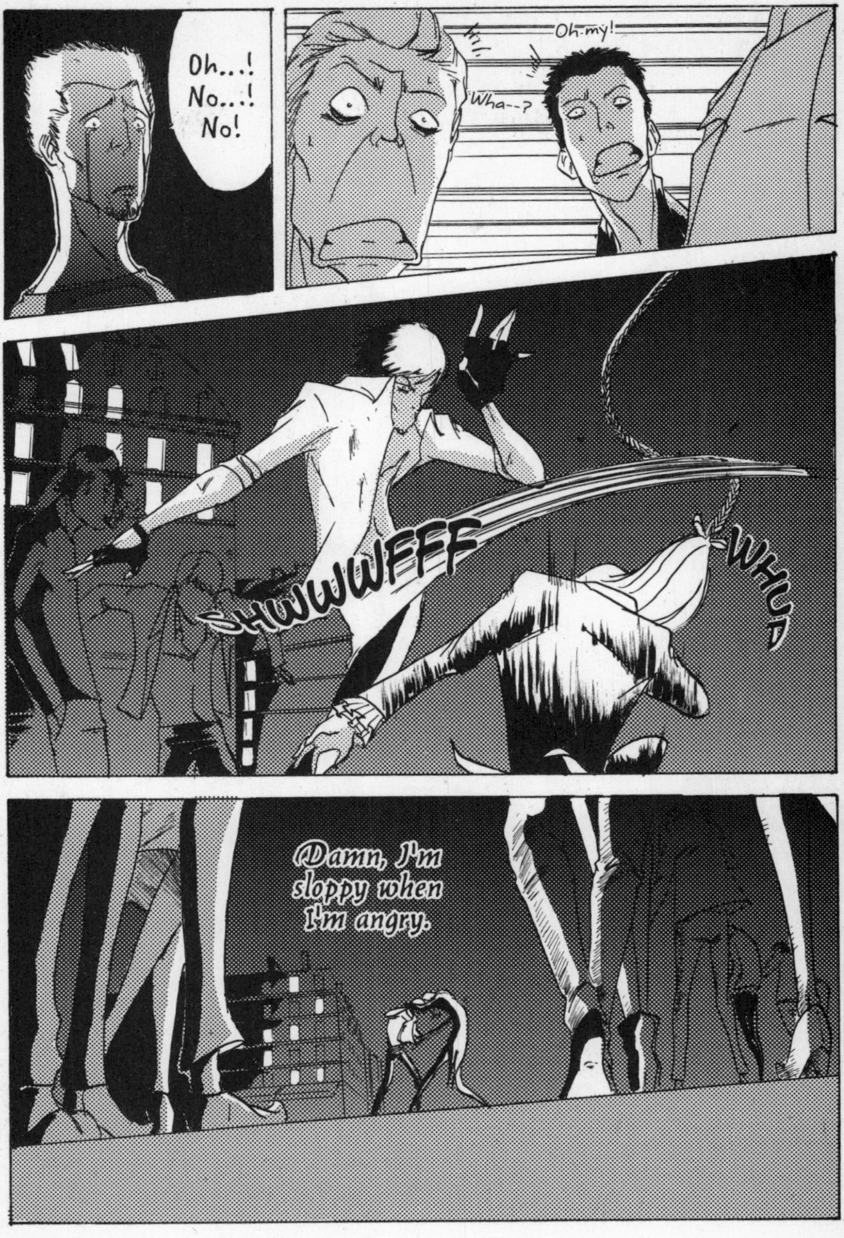
Oh-my!
Wha--?
Oh...! No...! No!
SHWWWFFF
WHUD
Damn, I'm sloppy when I'm angry.

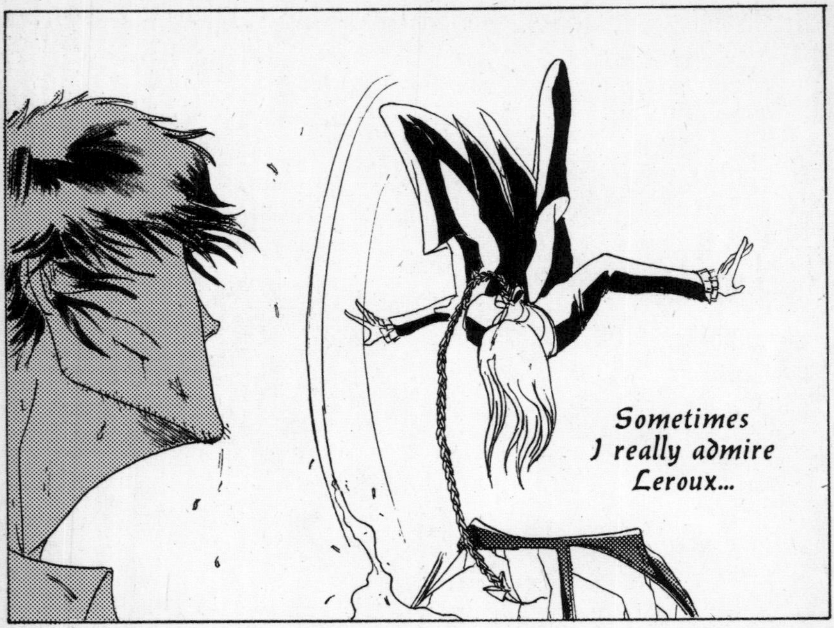
Sometimes
I really admire
Leroux...
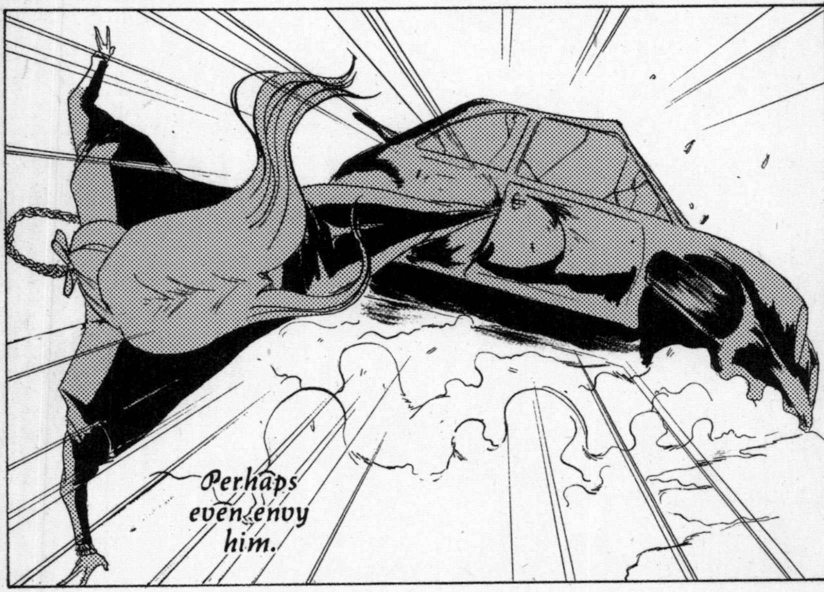
Perhaps
even envy
him.

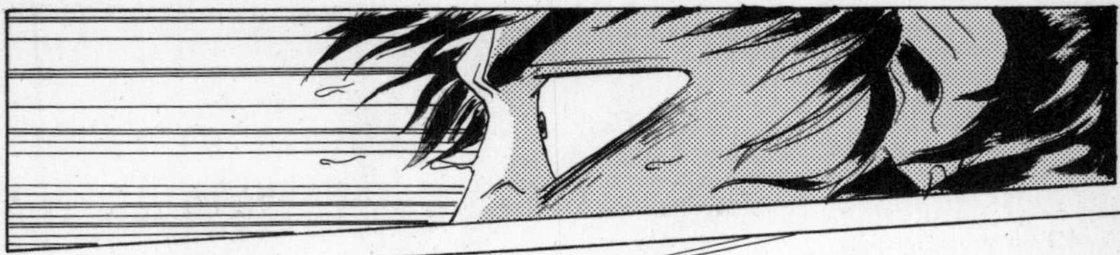

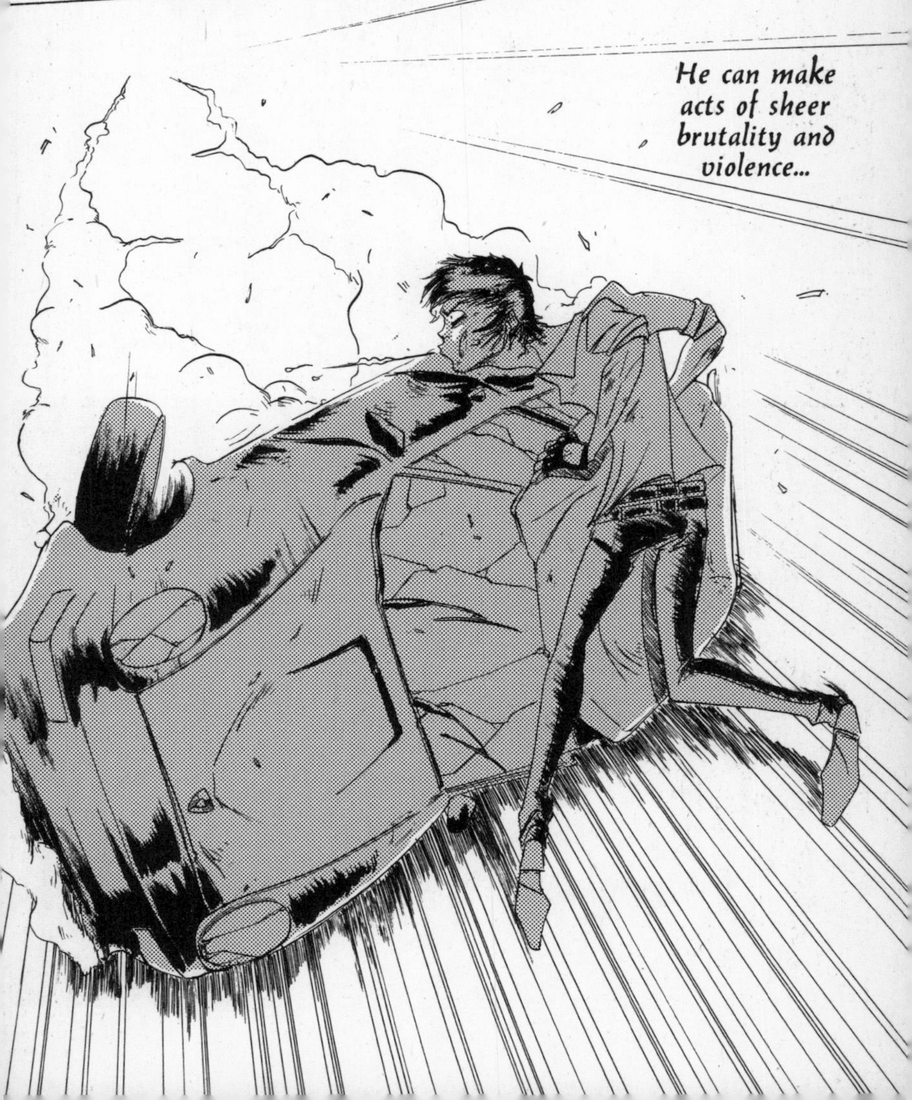
He can make acts of sheer brutality and violence...

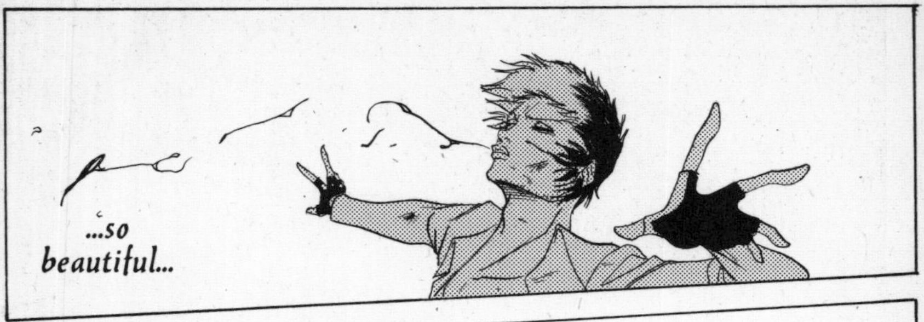
...so beautiful...

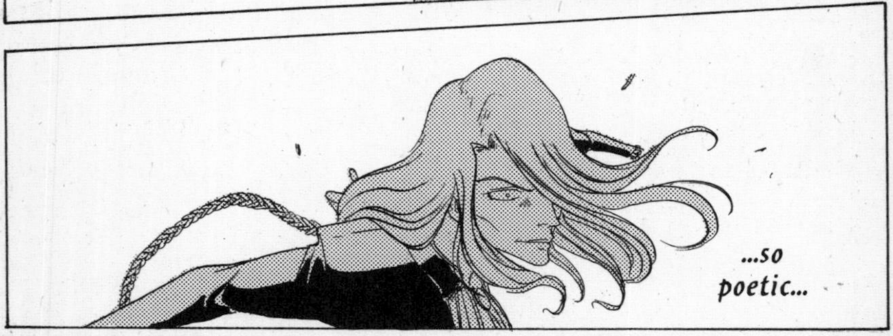
...so poetic...

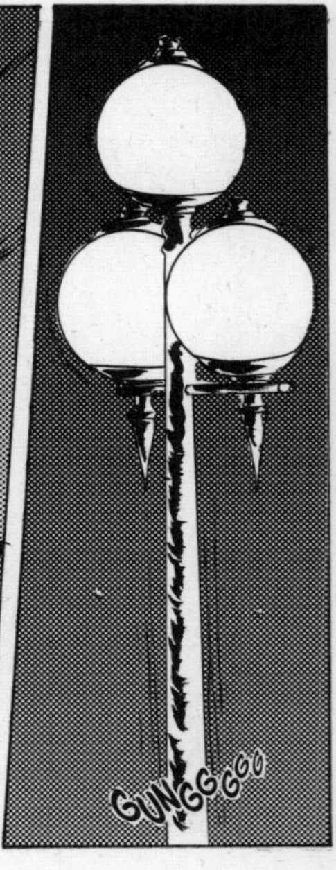
GUNGGGGG

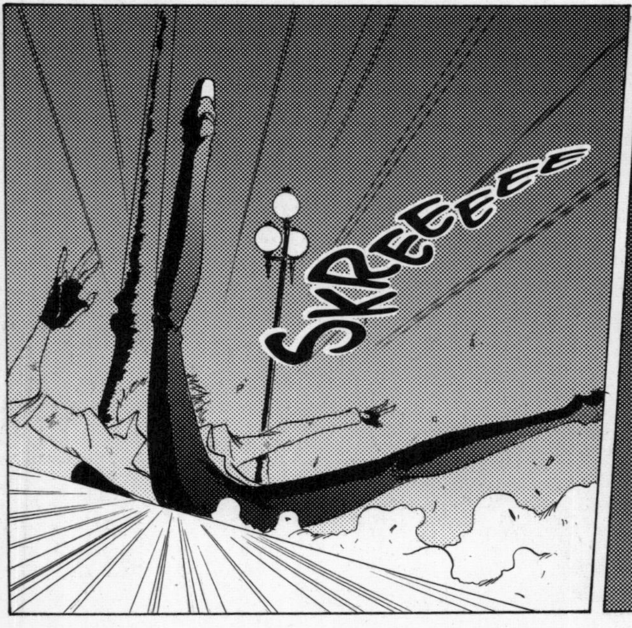
SKREEEEE

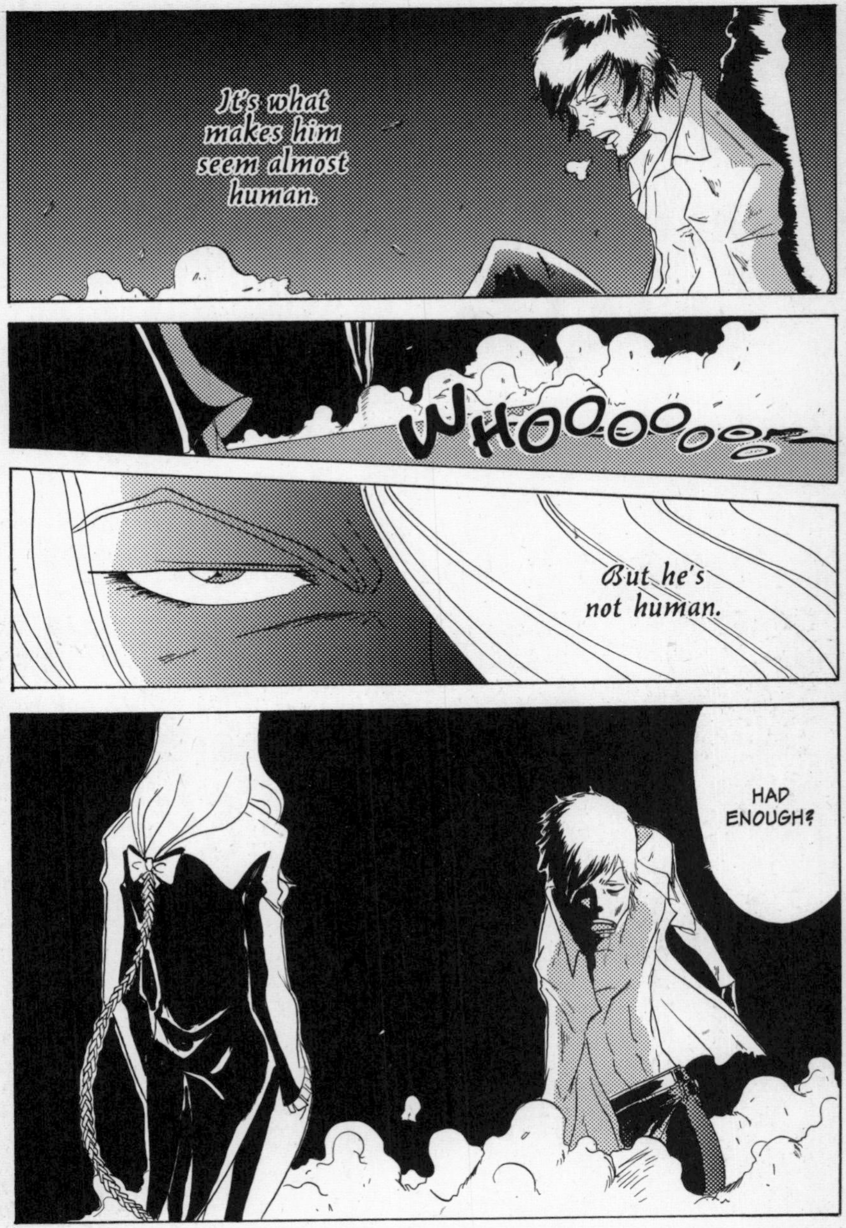
It's what makes him seem almost human.
WHOOOOOO
But he's not human.
HAD ENOUGH?

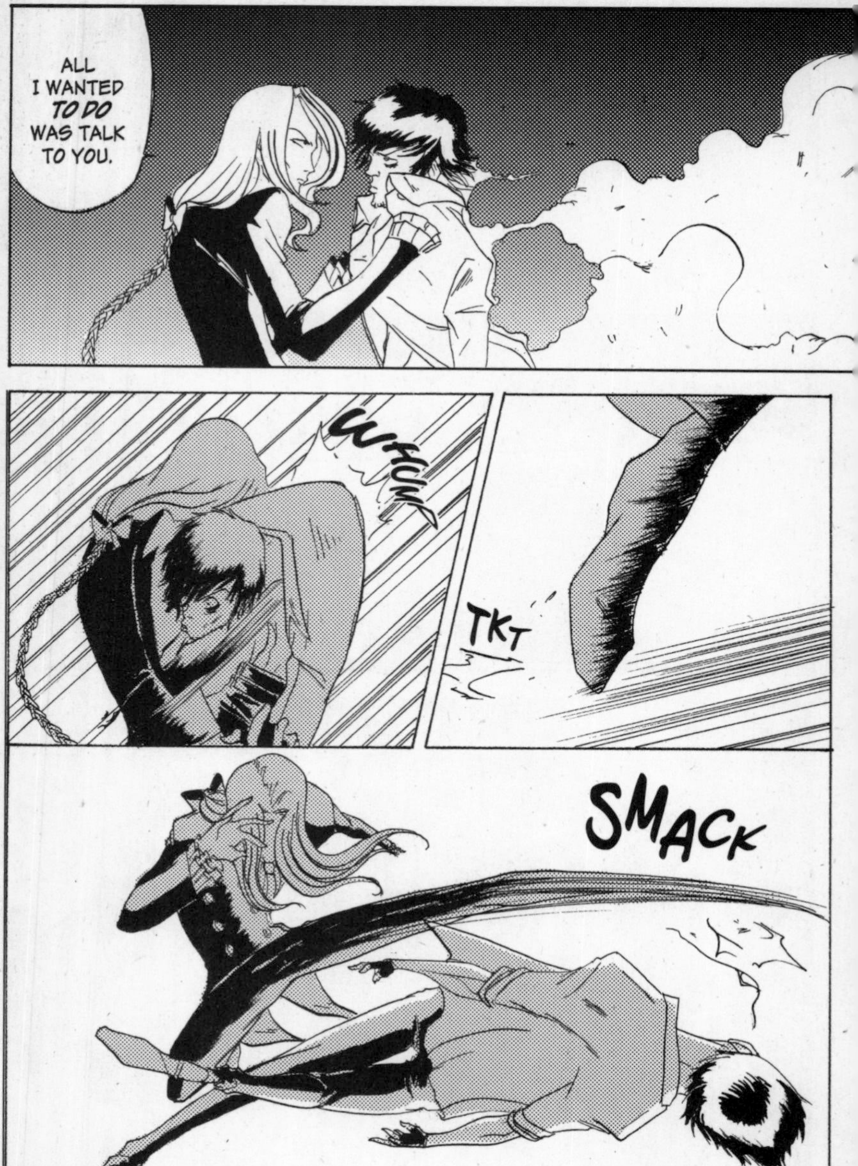
ALL I WANTED *TO DO* WAS TALK TO YOU.
TKT
WHUMP
SMACK

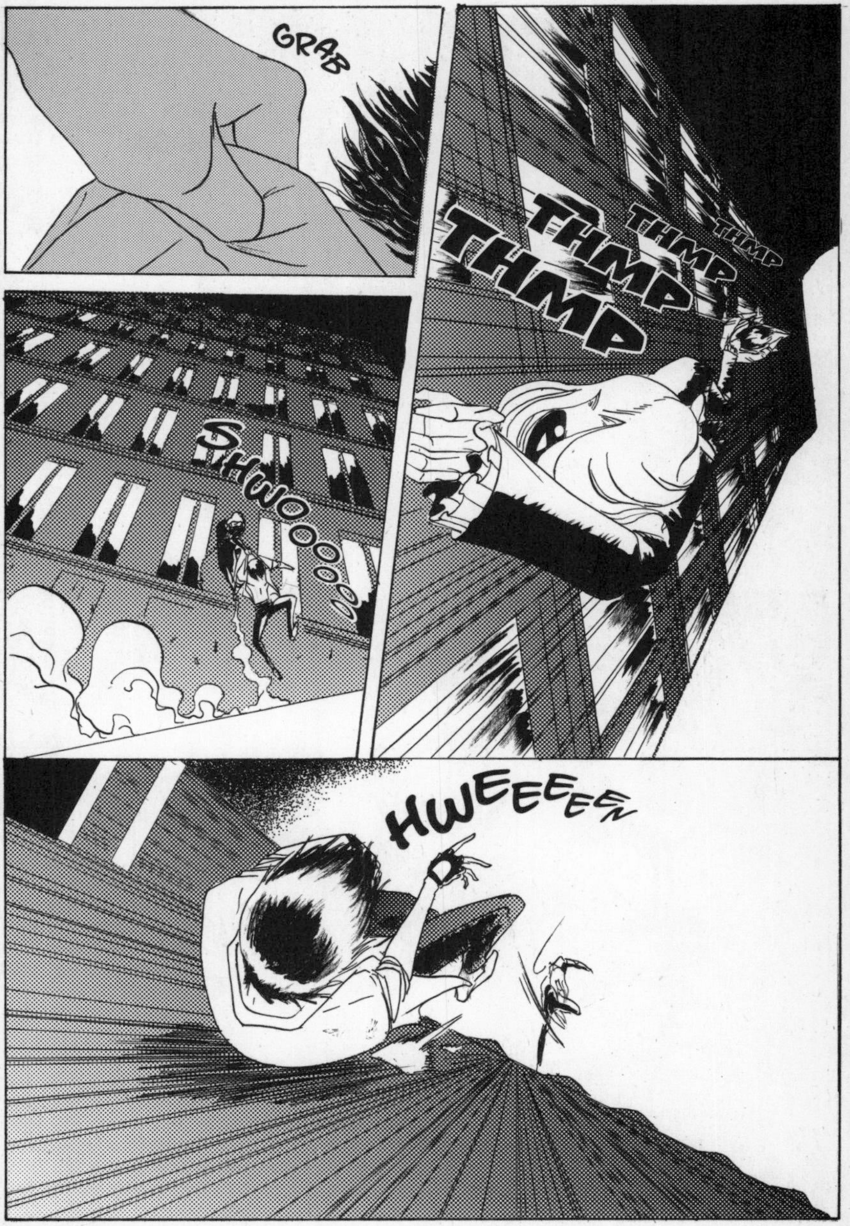
THMP
THMP
THMP
THMP
GRAB
SHWOOOOOOO
HWEEEEEN

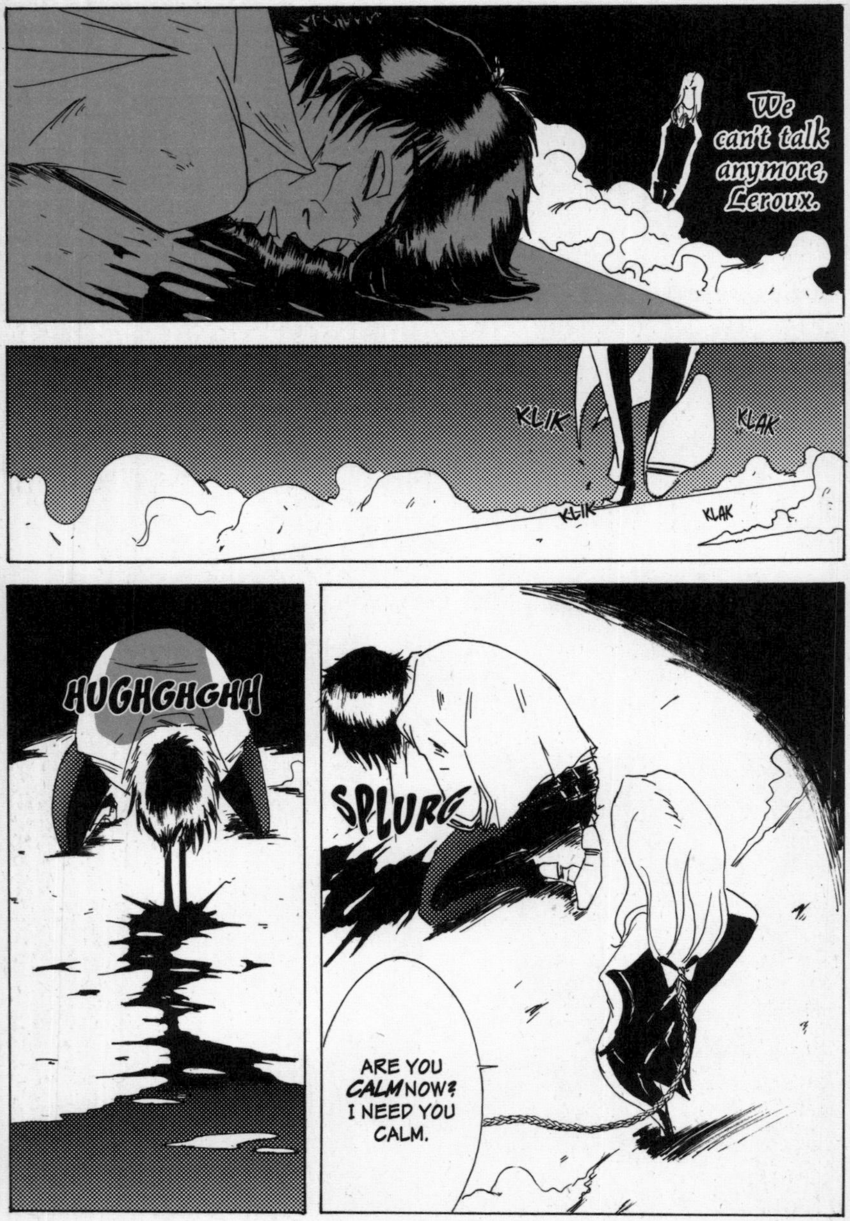
We can't talk anymore, Leroux.
KLIK
KLAK
KLIK
KLAK
SPLURG
ARE YOU CALM NOW? I NEED YOU CALM.
HUGHGHGHH

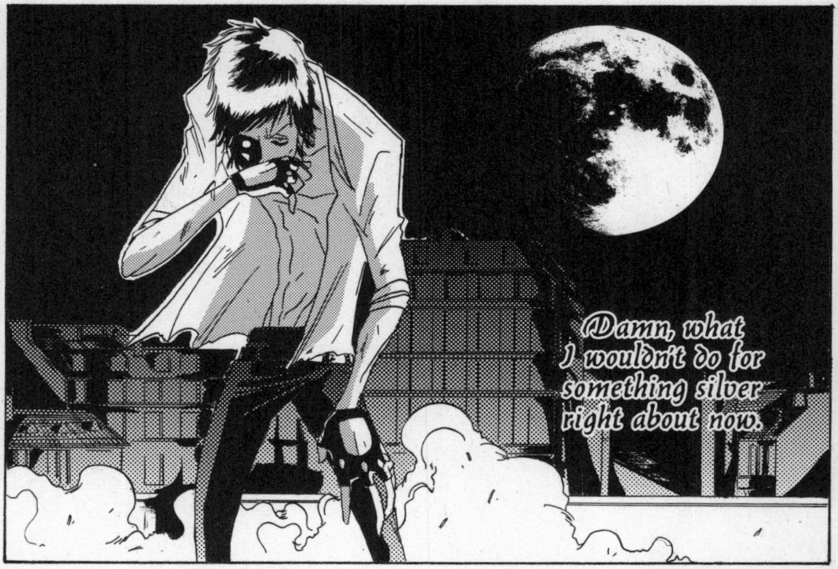
Damn, what I wouldn't do for something silver right about now.
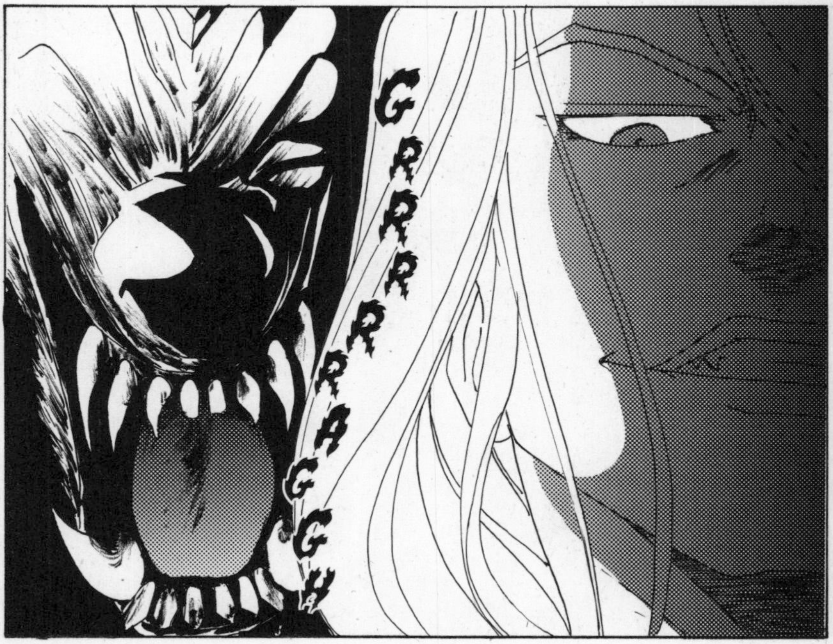
GRRRRRRAGGGH

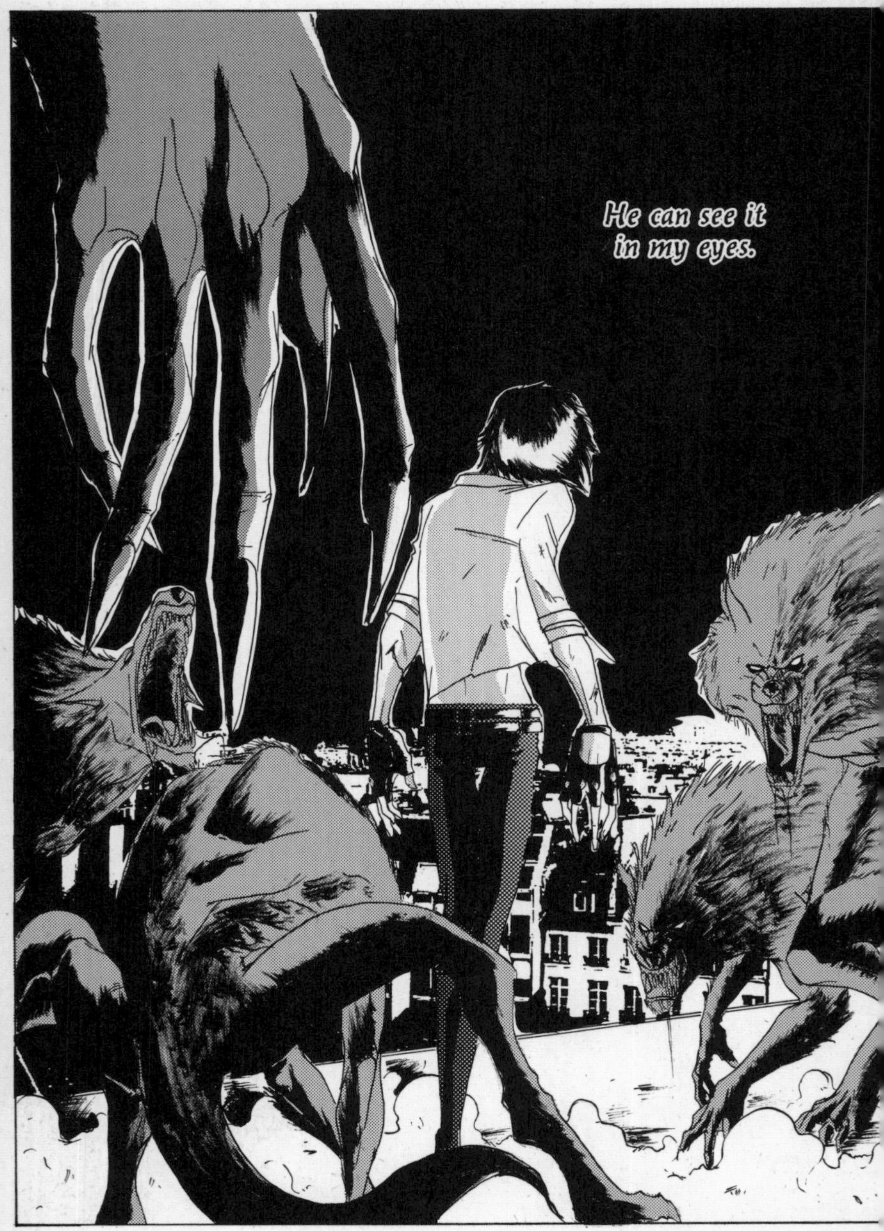
He can see it
in my eyes.

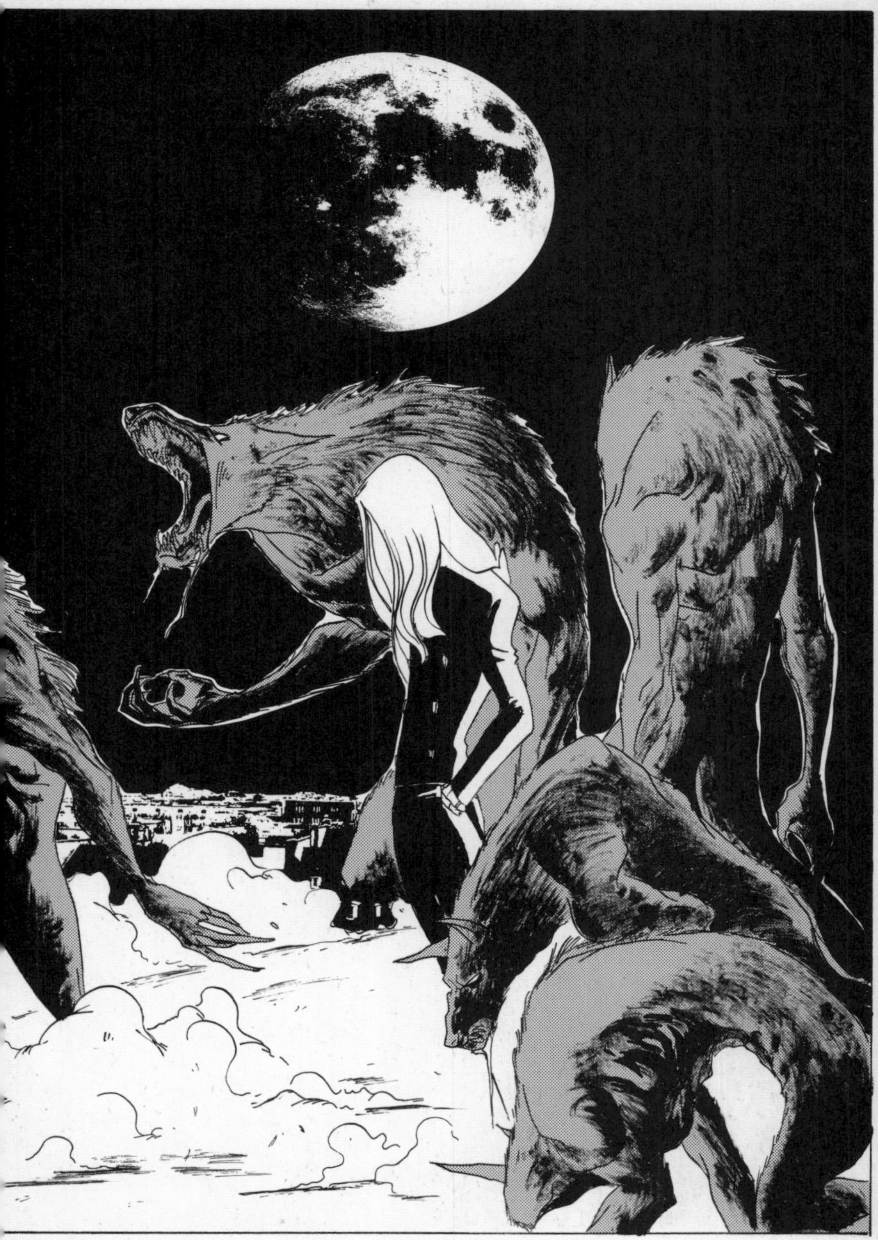

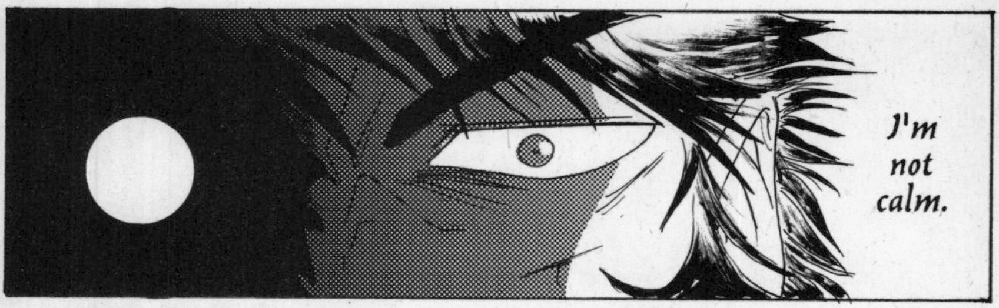
I'm not calm.
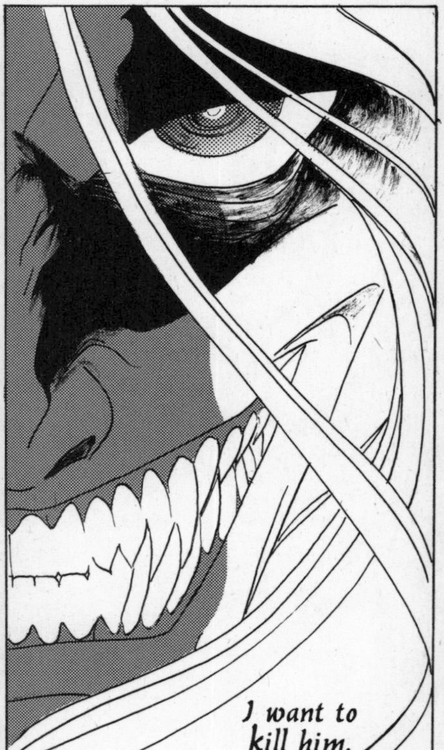
I want to kill him.
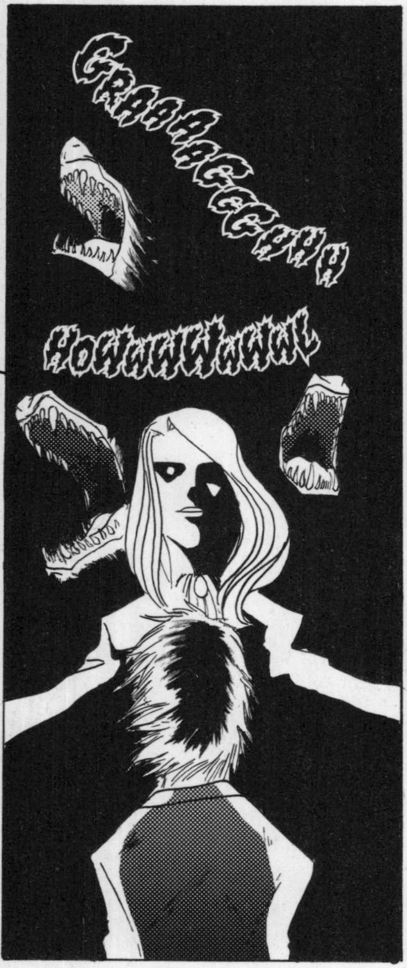
GRAAACCCHHH
HOWWWWWWWL

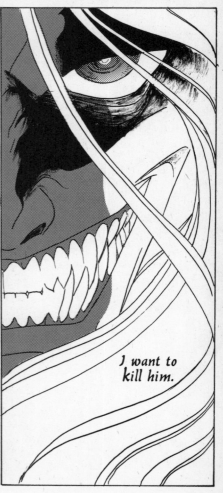

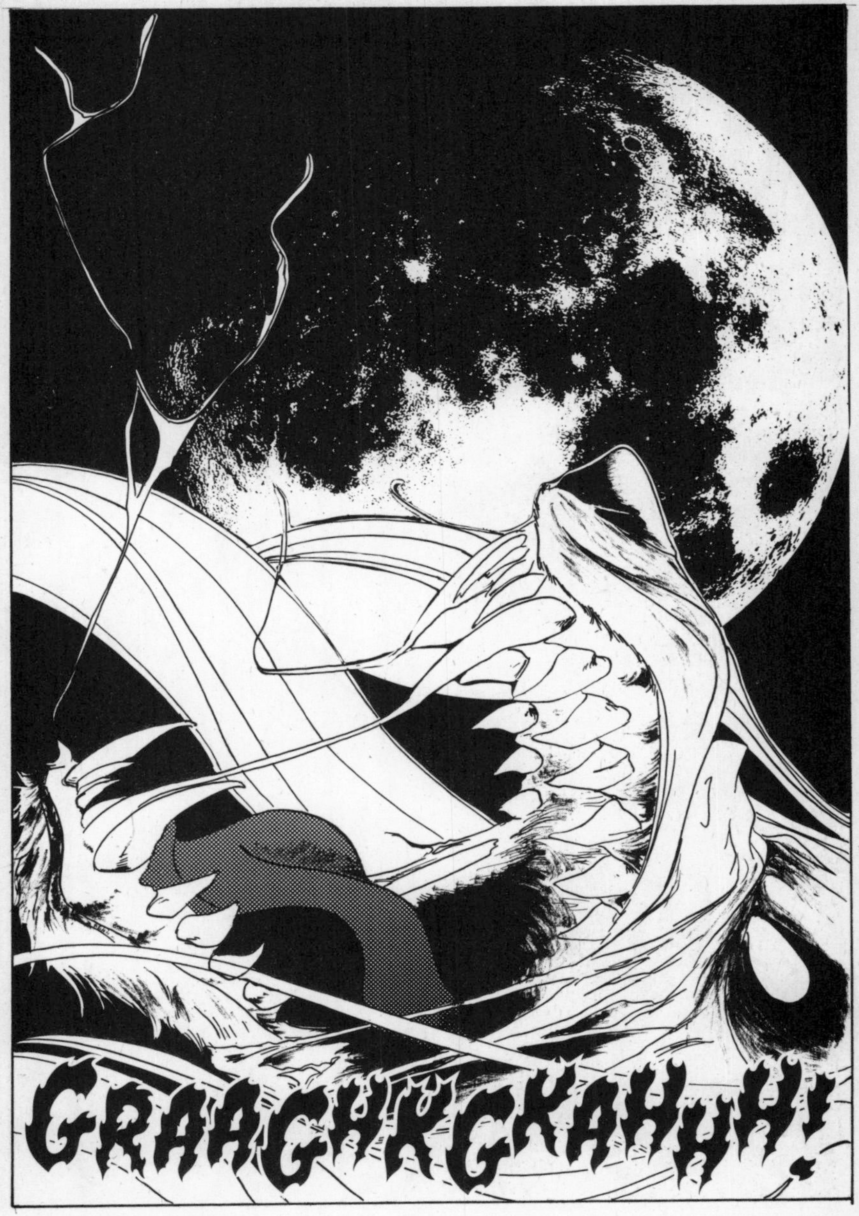
GRAAGHRGKAHHH!

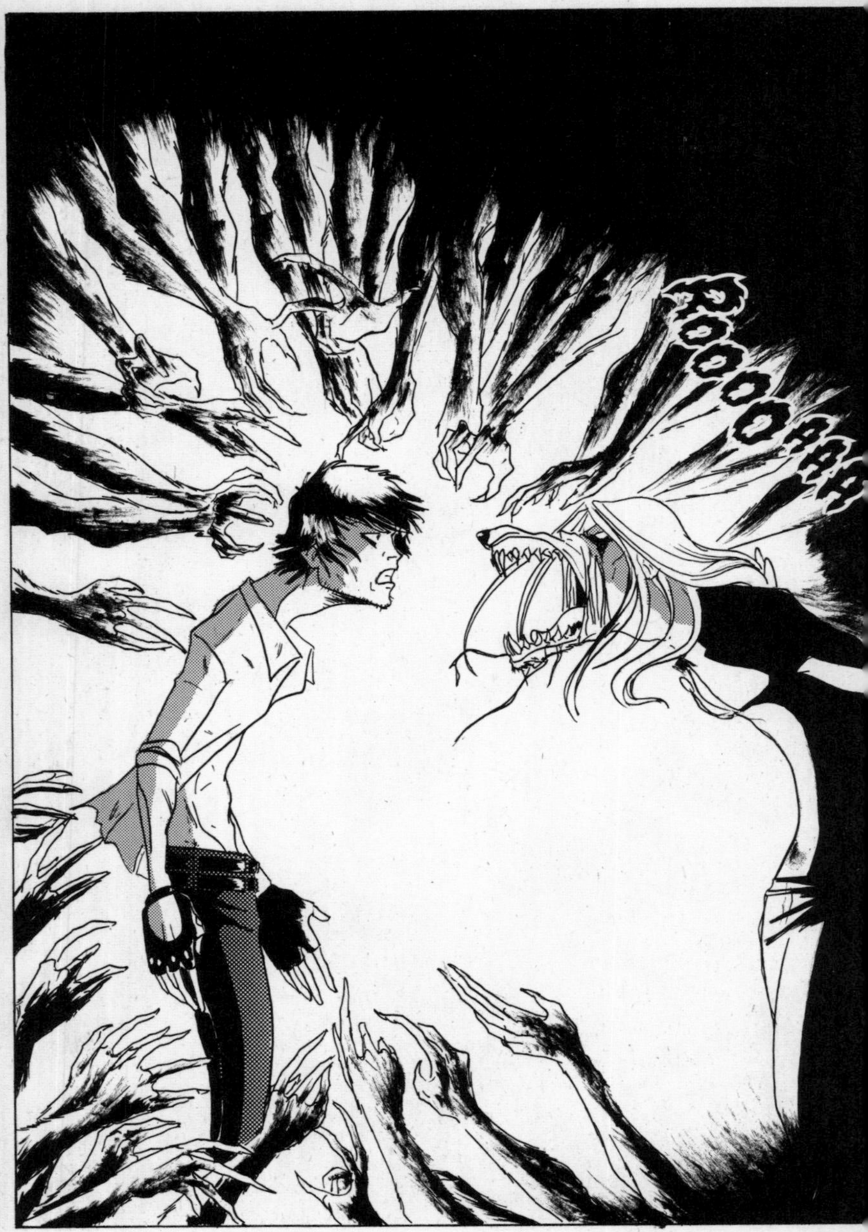
ROOOOAAA

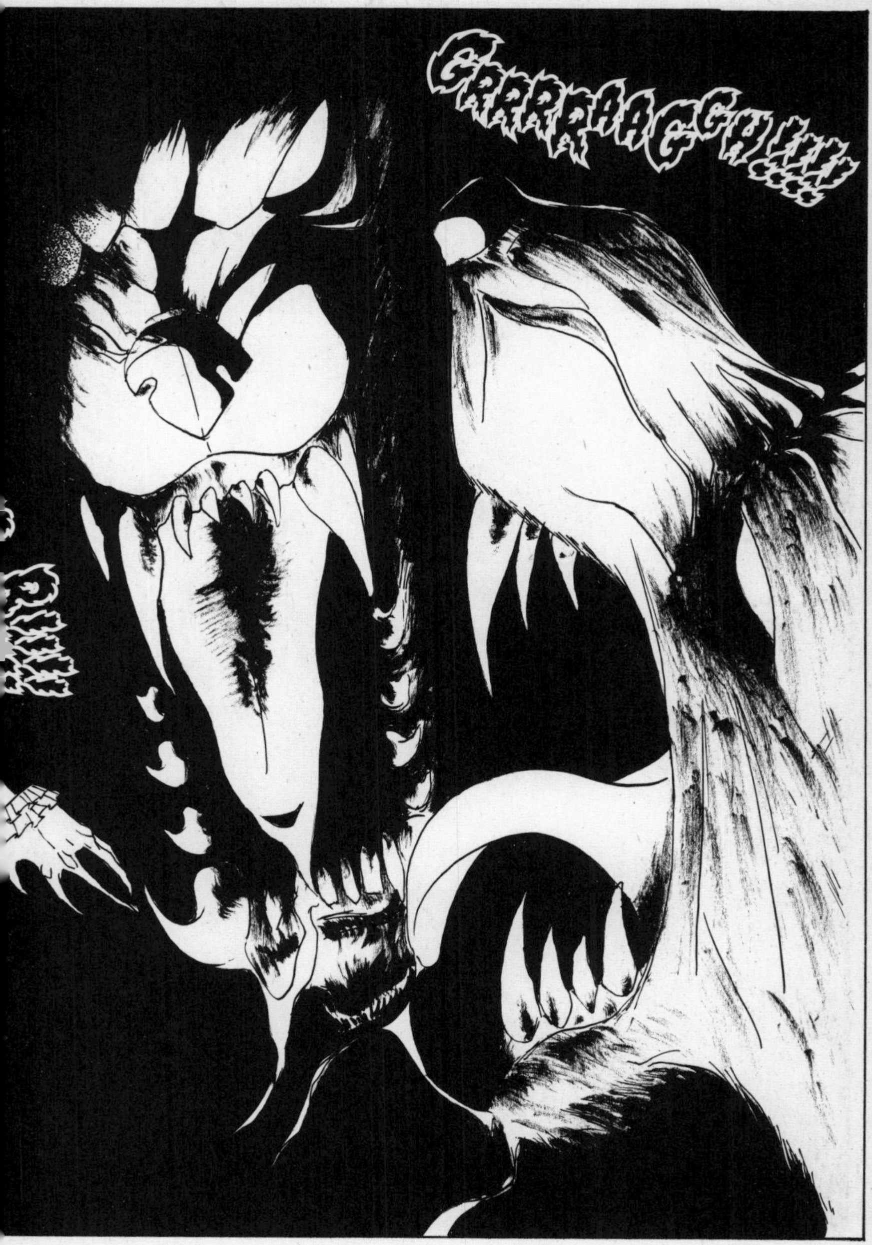
GRRRRAAGGHHH...!!

*Wait.
Something's
happened...*

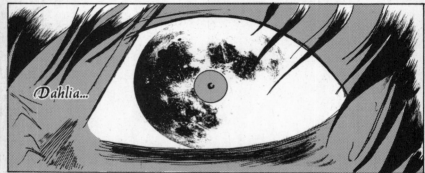

*Dahlia...*

*Christine...*

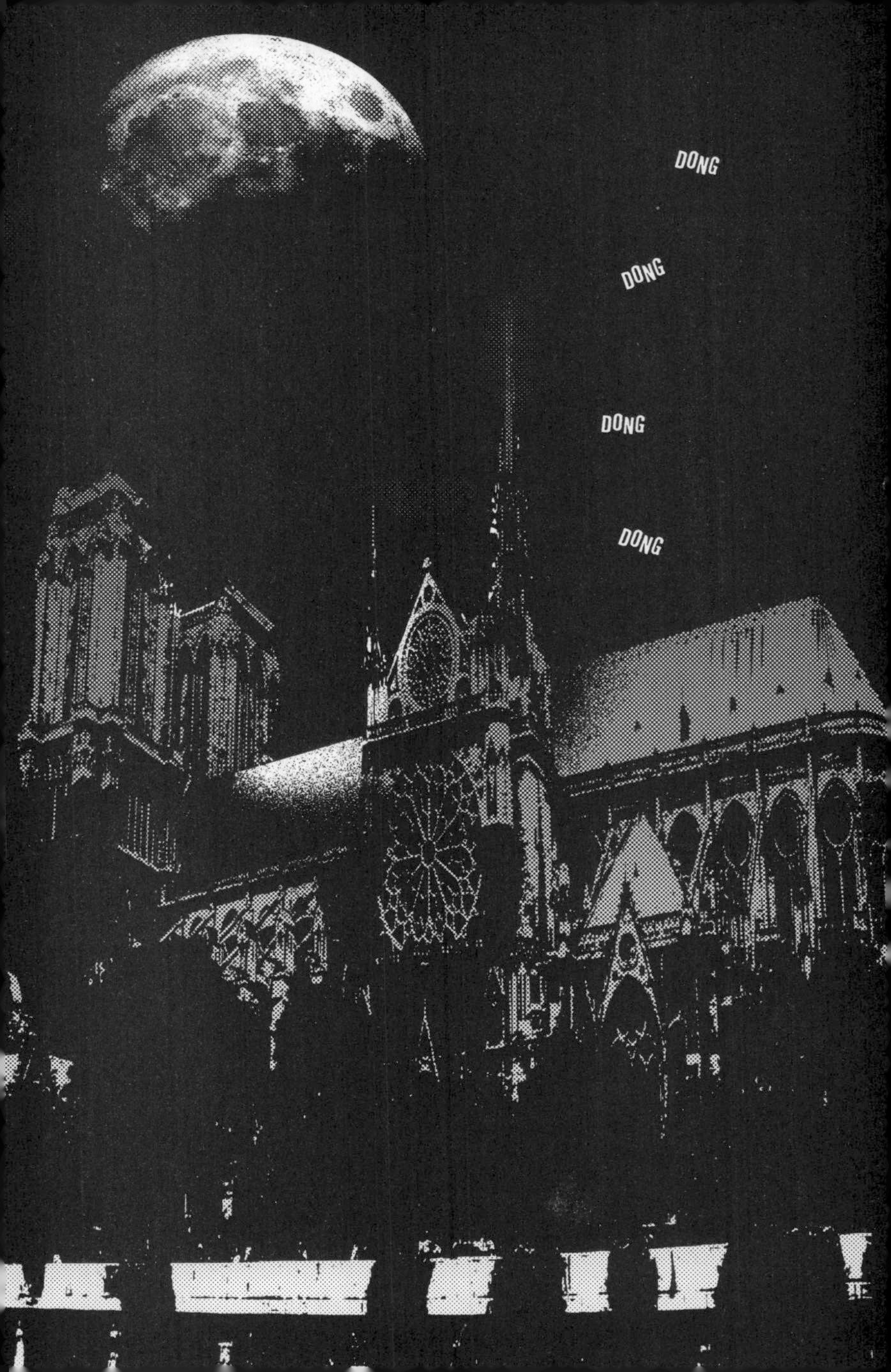
DONG
DONG
DONG
DONG

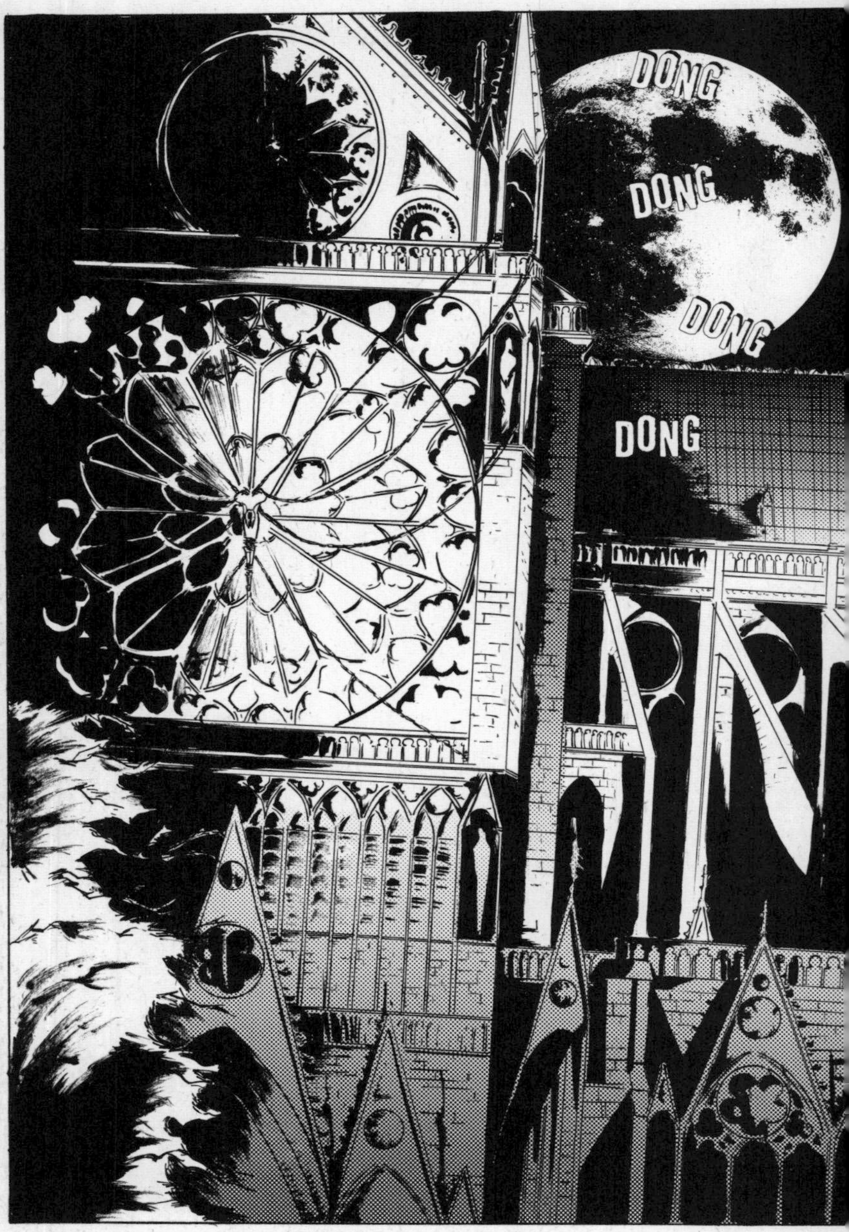
DONG
DONG
DONG
DONG

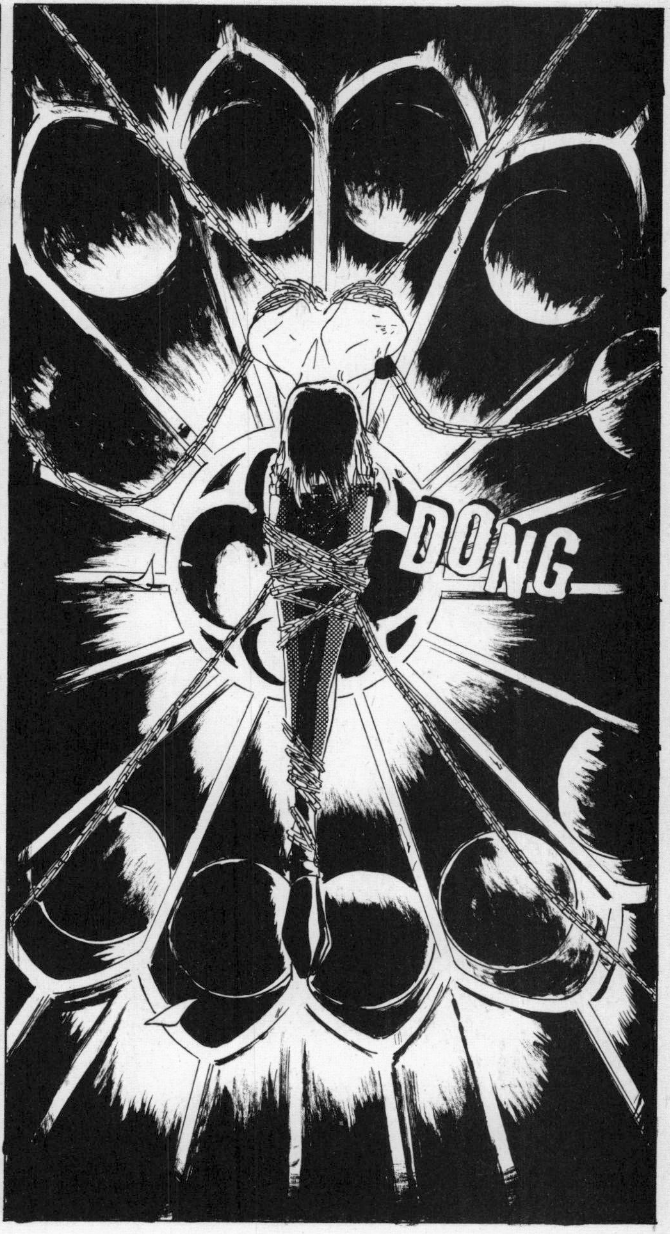
DONG
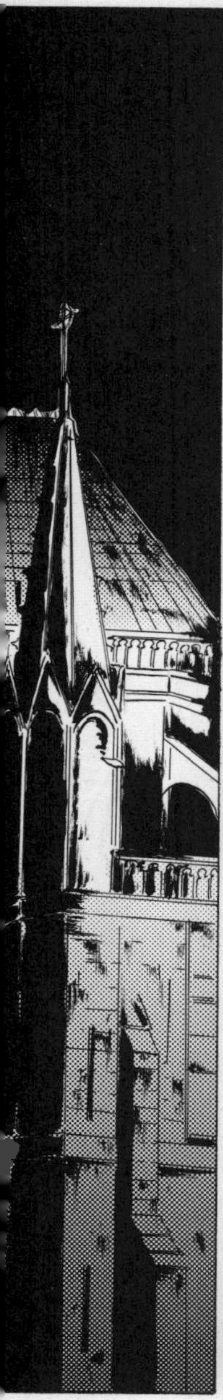

That's right, Leroux.

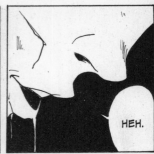

HEH.

Now I am the beast who must be caged.

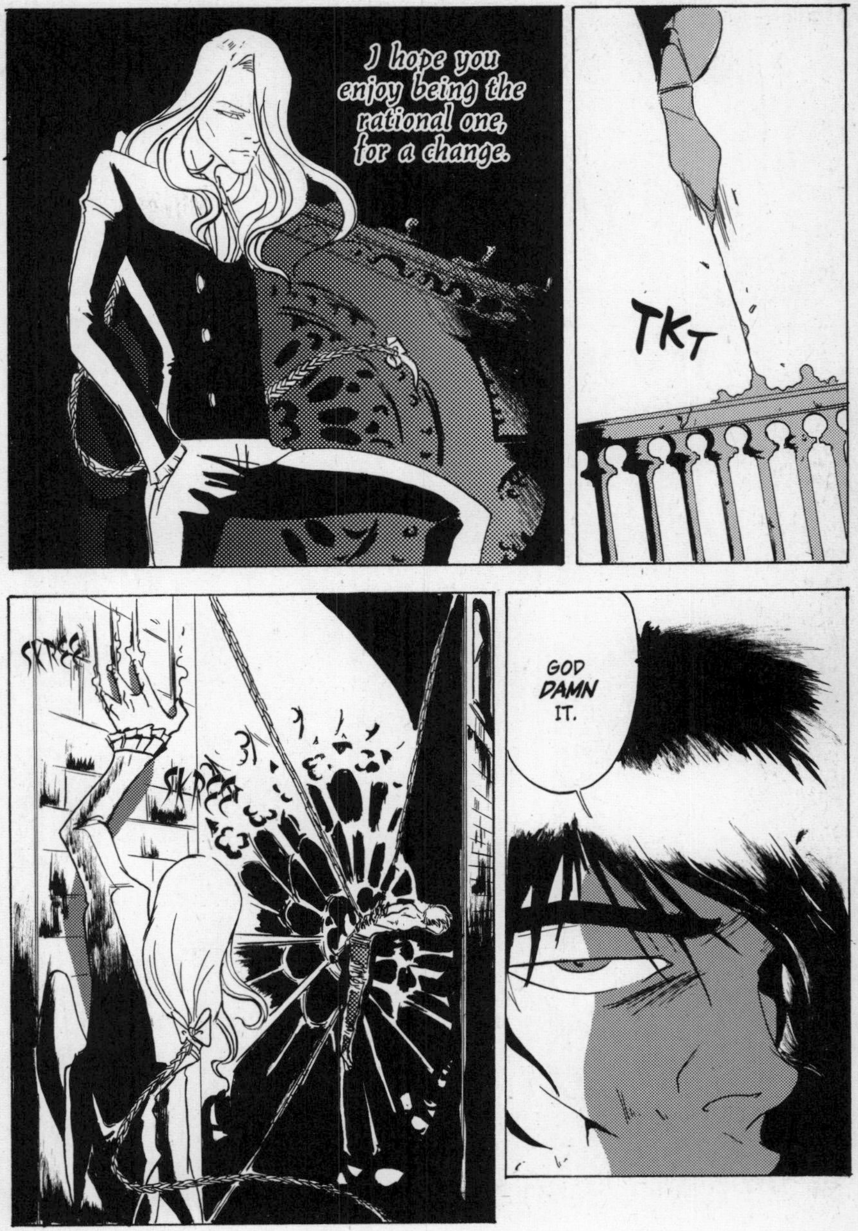
I hope you enjoy being the rational one, for a change.
TKT
SKREE
SKREE
GOD DAMN IT.

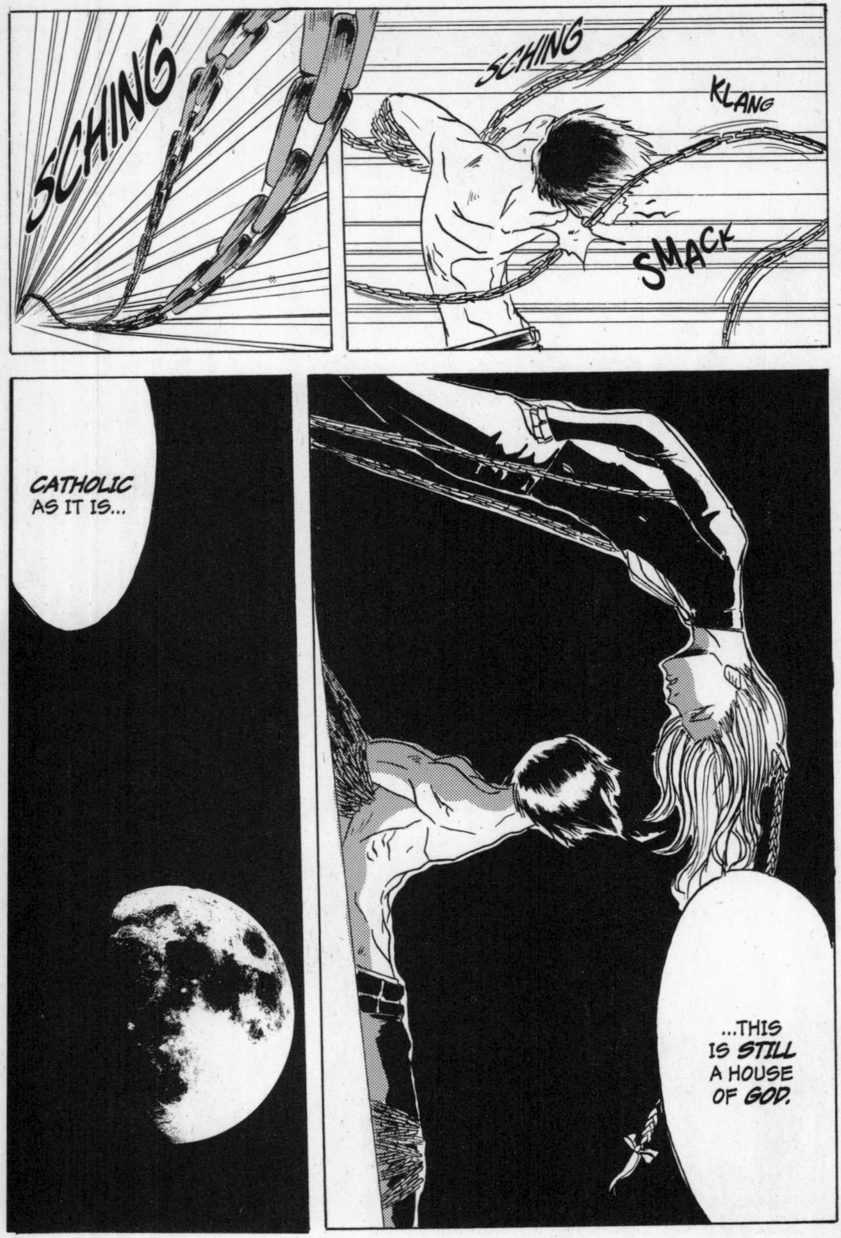
SCHING
SCHING
KLANG
SMACK
CATHOLIC AS IT IS...
...THIS IS STILL A HOUSE OF GOD.

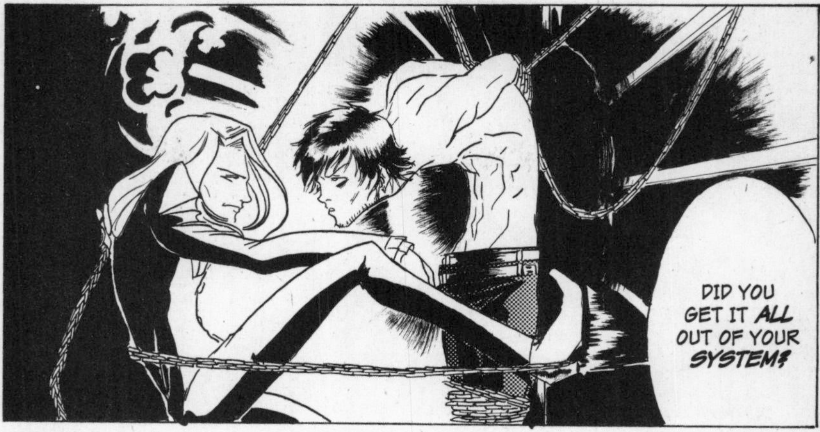
DID YOU GET IT ALL OUT OF YOUR SYSTEM?
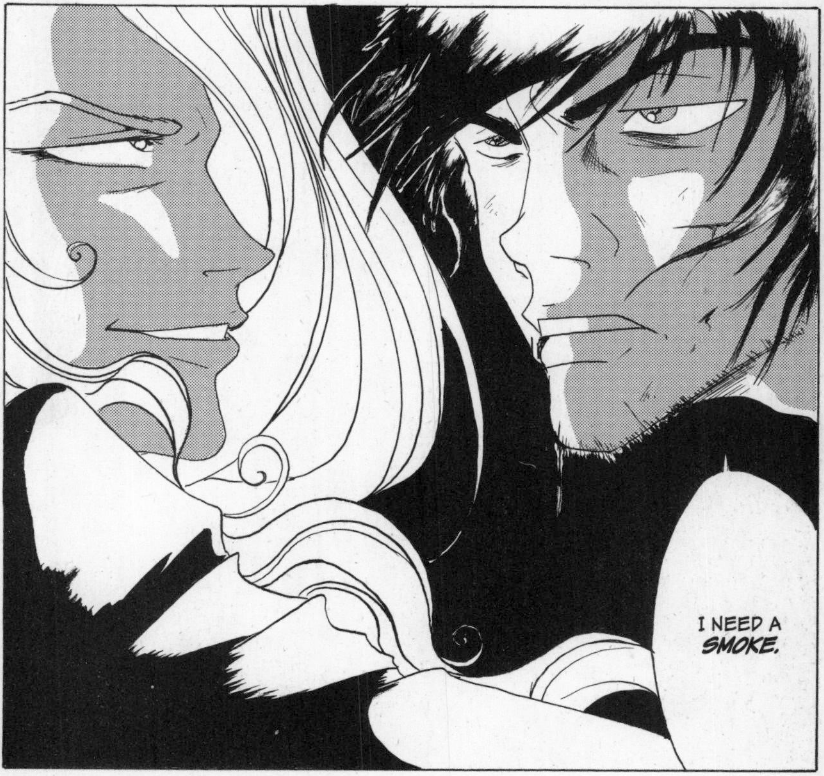
I NEED A SMOKE.

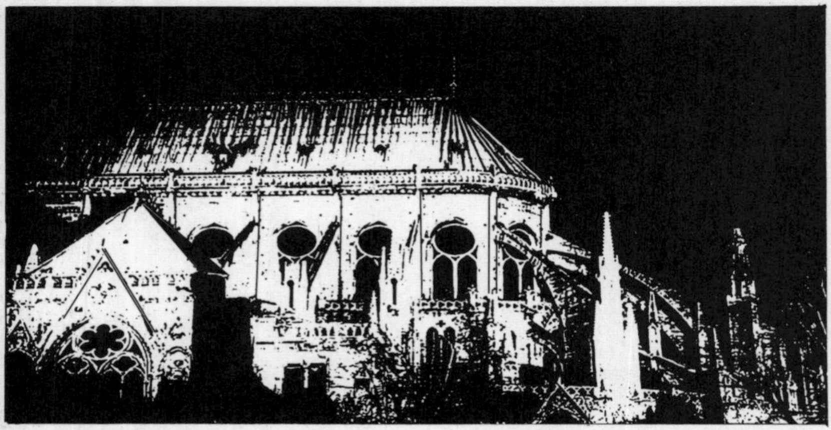
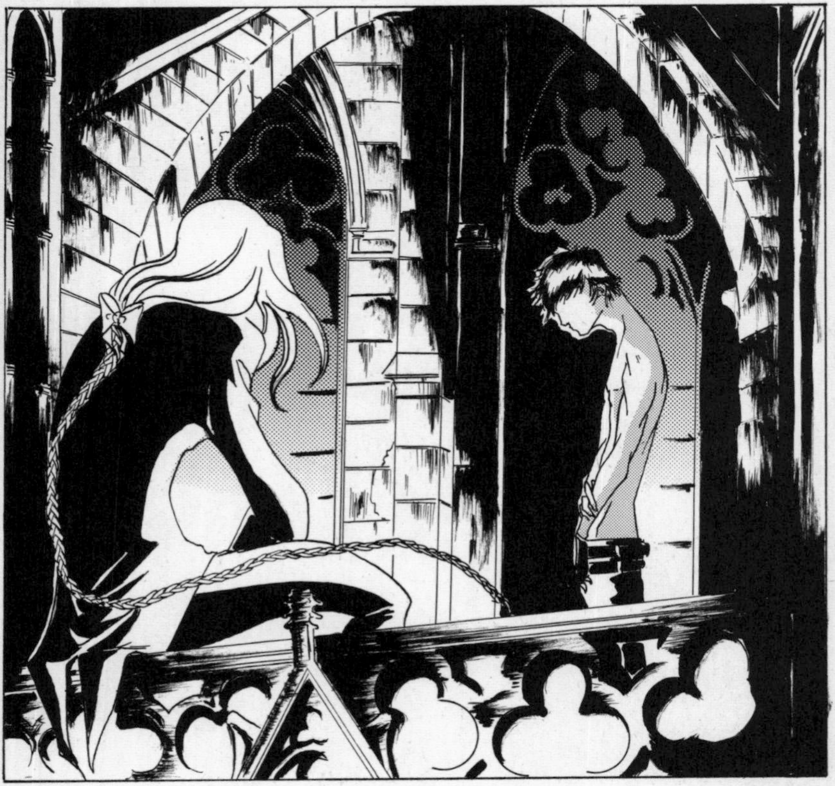

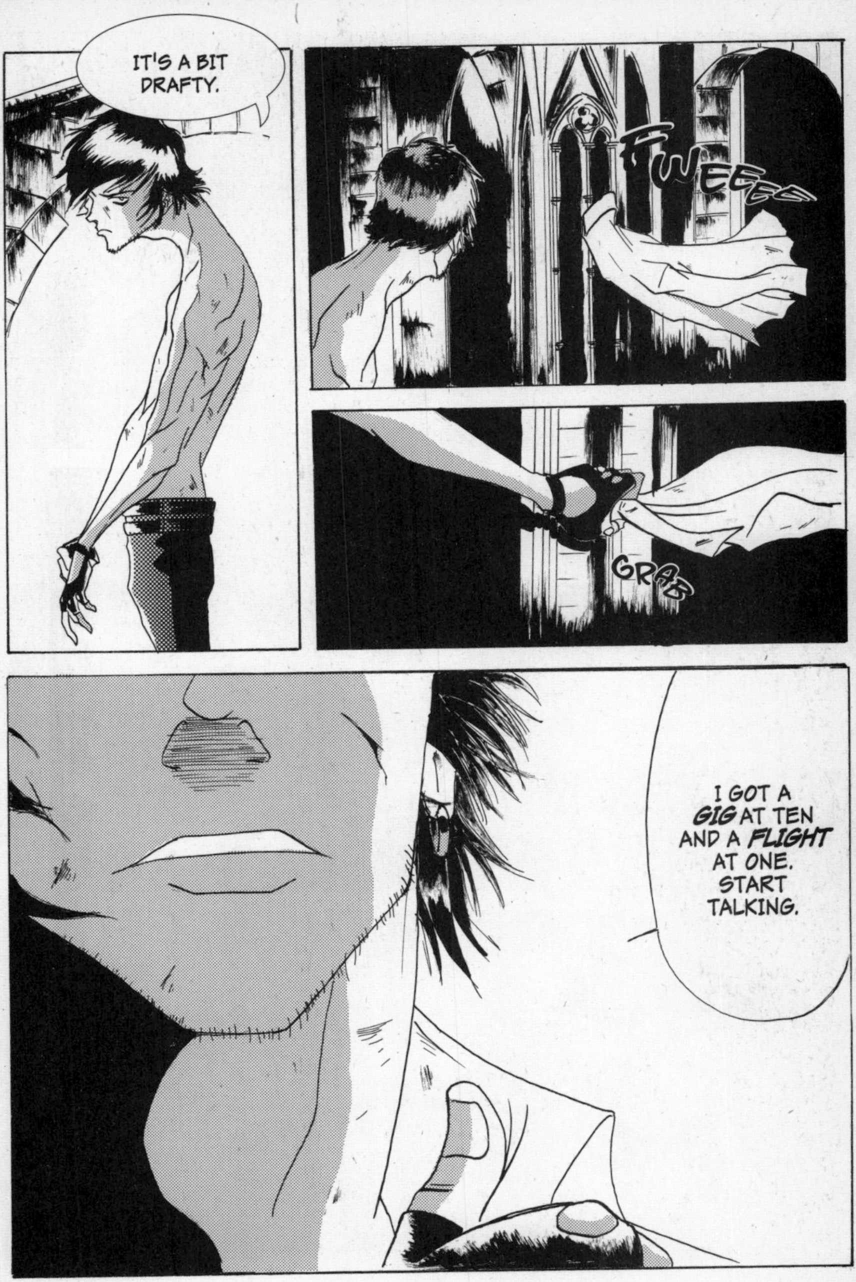
IT'S A BIT DRAFTY.
FWEEEEE
GRAB
I GOT A *GIG* AT TEN AND A *FLIGHT* AT ONE. START TALKING.

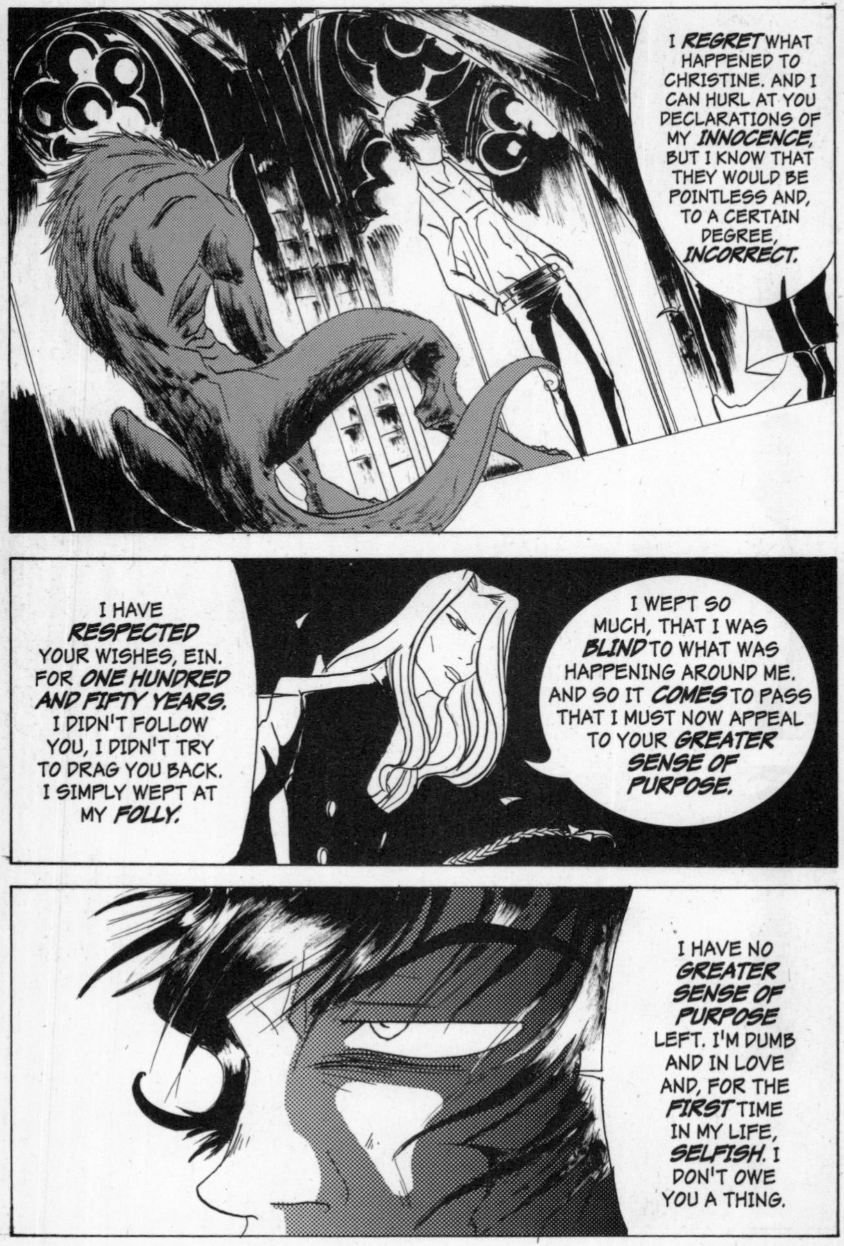
I REGRET WHAT HAPPENED TO CHRISTINE. AND I CAN HURL AT YOU DECLARATIONS OF MY INNOCENCE, BUT I KNOW THAT THEY WOULD BE POINTLESS AND, TO A CERTAIN DEGREE, INCORRECT.
I WEPT SO MUCH, THAT I WAS BLIND TO WHAT WAS HAPPENING AROUND ME. AND SO IT COMES TO PASS THAT I MUST NOW APPEAL TO YOUR GREATER SENSE OF PURPOSE.
I HAVE RESPECTED YOUR WISHES, EIN. FOR ONE HUNDRED AND FIFTY YEARS. I DIDN'T FOLLOW YOU, I DIDN'T TRY TO DRAG YOU BACK. I SIMPLY WEPT AT MY FOLLY.
I HAVE NO GREATER SENSE OF PURPOSE LEFT. I'M DUMB AND IN LOVE AND, FOR THE FIRST TIME IN MY LIFE, SELFISH. I DON'T OWE YOU A THING.

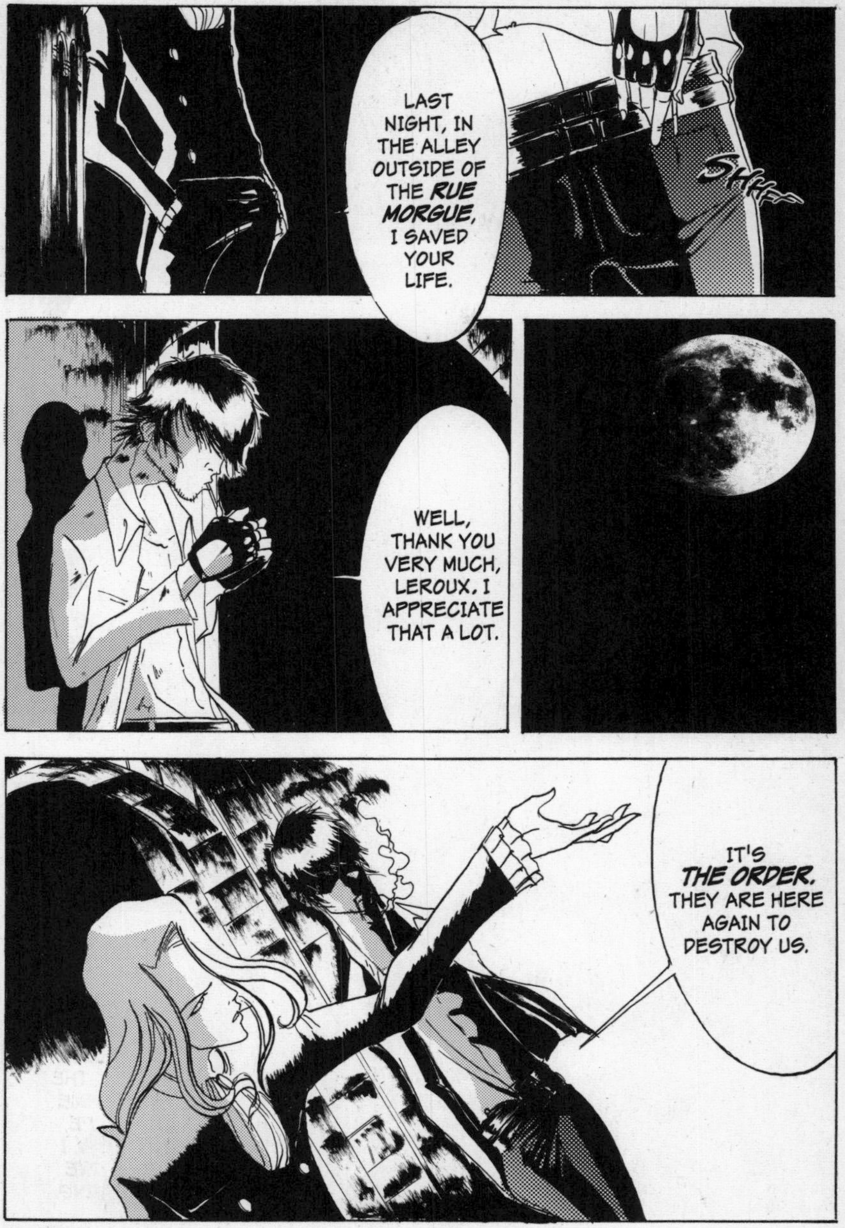
LAST NIGHT, IN THE ALLEY OUTSIDE OF THE *RUE MORGUE,* I SAVED YOUR LIFE.
WELL, THANK YOU VERY MUCH, LEROUX. I APPRECIATE THAT A LOT.
IT'S *THE ORDER.* THEY ARE HERE AGAIN TO DESTROY US.

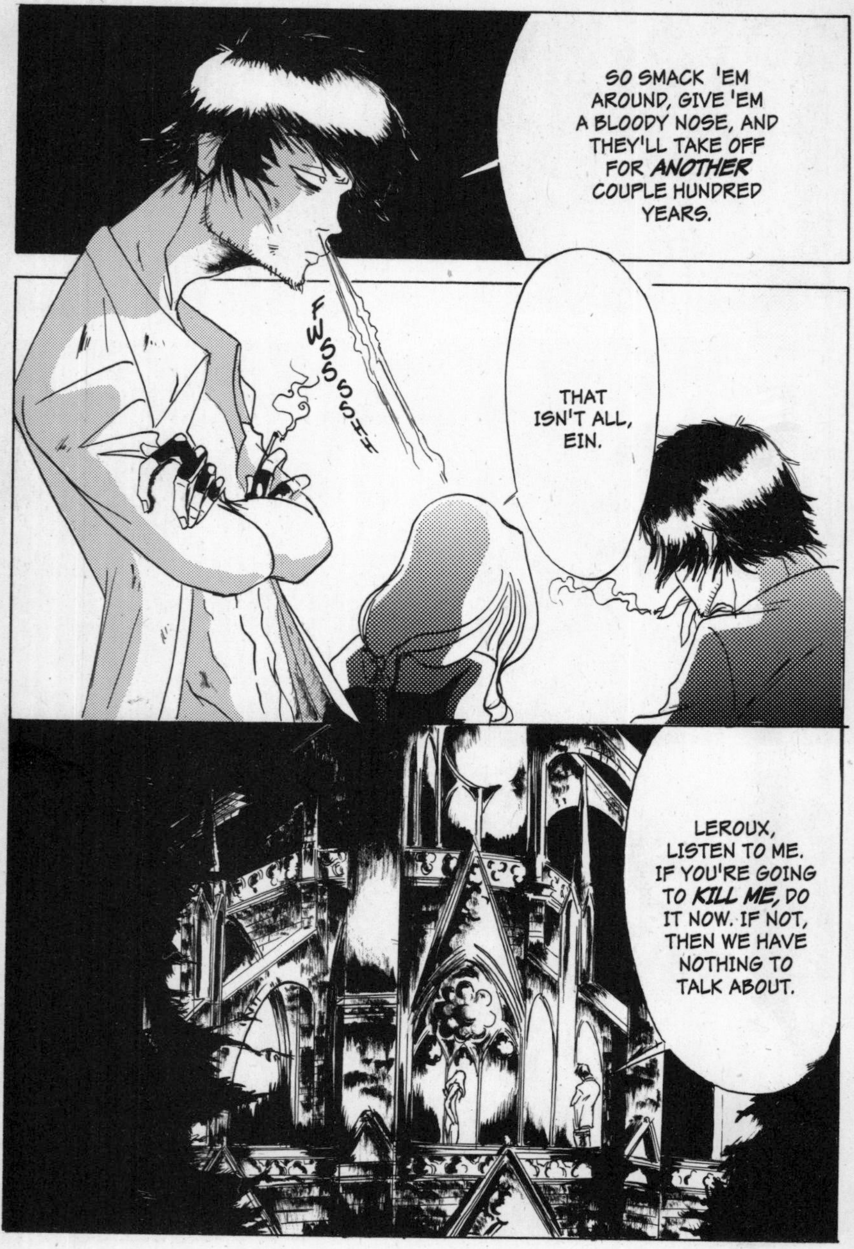
SO SMACK 'EM AROUND, GIVE 'EM A BLOODY NOSE, AND THEY'LL TAKE OFF FOR ANOTHER COUPLE HUNDRED YEARS.
THAT ISN'T ALL, EIN.
FWSSSSHH
LEROUX, LISTEN TO ME. IF YOU'RE GOING TO KILL ME, DO IT NOW. IF NOT, THEN WE HAVE NOTHING TO TALK ABOUT.

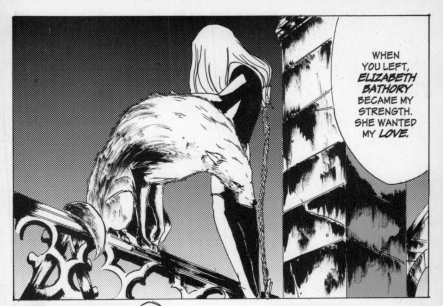

WHEN YOU LEFT, *ELIZABETH BATHORY* BECAME MY STRENGTH. SHE WANTED MY *LOVE.*

I COULD NOT *GIVE* HER THAT.

BUT I COULD GIVE HER MY *TRUST,* AND WITH IT, SHE TOOK YOUR PLACE AS *LEADER.*

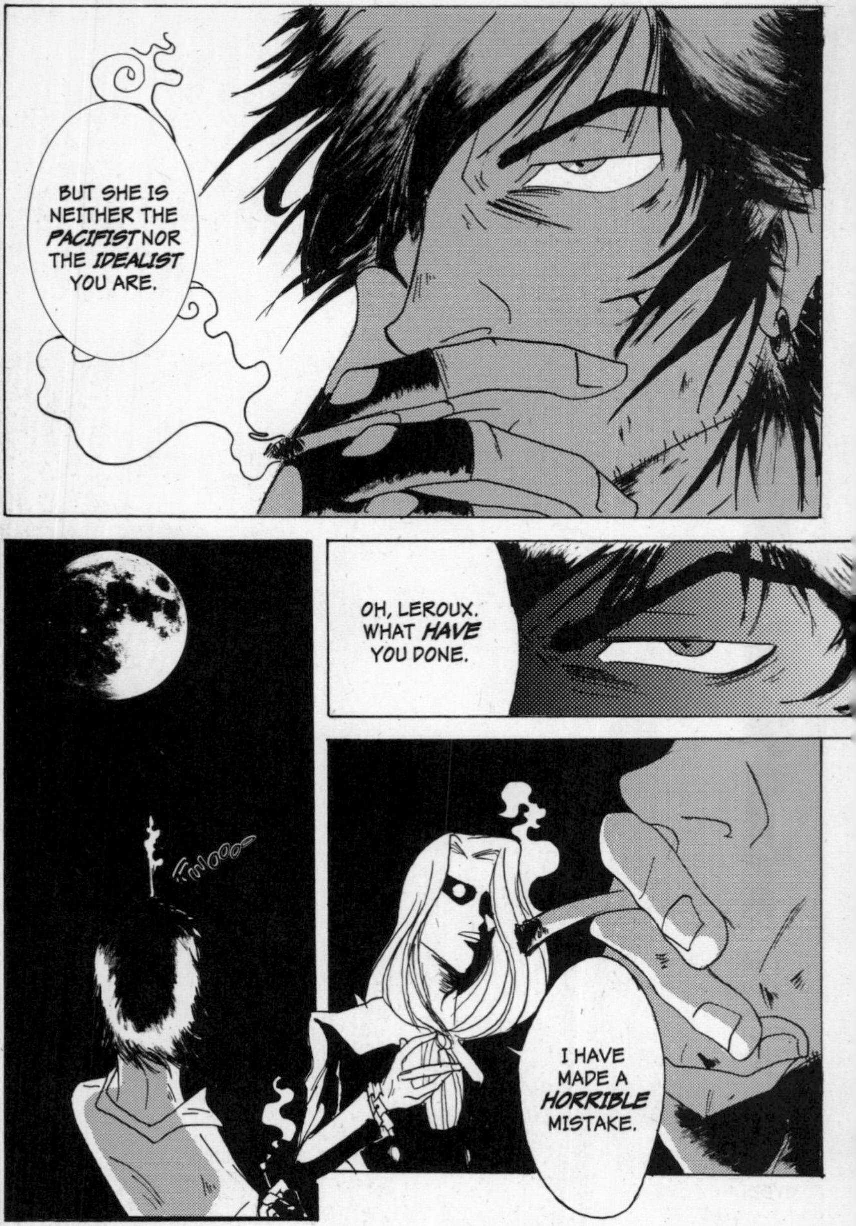
BUT SHE IS NEITHER THE *PACIFIST* NOR THE *IDEALIST* YOU ARE.
OH, LEROUX. WHAT *HAVE* YOU DONE.
I HAVE MADE A *HORRIBLE* MISTAKE.

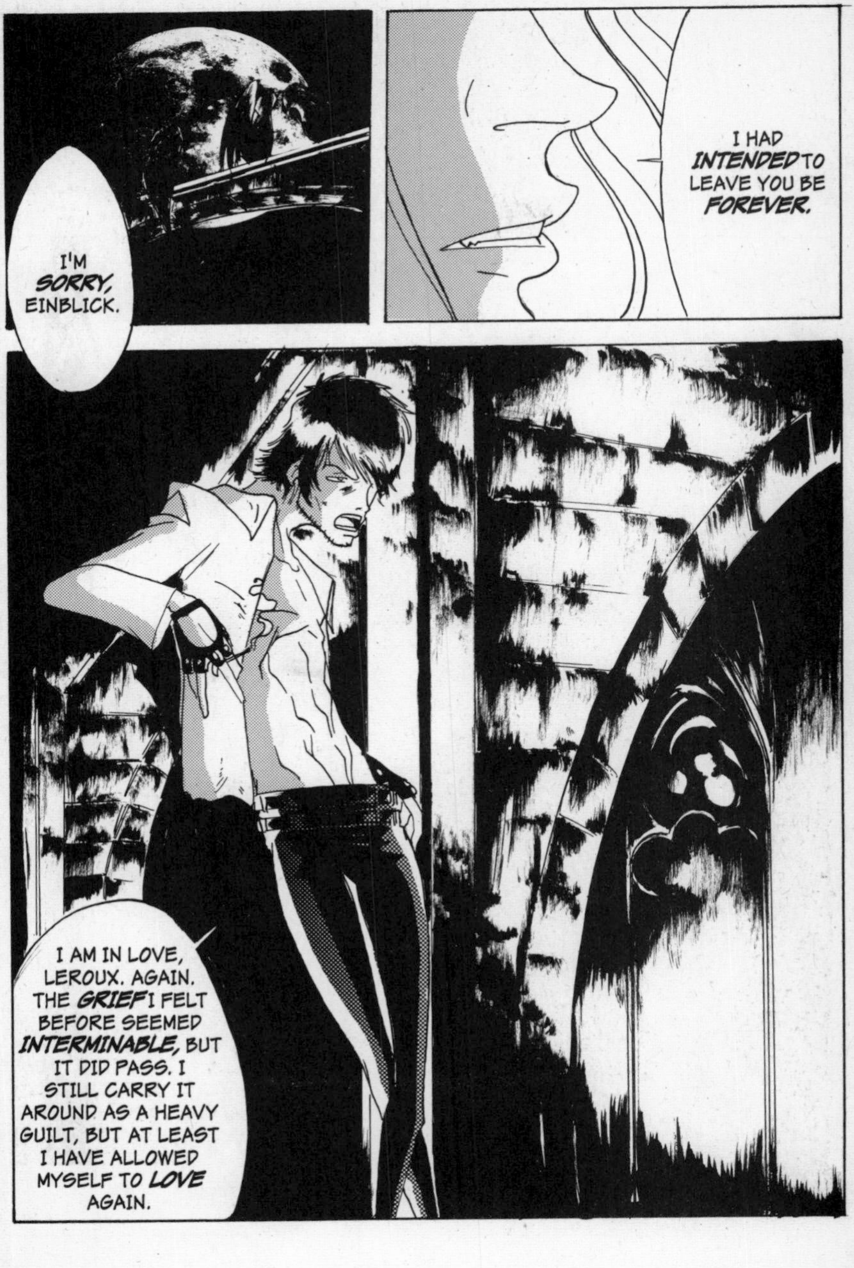
I HAD INTENDED TO LEAVE YOU BE FOREVER.
I'M SORRY, EINBLICK.
I AM IN LOVE, LEROUX. AGAIN. THE GRIEF I FELT BEFORE SEEMED INTERMINABLE, BUT IT DID PASS. I STILL CARRY IT AROUND AS A HEAVY GUILT, BUT AT LEAST I HAVE ALLOWED MYSELF TO LOVE AGAIN.

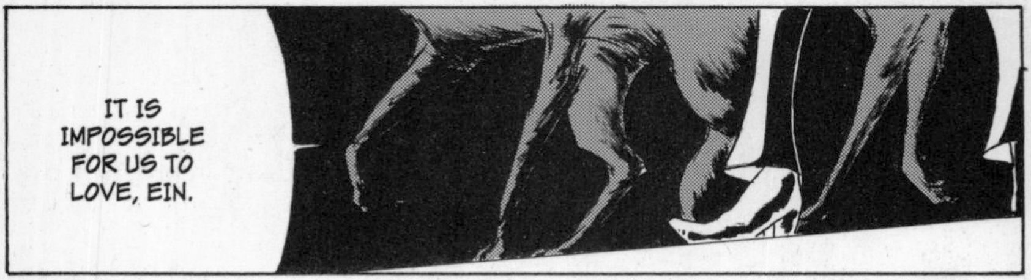
IT IS IMPOSSIBLE FOR US TO LOVE, EIN.

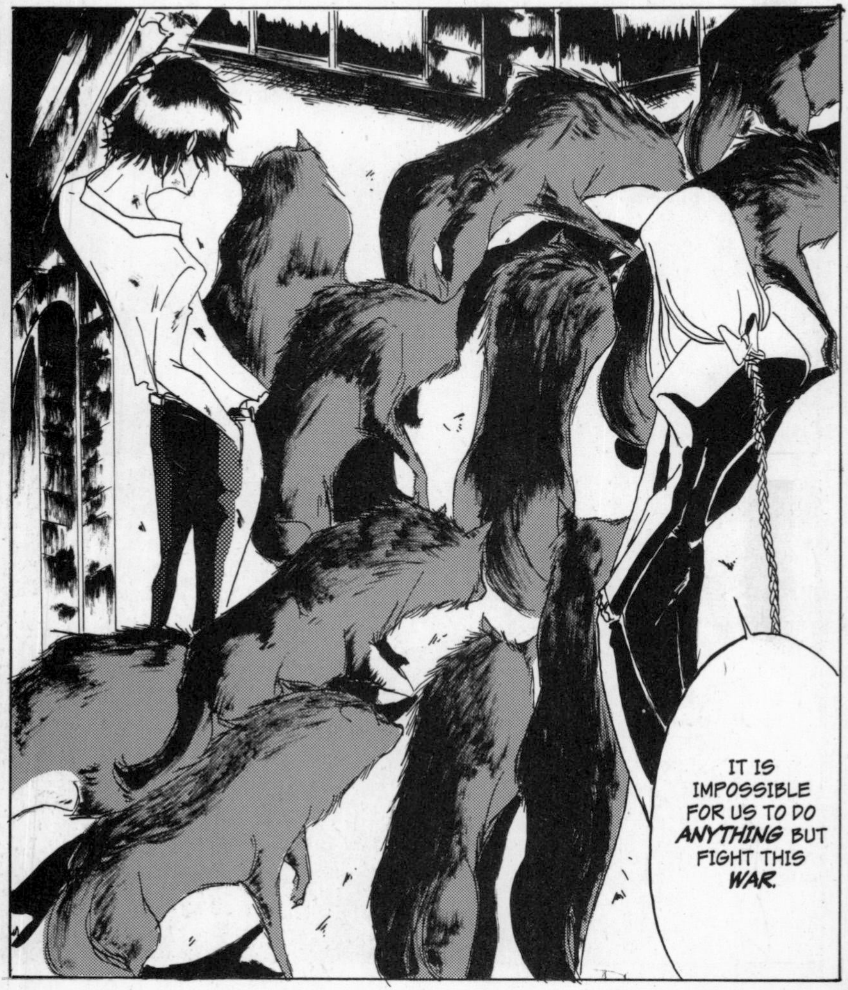
IT IS IMPOSSIBLE FOR US TO DO *ANYTHING* BUT FIGHT THIS *WAR*.

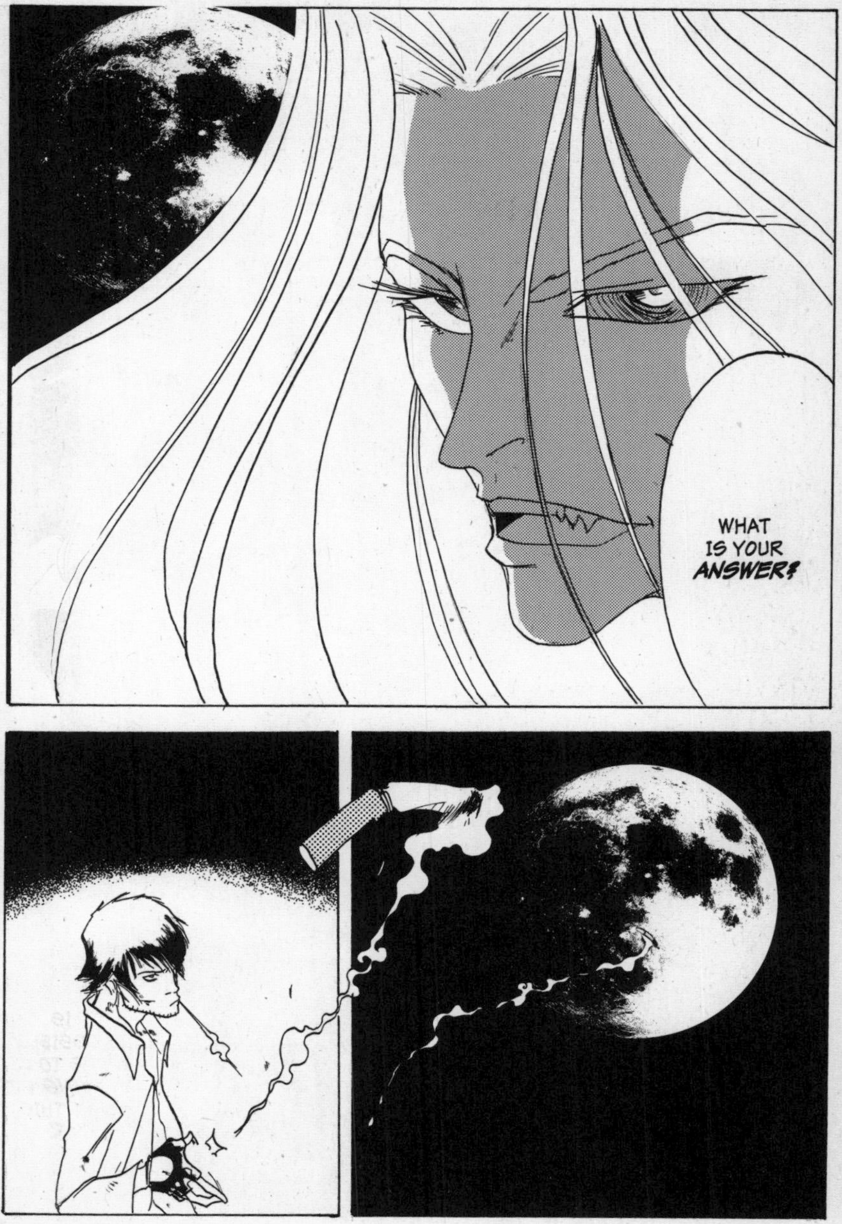
WHAT IS YOUR ANSWER?

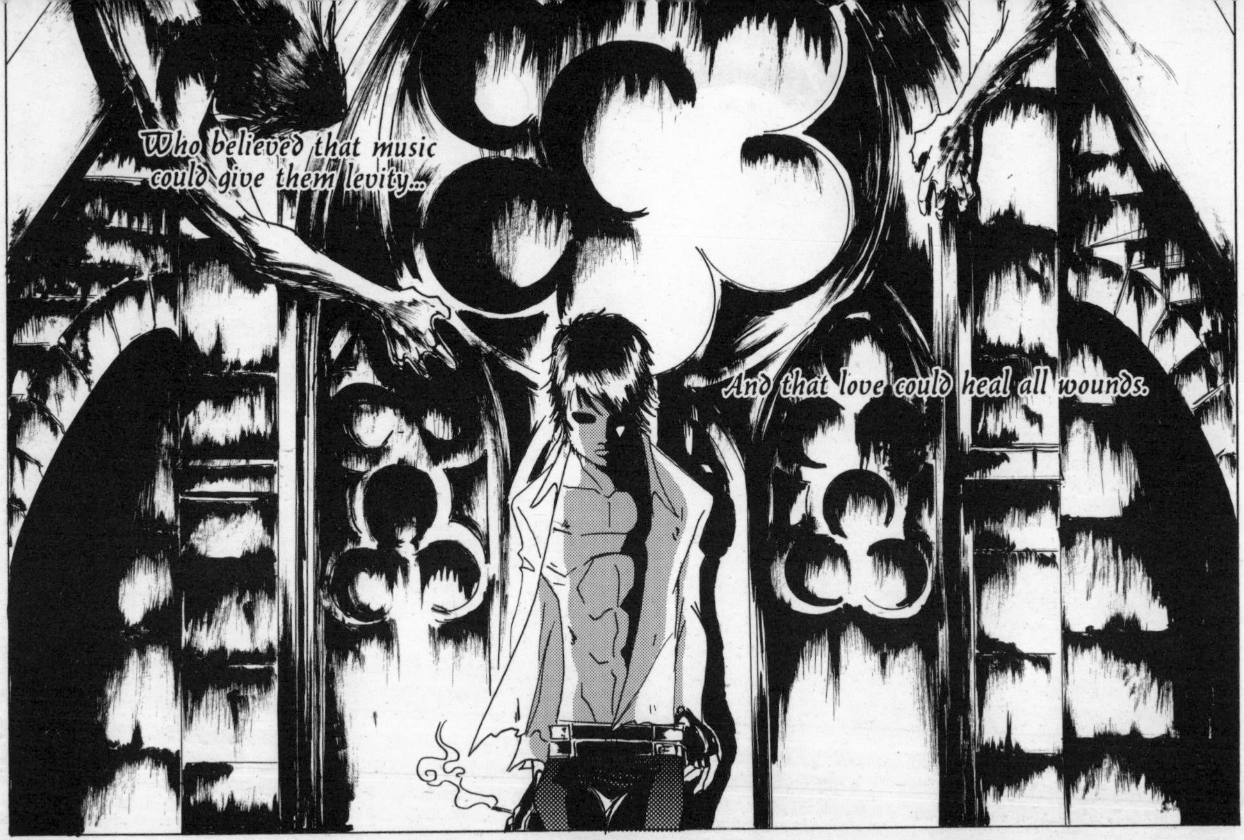
Who believed that music could give them levity...
And that love could heal all wounds.

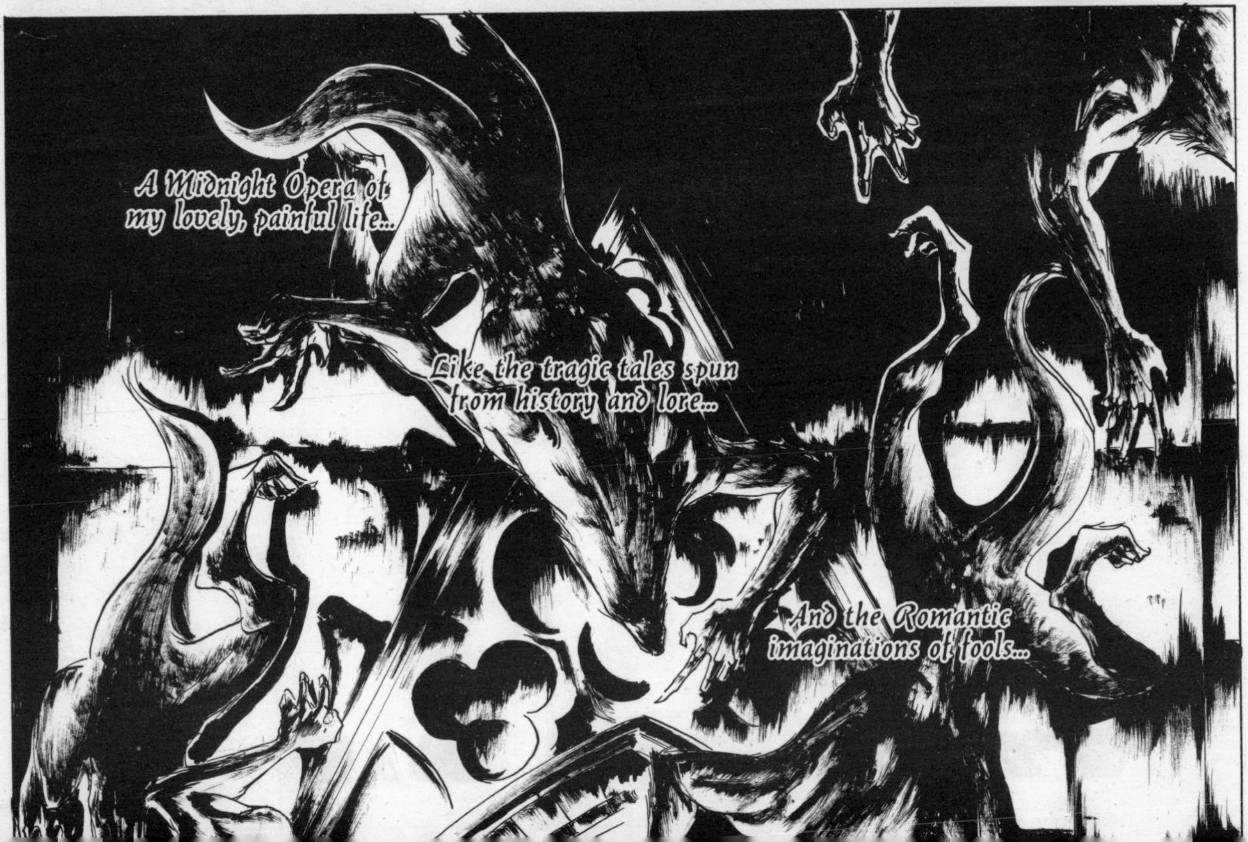
A Midnight Opera of my lovely, painful life...
Like the tragic tales spun from history and lore...
And the Romantic imaginations of fools...

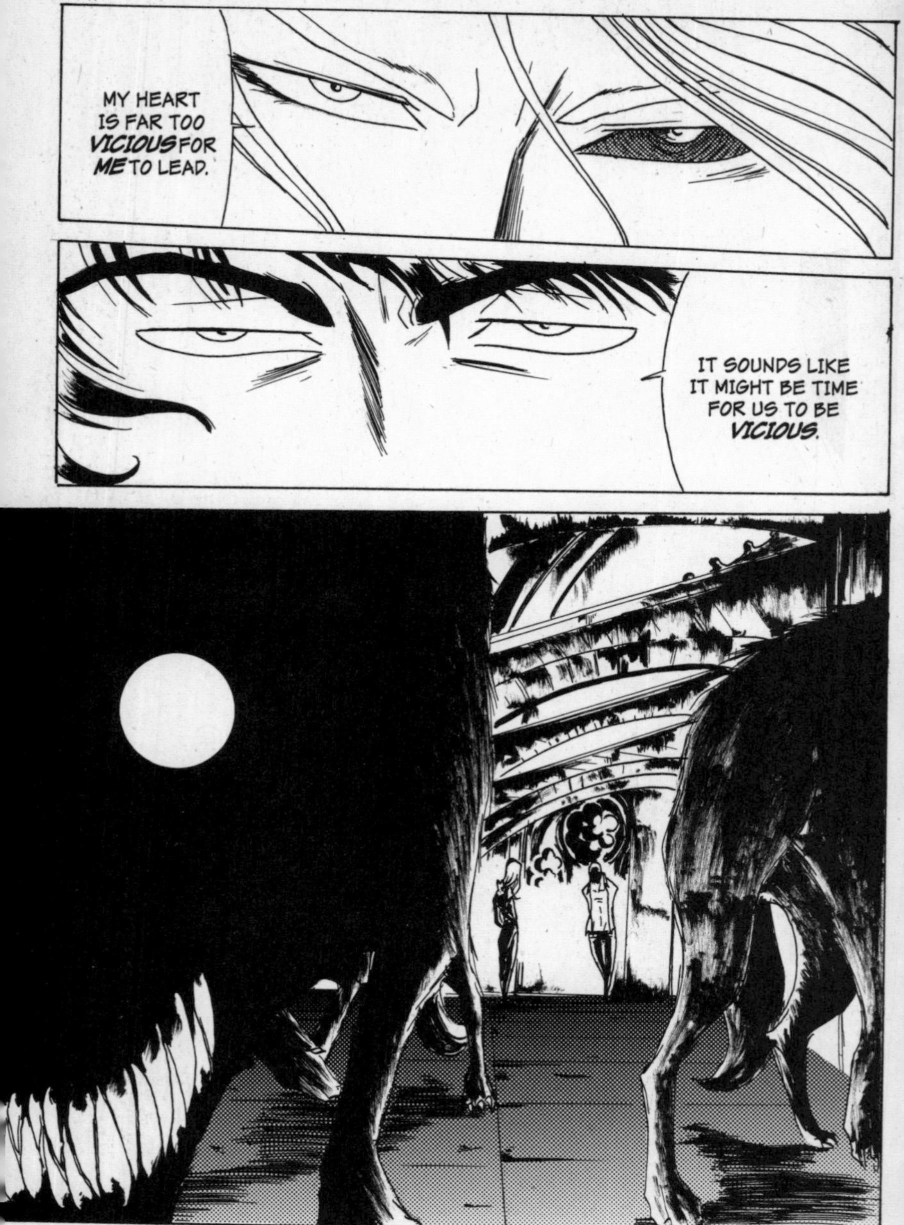
MY HEART IS FAR TOO VICIOUS FOR ME TO LEAD.
IT SOUNDS LIKE IT MIGHT BE TIME FOR US TO BE VICIOUS.

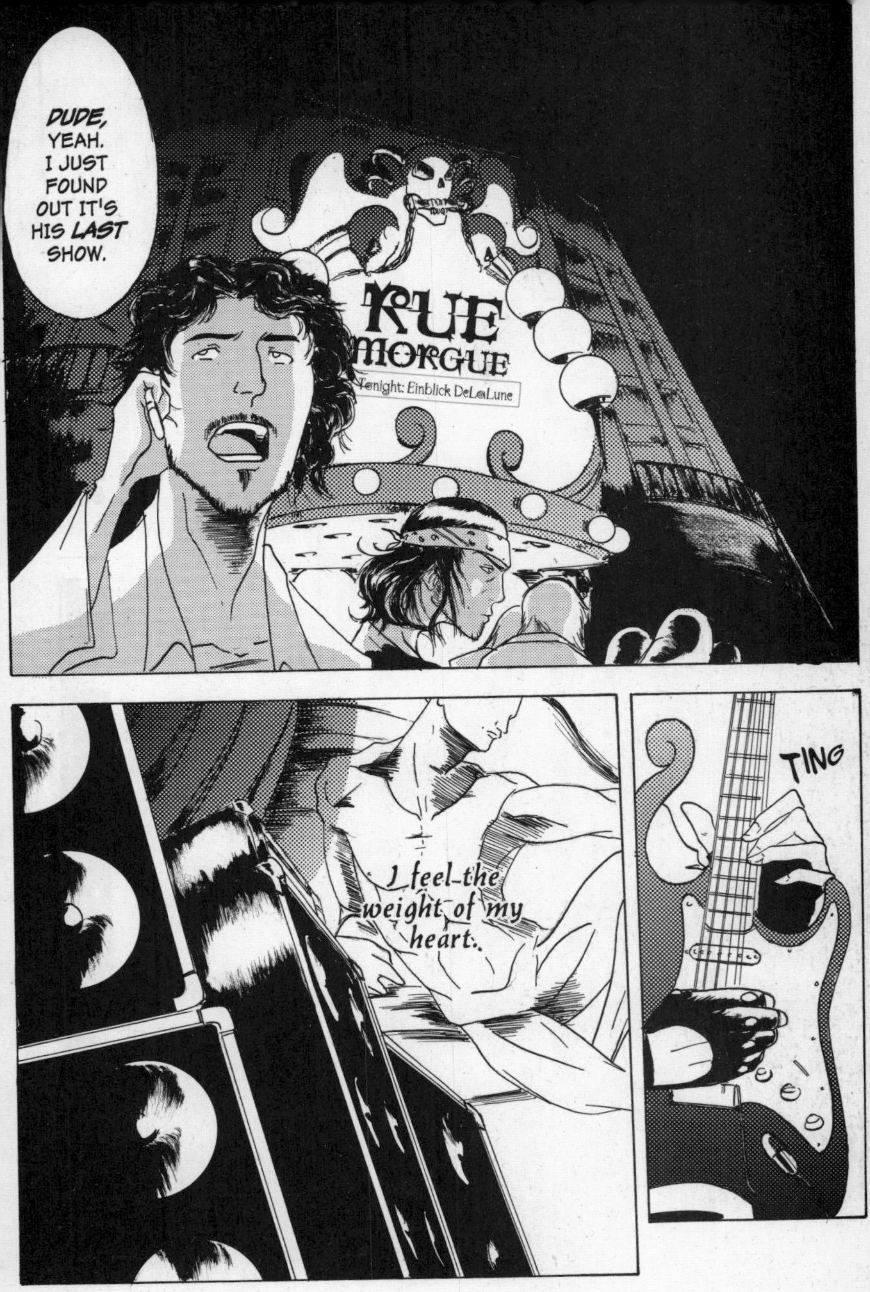
DUDE, YEAH. I JUST FOUND OUT IT'S HIS LAST SHOW.
RUE MORGUE
Tonight: Einblick DeLaLune
TING
I feel the weight of my heart..

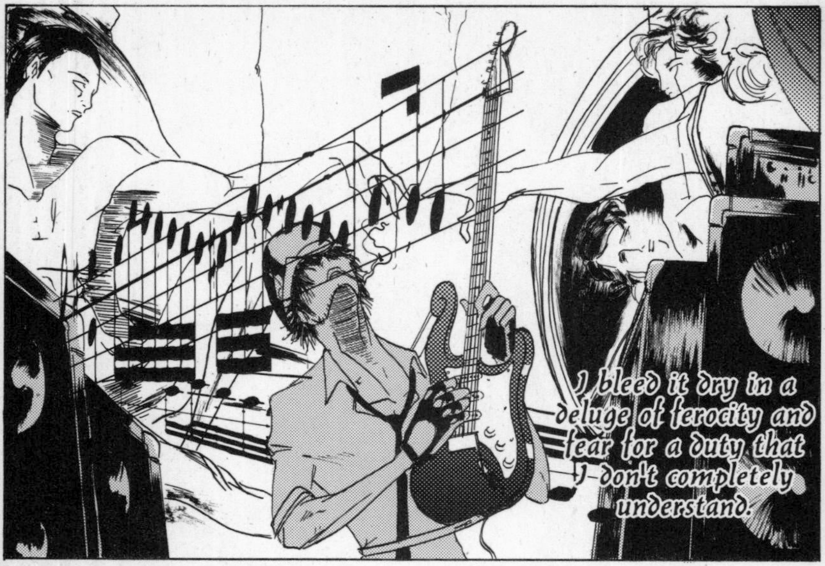
I bleed it dry in a deluge of ferocity and fear for a duty that I don't completely understand.
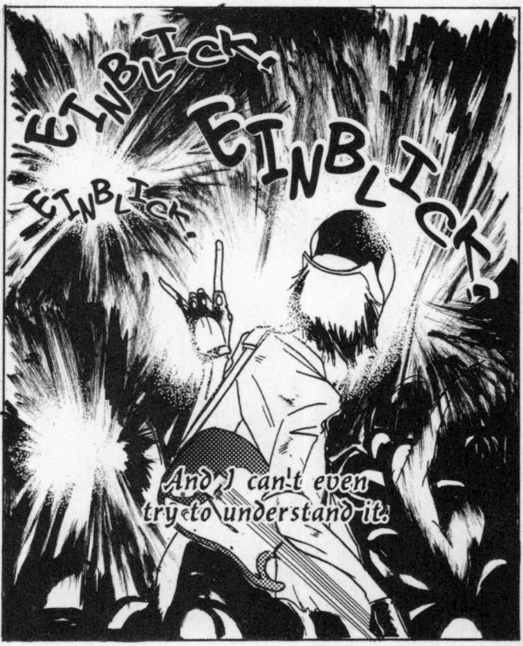
EINBLICK,
EINBLICK,
EINBLICK,
EINBLICK,
And I can't even try to understand it.
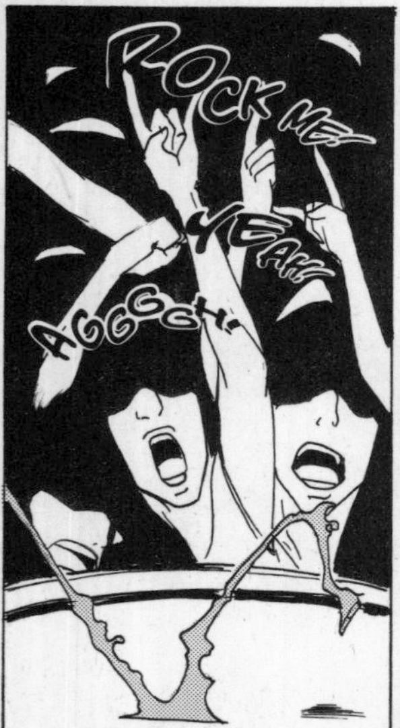
ROCK ME!
YEAH!
AGGGGH!
PMMF

STZZZZZZZT

*Because then I'll realize that my love for her...*

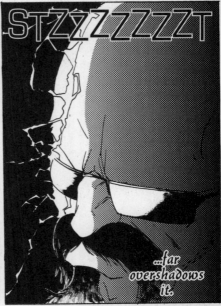

STZZZZZZZT

*...far overshadows it.*

*Is it so dangerous to love me?*

STZZZZZZZT

CREAK

*Is it so...*

CREAK

*...useless?*

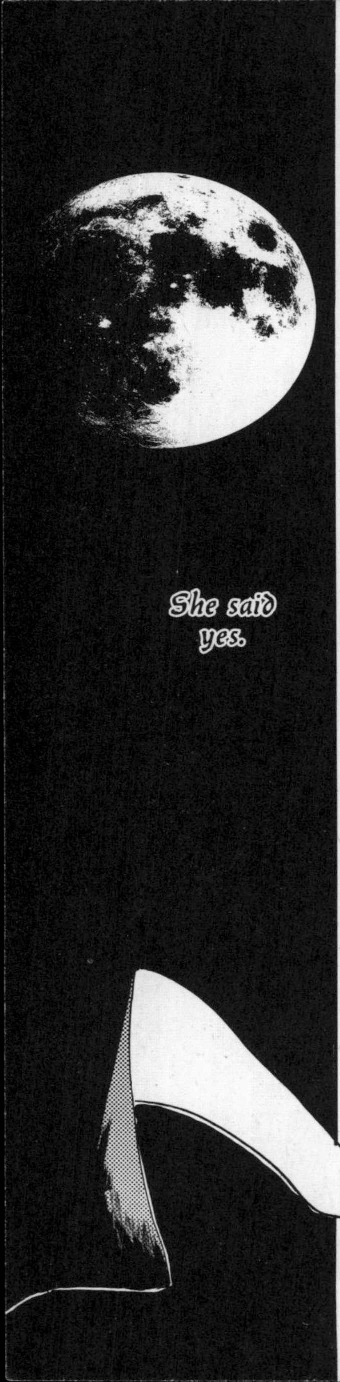
She said yes.
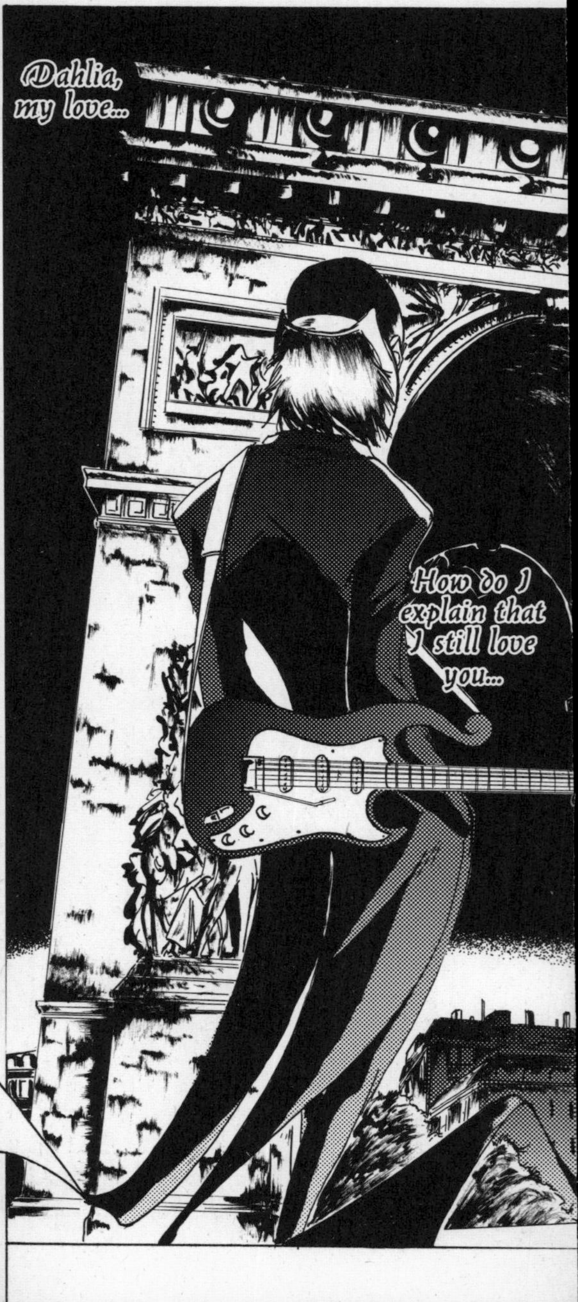
Dahlia, my love...
How do I explain that I still love you...

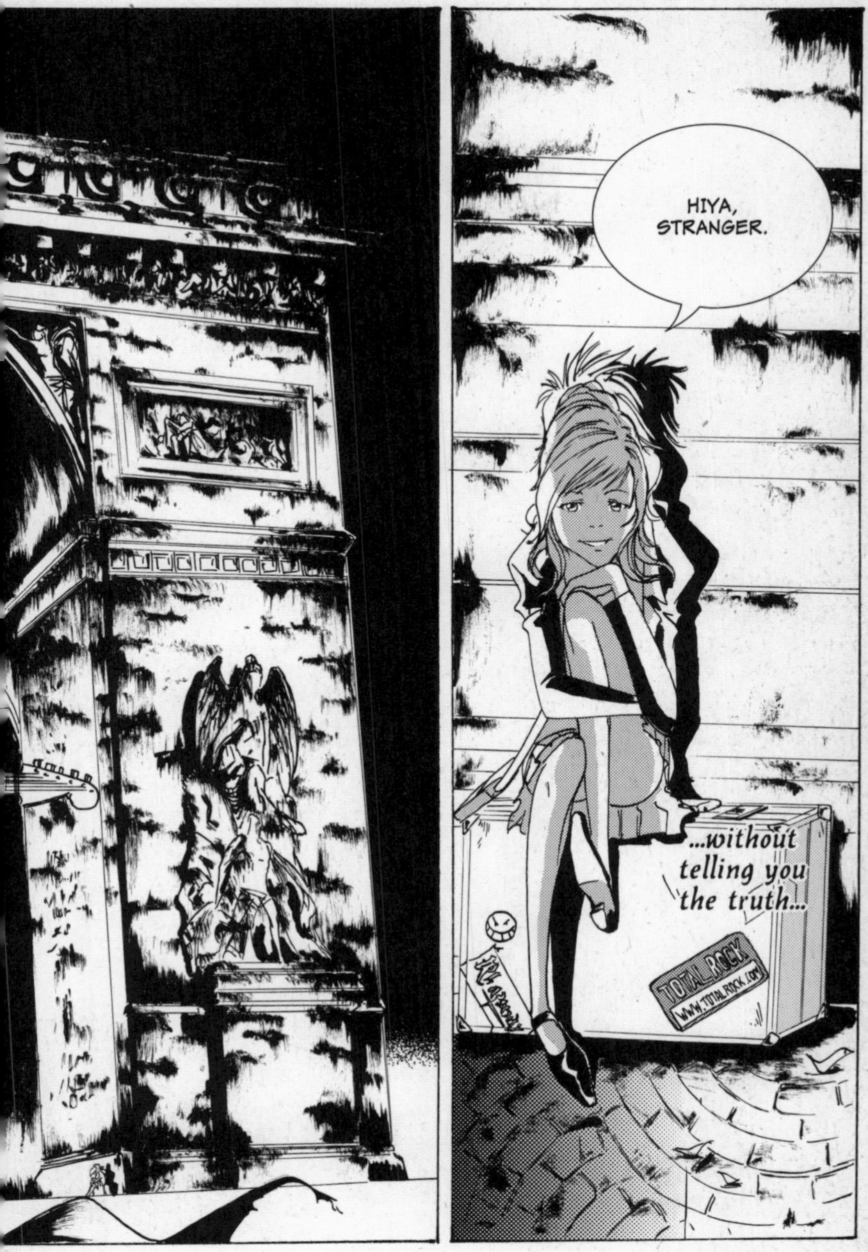
HIYA, STRANGER.
...without telling you the truth...
TOTAL ROCK
WWW.TOTALROCK.COM

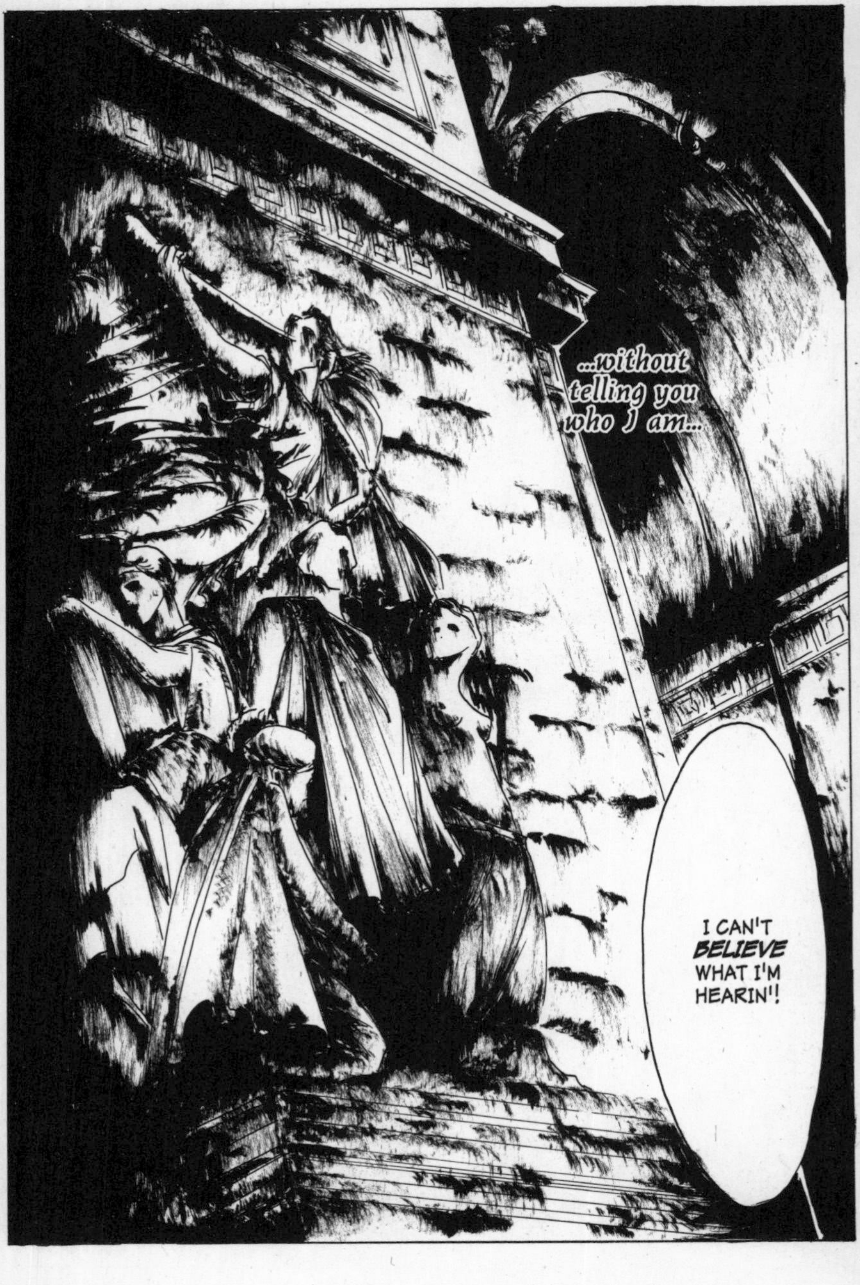
...without telling you who I am...
I CAN'T BELIEVE WHAT I'M HEARIN'!

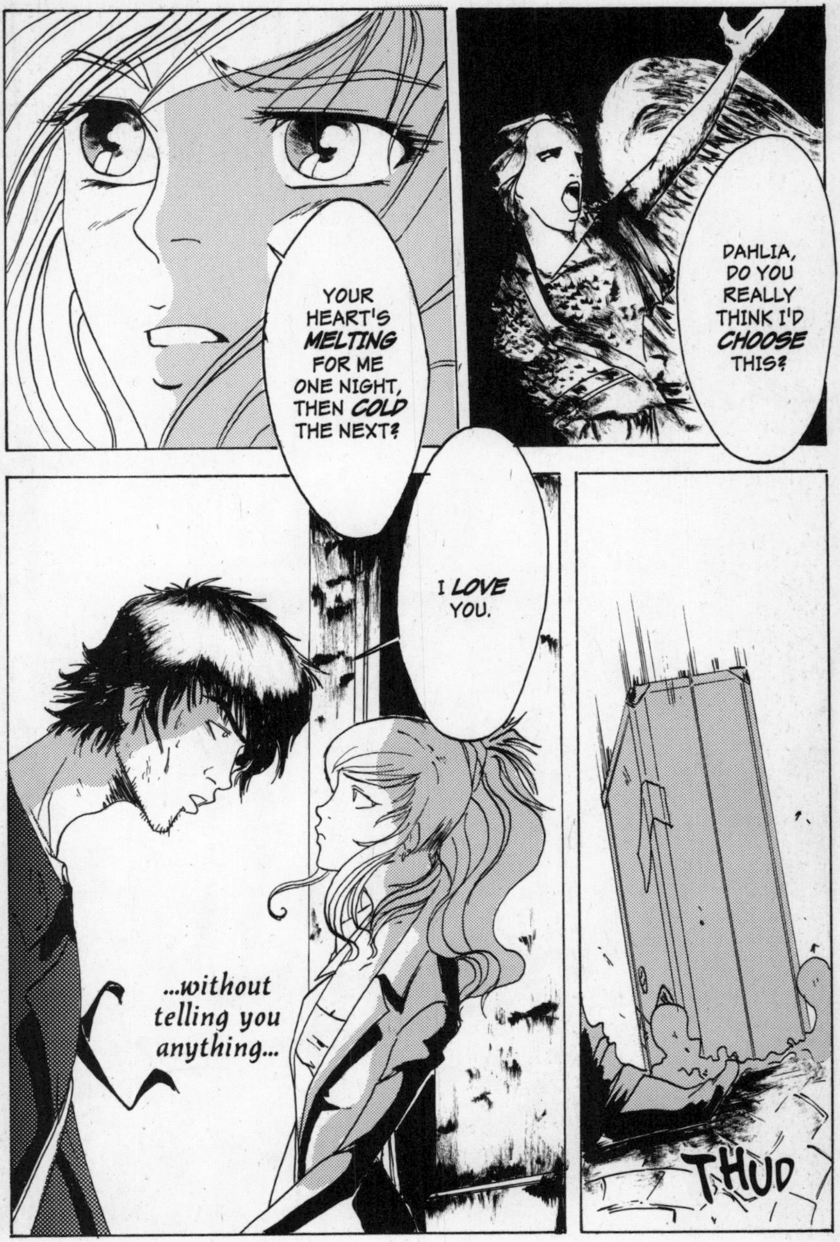
DAHLIA, DO YOU REALLY THINK I'D CHOOSE THIS?
YOUR HEART'S MELTING FOR ME ONE NIGHT, THEN COLD THE NEXT?
THUD
I LOVE YOU.
...without telling you anything...

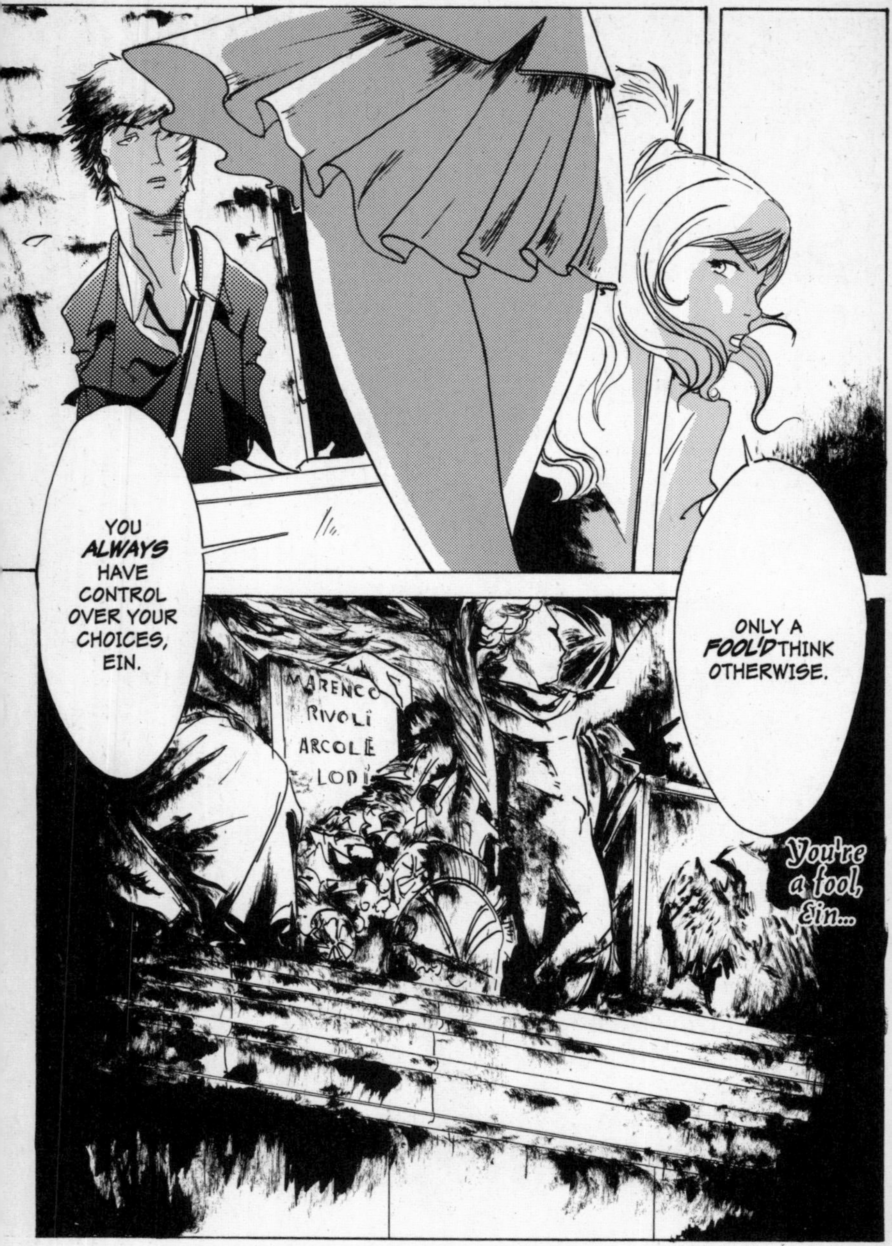
YOU ALWAYS HAVE CONTROL OVER YOUR CHOICES, EIN.
ONLY A FOOL'D THINK OTHERWISE.
MARENCO RIVOLI ARCOLE LODI
You're a fool, Ein...

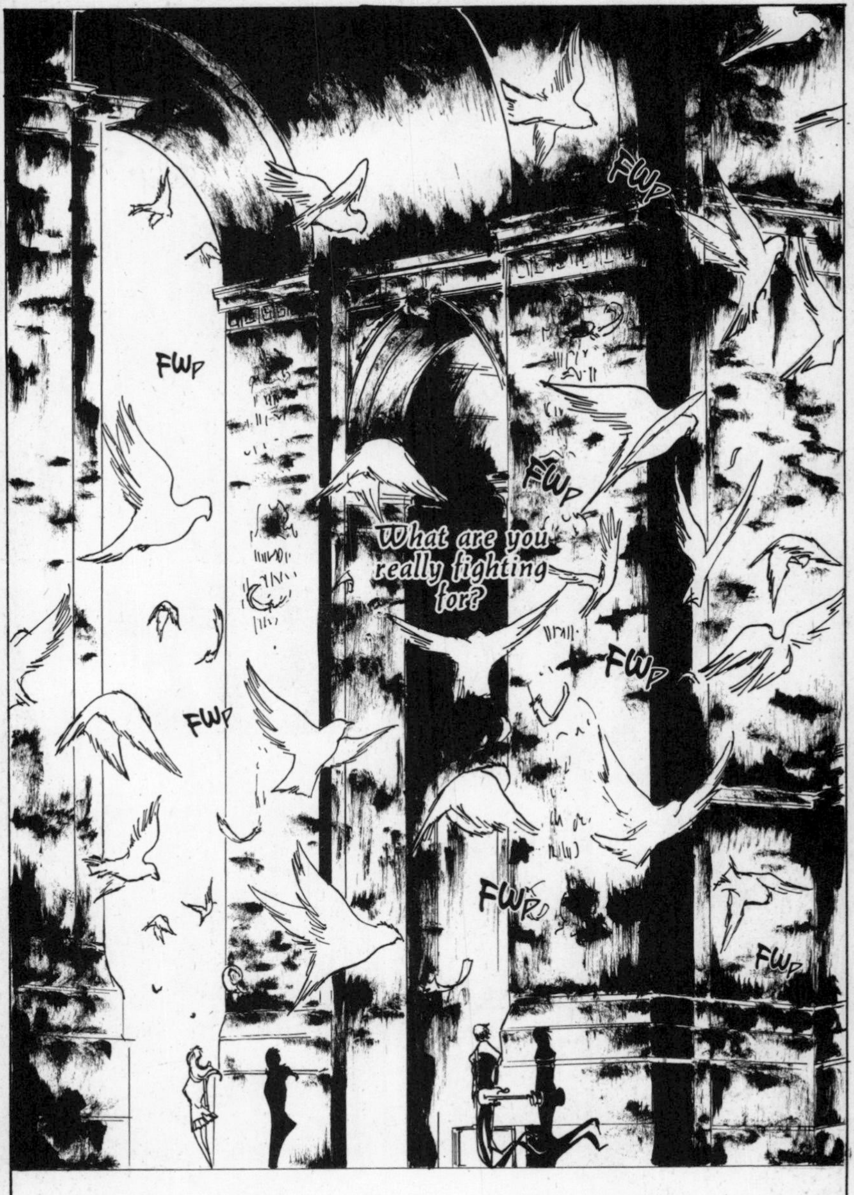
FWP
FWP
What are you really fighting for?
FWP
FWP
FWP
FWP
FWP

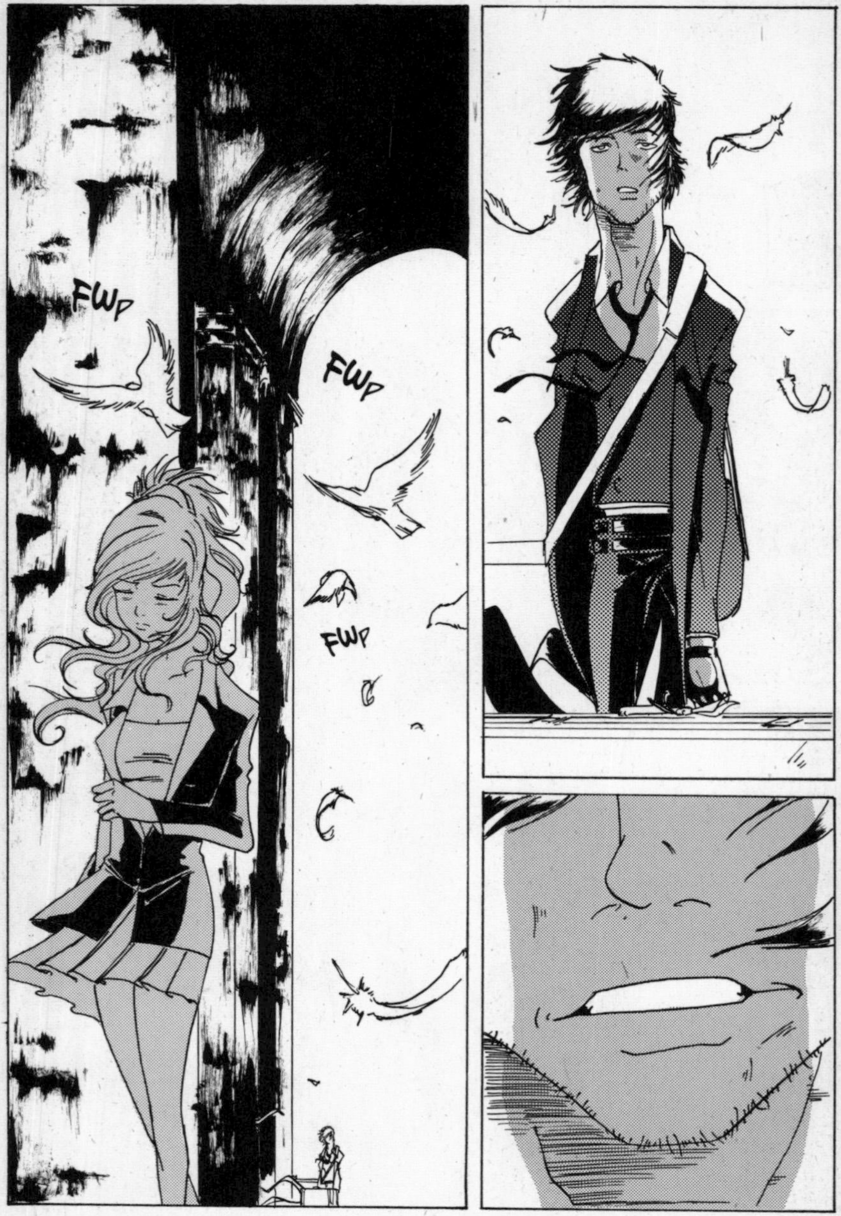
FWP
FWP
FWP

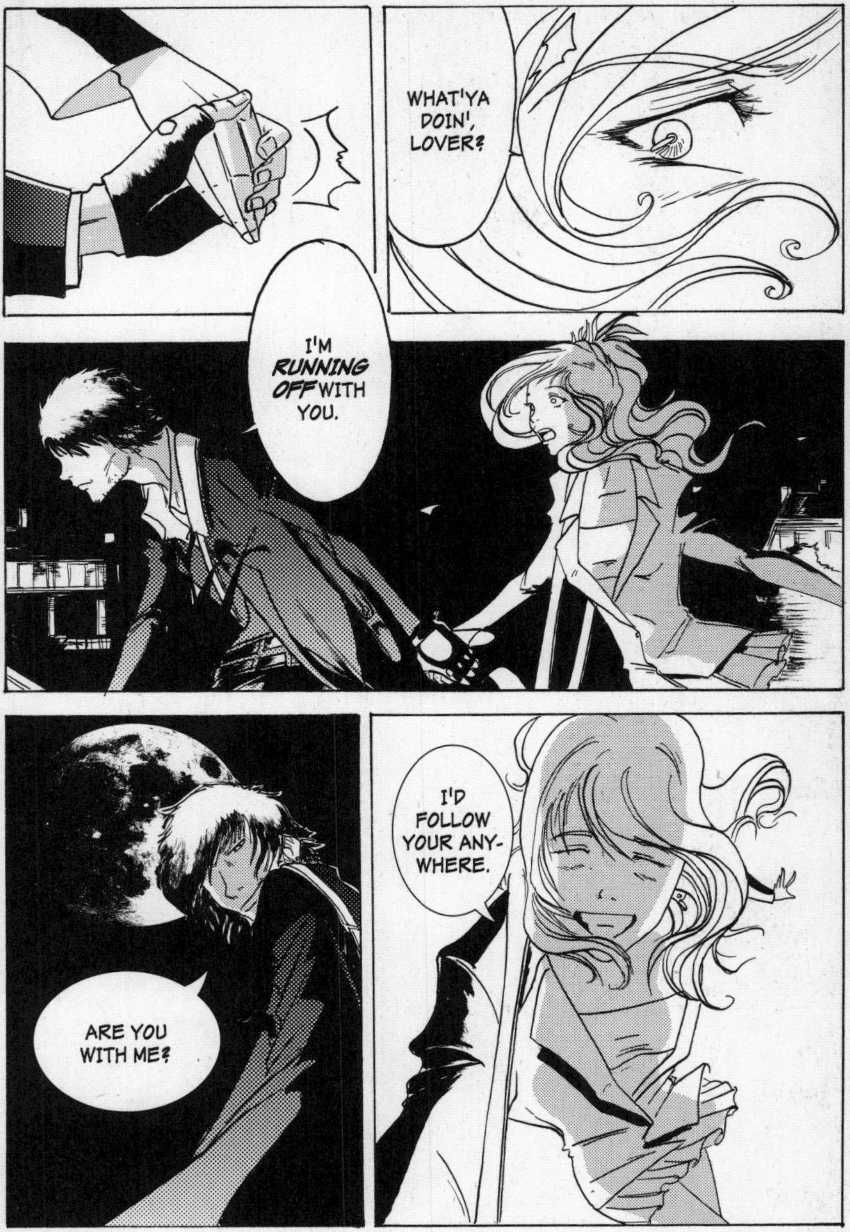
WHAT'YA DOIN', LOVER?
I'M *RUNNING OFF* WITH YOU.
ARE YOU WITH ME?
I'D FOLLOW YOUR ANY-WHERE.

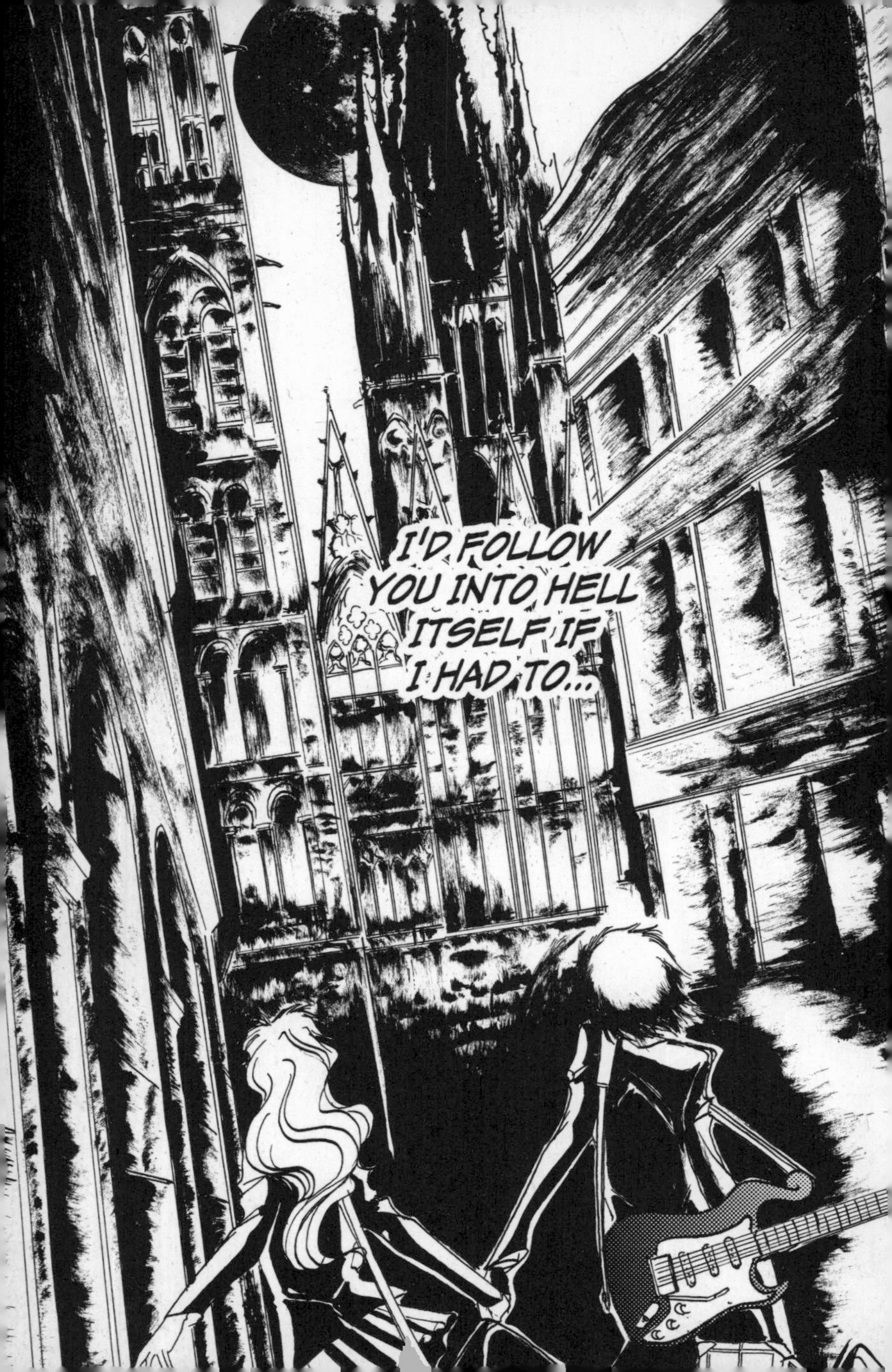
I'D FOLLOW YOU INTO HELL ITSELF IF I HAD TO...

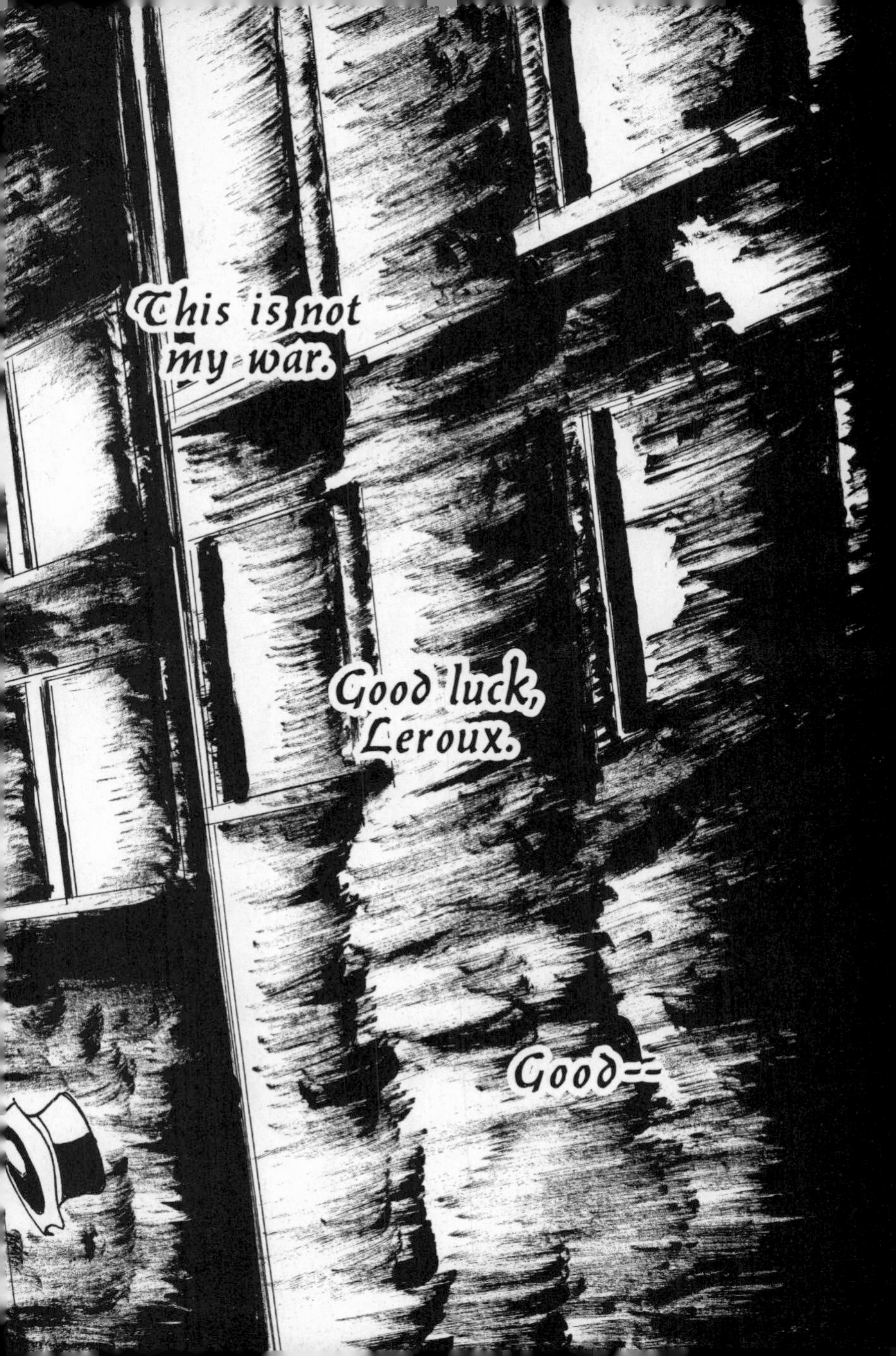
This is not my war.
Good luck, Leroux.
Good--

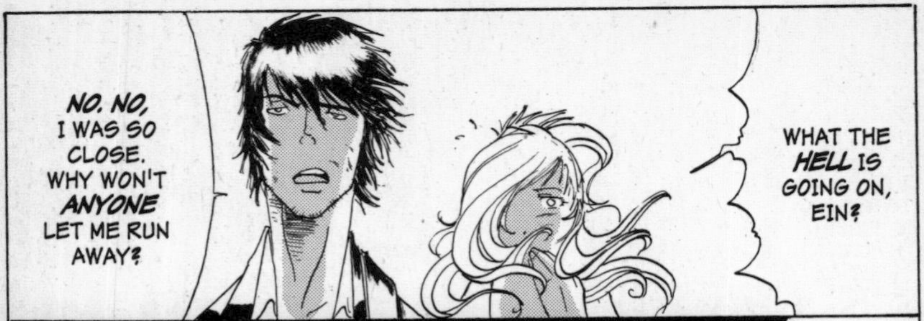
WHAT THE HELL IS GOING ON, EIN?
NO. NO, I WAS SO CLOSE. WHY WON'T ANYONE LET ME RUN AWAY?

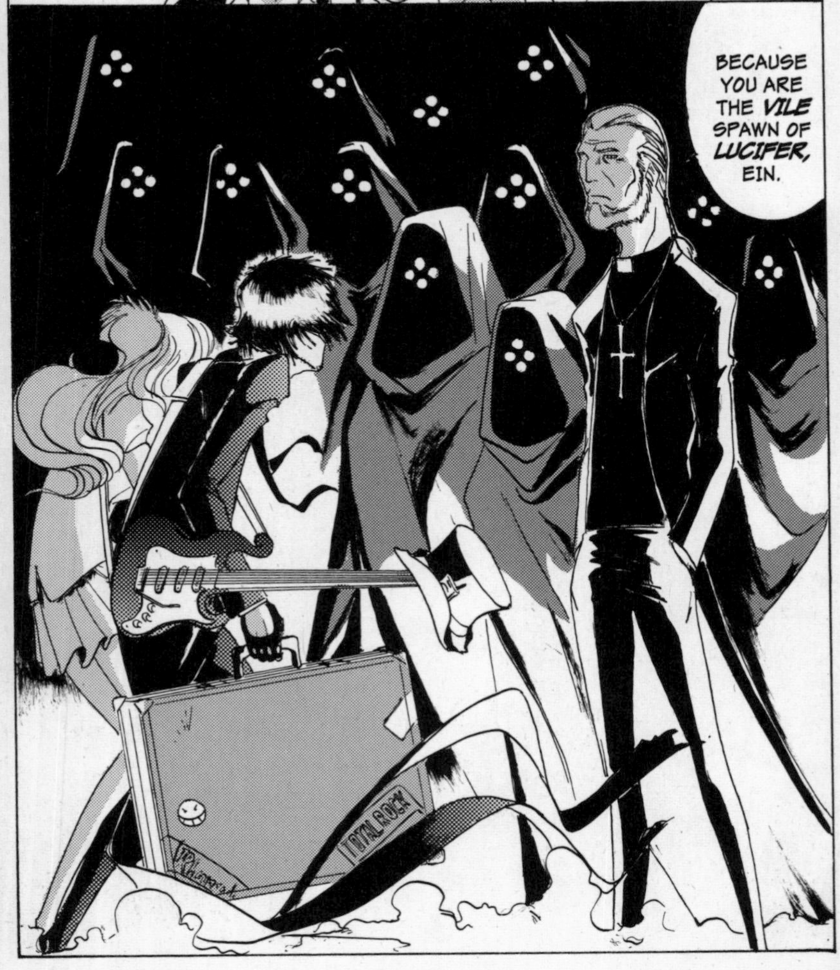
BECAUSE YOU ARE THE VILE SPAWN OF LUCIFER, EIN.
TOTAL ROCK

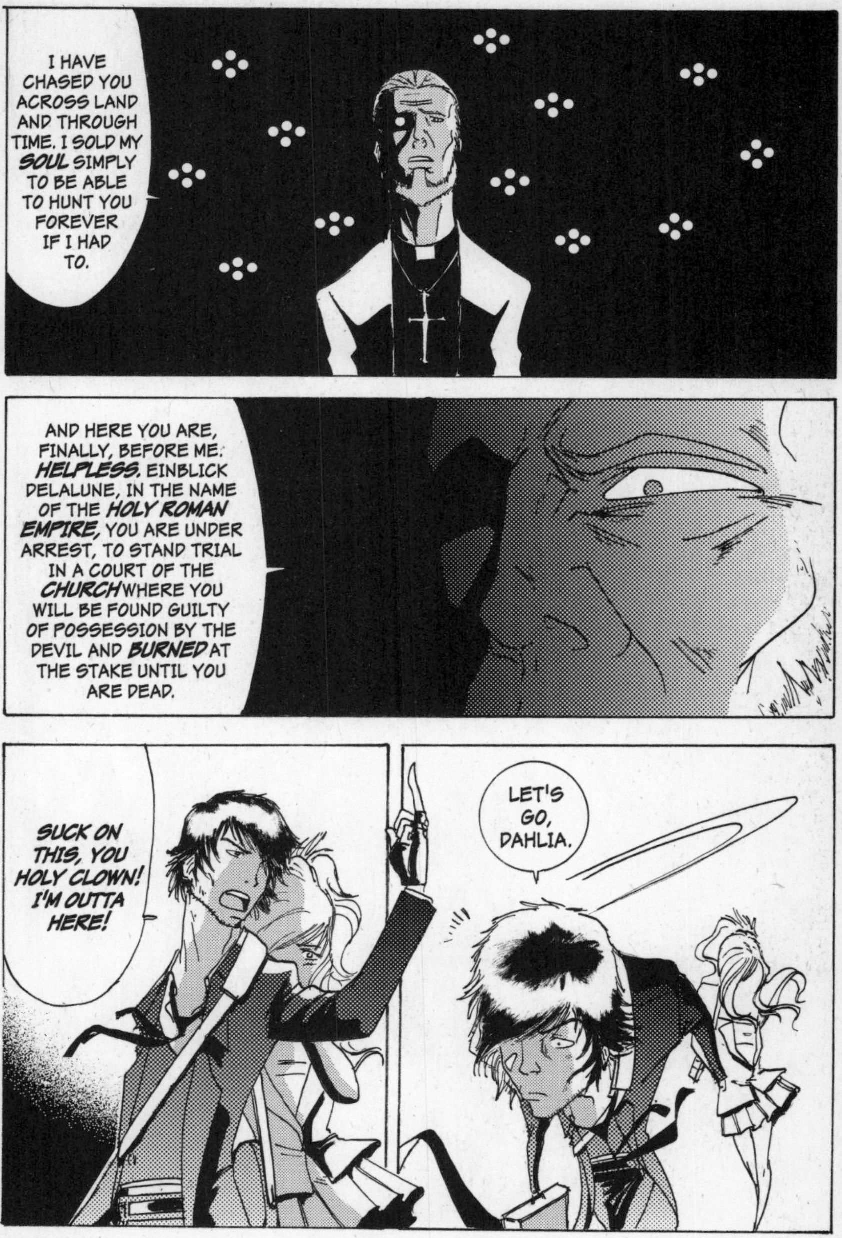
I HAVE CHASED YOU ACROSS LAND AND THROUGH TIME. I SOLD MY SOUL SIMPLY TO BE ABLE TO HUNT YOU FOREVER IF I HAD TO.
AND HERE YOU ARE, FINALLY, BEFORE ME. HELPLESS. EINBLICK DELALUNE, IN THE NAME OF THE HOLY ROMAN EMPIRE, YOU ARE UNDER ARREST, TO STAND TRIAL IN A COURT OF THE CHURCH WHERE YOU WILL BE FOUND GUILTY OF POSSESSION BY THE DEVIL AND BURNED AT THE STAKE UNTIL YOU ARE DEAD.
SUCK ON THIS, YOU HOLY CLOWN! I'M OUTTA HERE!
LET'S GO, DAHLIA.

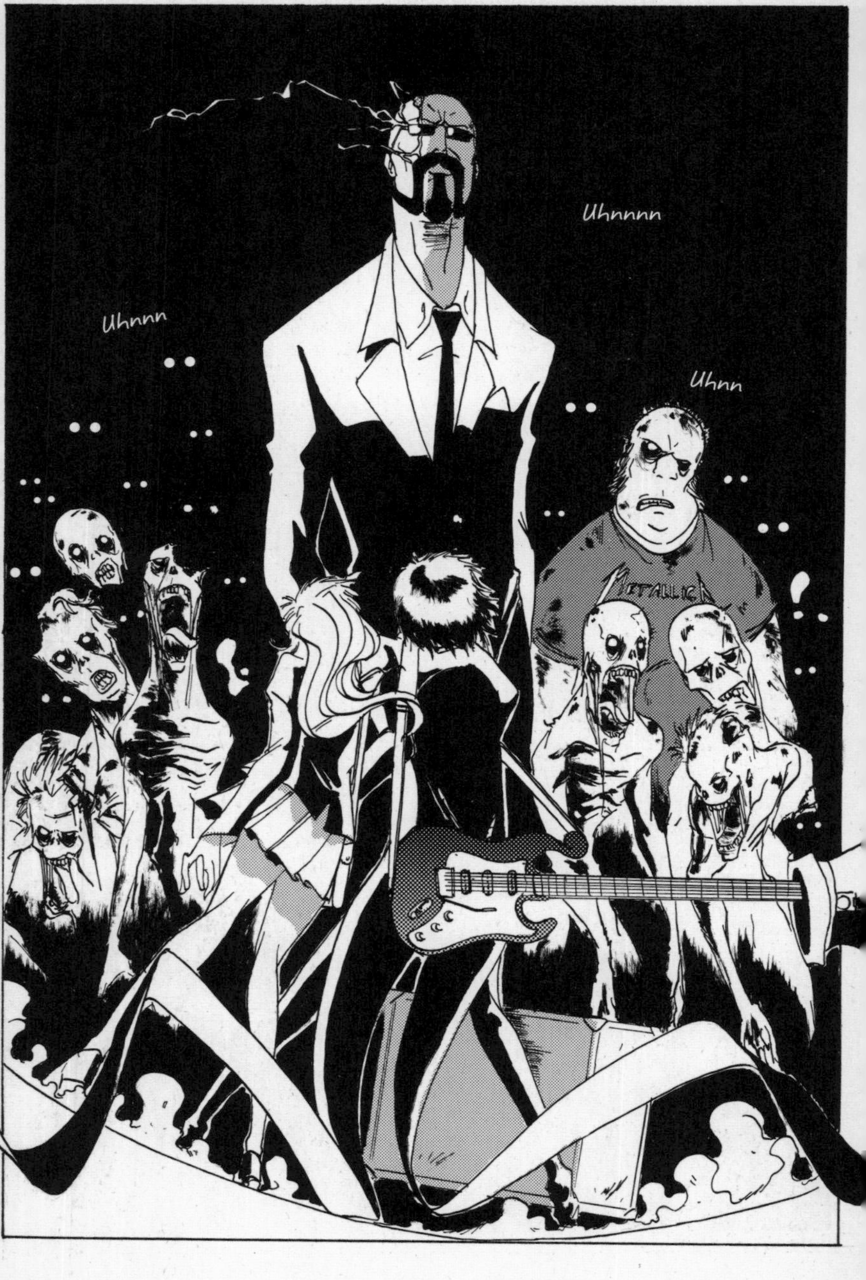
Uhnnnn
Uhnnn
Uhnn
METALLICA

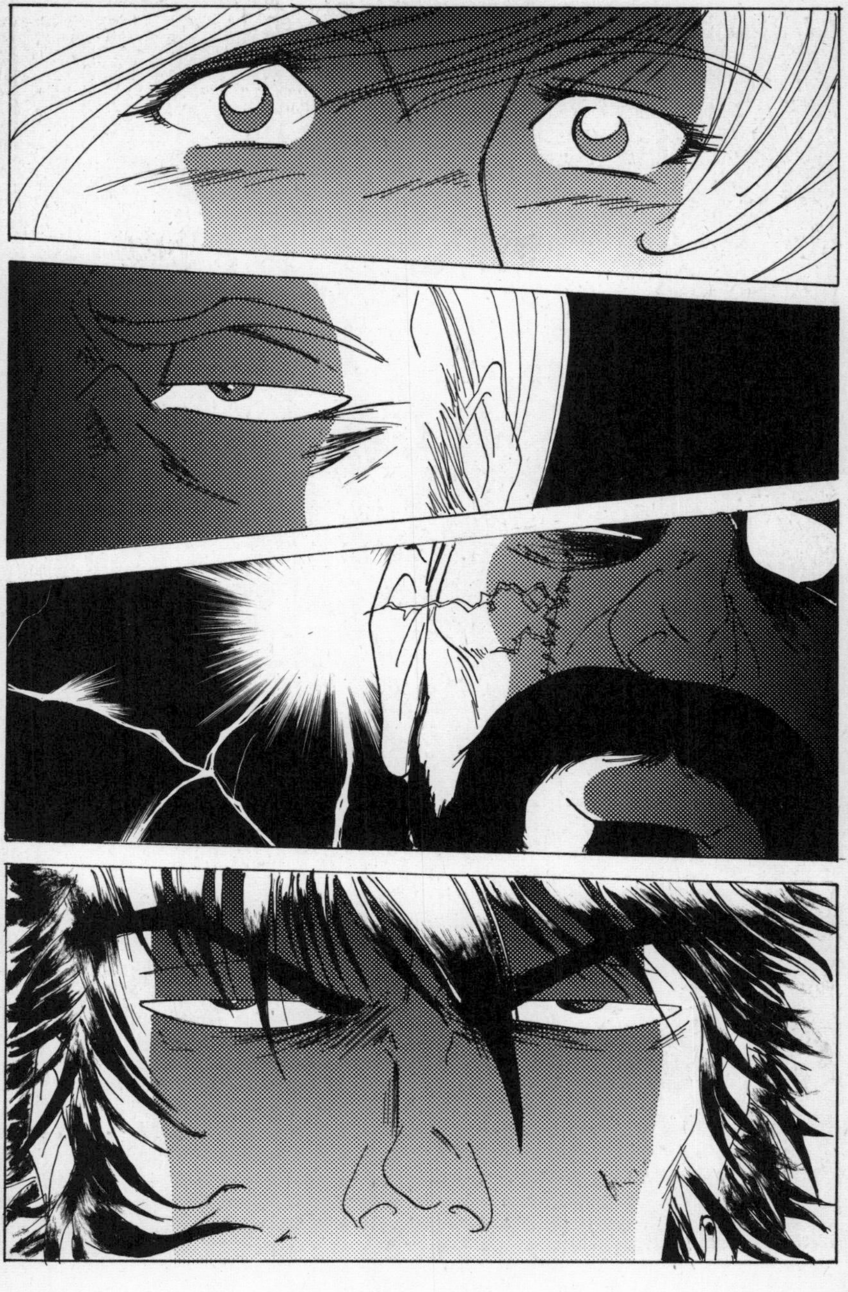

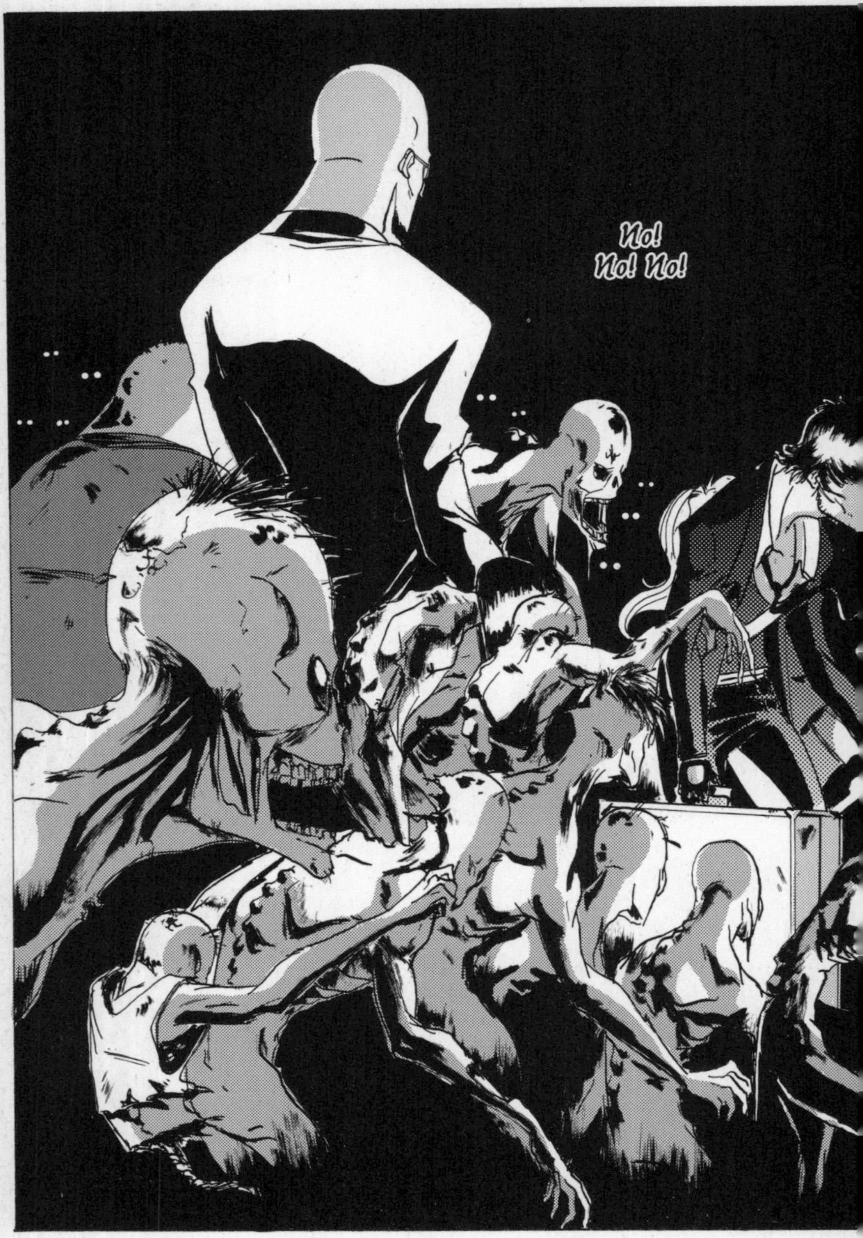
No!
No! No!

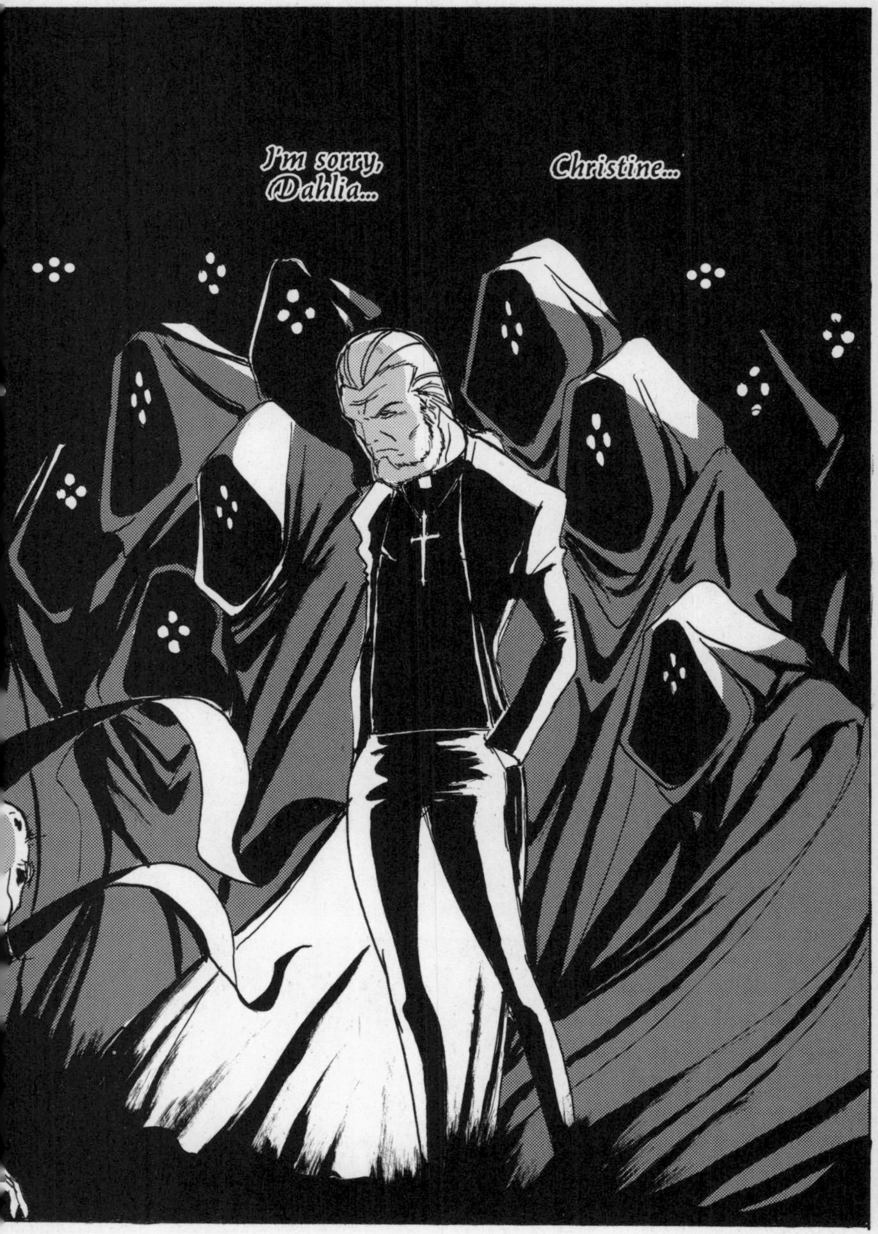
Christine...
I'm sorry, Dahlia...

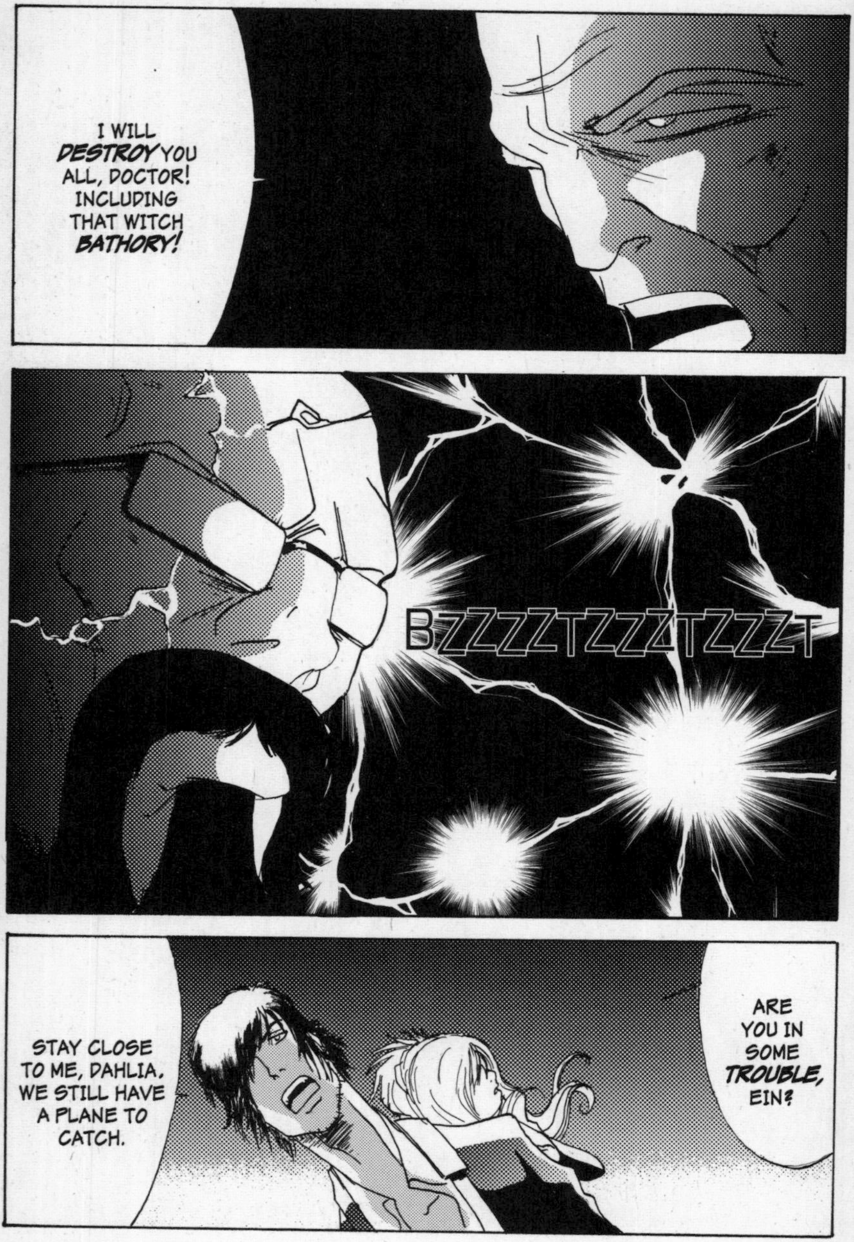
I WILL DESTROY YOU ALL, DOCTOR! INCLUDING THAT WITCH BATHORY!
BZZZZZTZZZZTZZZZT
ARE YOU IN SOME TROUBLE, EIN?
STAY CLOSE TO ME, DAHLIA, WE STILL HAVE A PLANE TO CATCH.

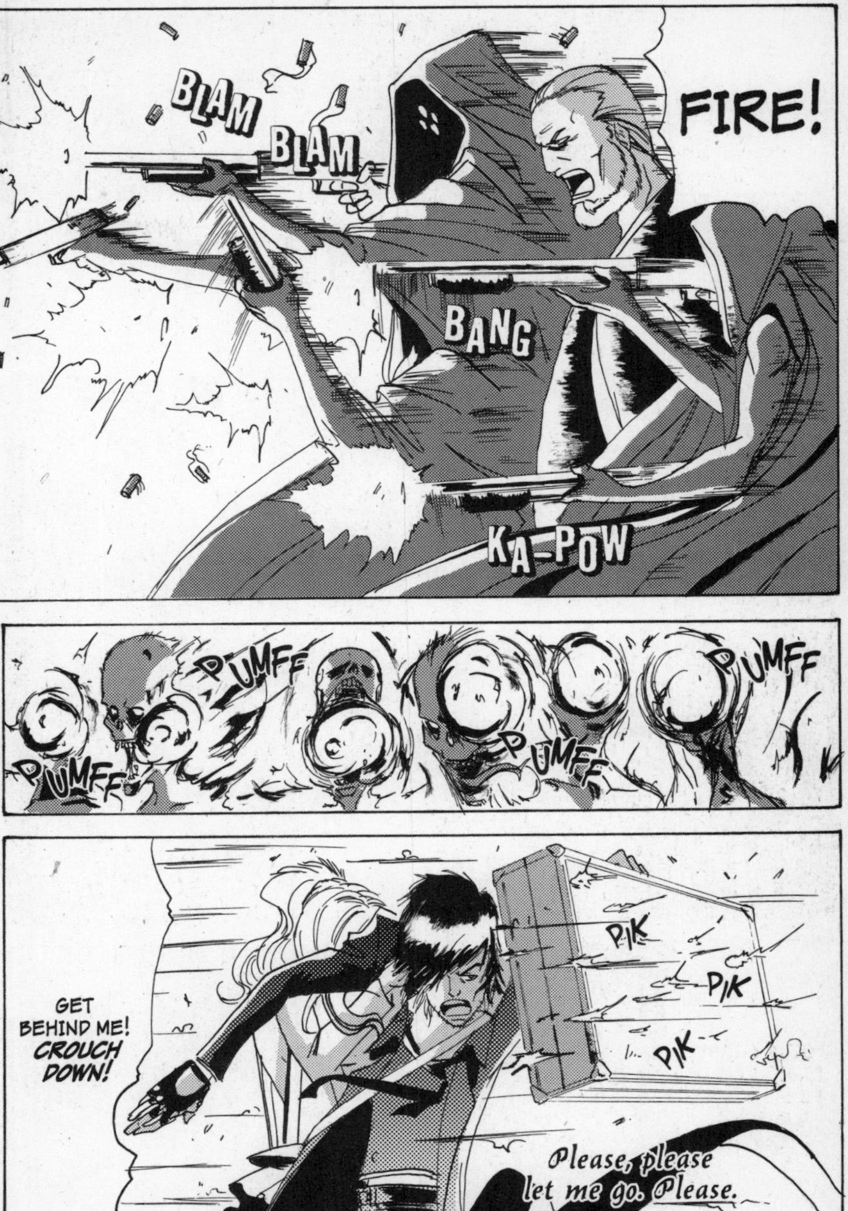
FIRE!
BLAM
BLAM
BANG
KA-POW
PUMFF
PUMFF
PUMFF
PUMFF
PIK
PIK
PIK
Please, please let me go. Please.
GET BEHIND ME! CROUCH DOWN!

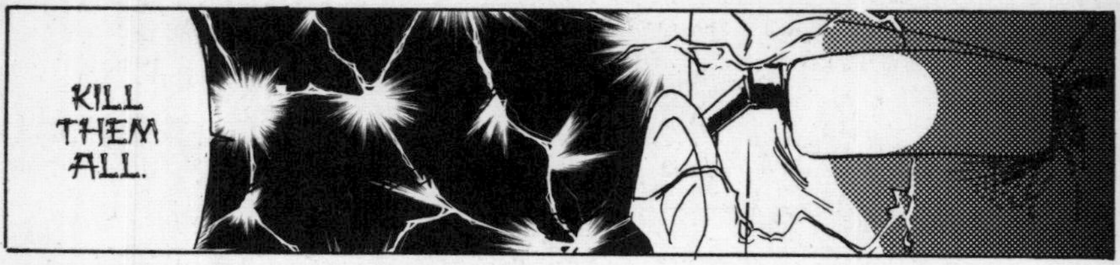
KILL THEM ALL.
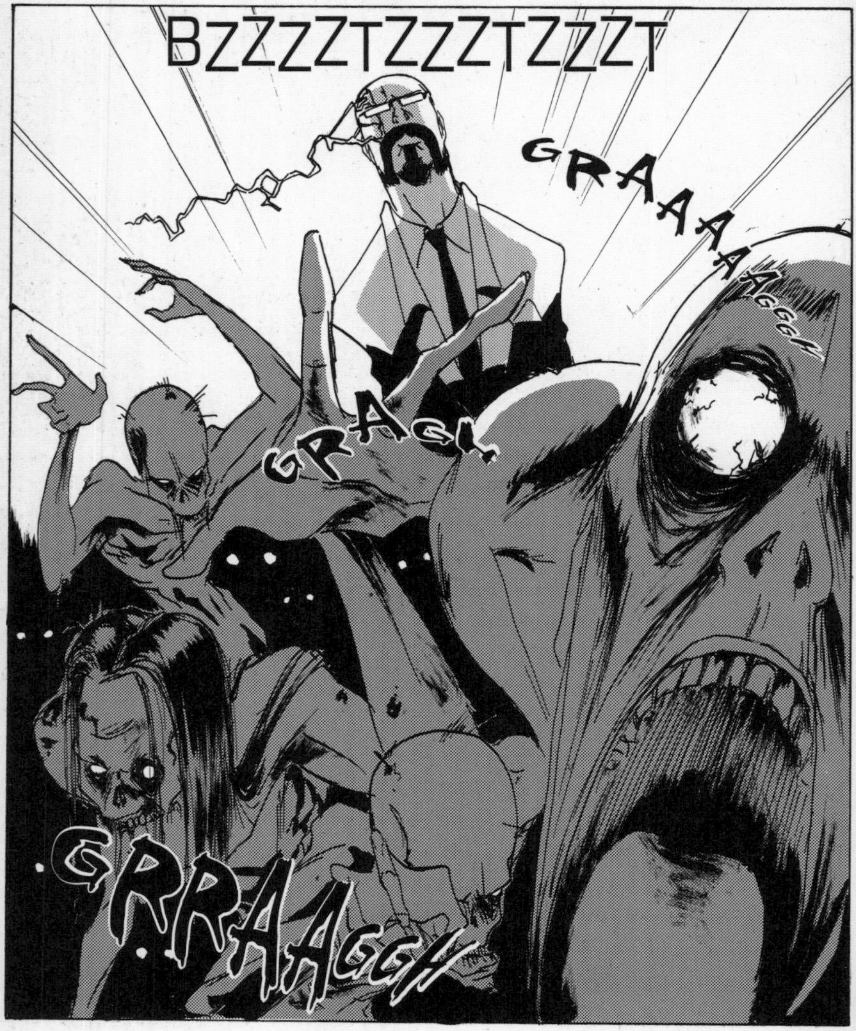
BZZZZZTZZZZTZZZZT
GRAAAAAGGGH
GRAGH
GRRAAGGGH

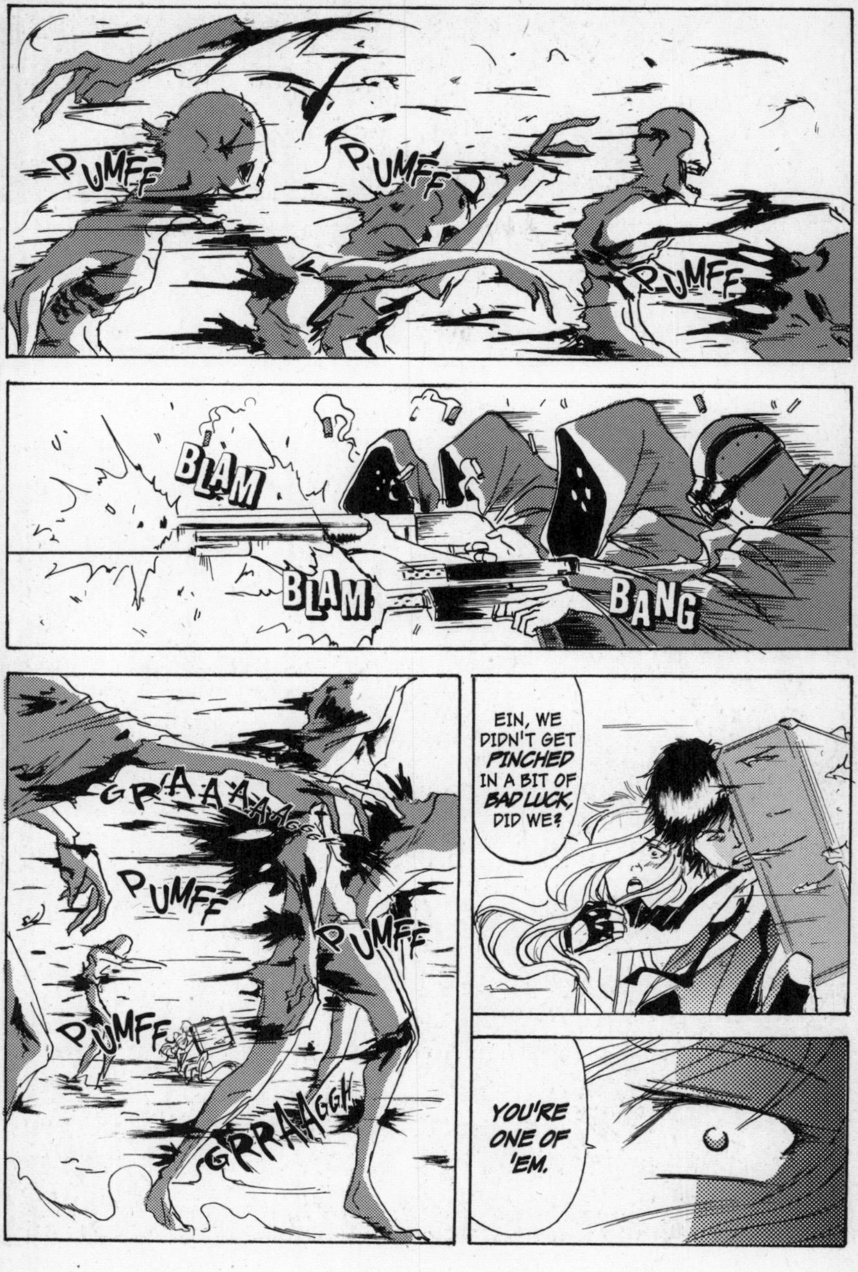
PUMFF
PUMFF
PUMFF
BANG
BLAM
BLAM
EIN, WE DIDN'T GET *PINCHED* IN A BIT OF *BAD LUCK*, DID WE?
*YOU'RE ONE OF 'EM.*
PUMFF
PUMFF
PUMFF
GRRAAGGH

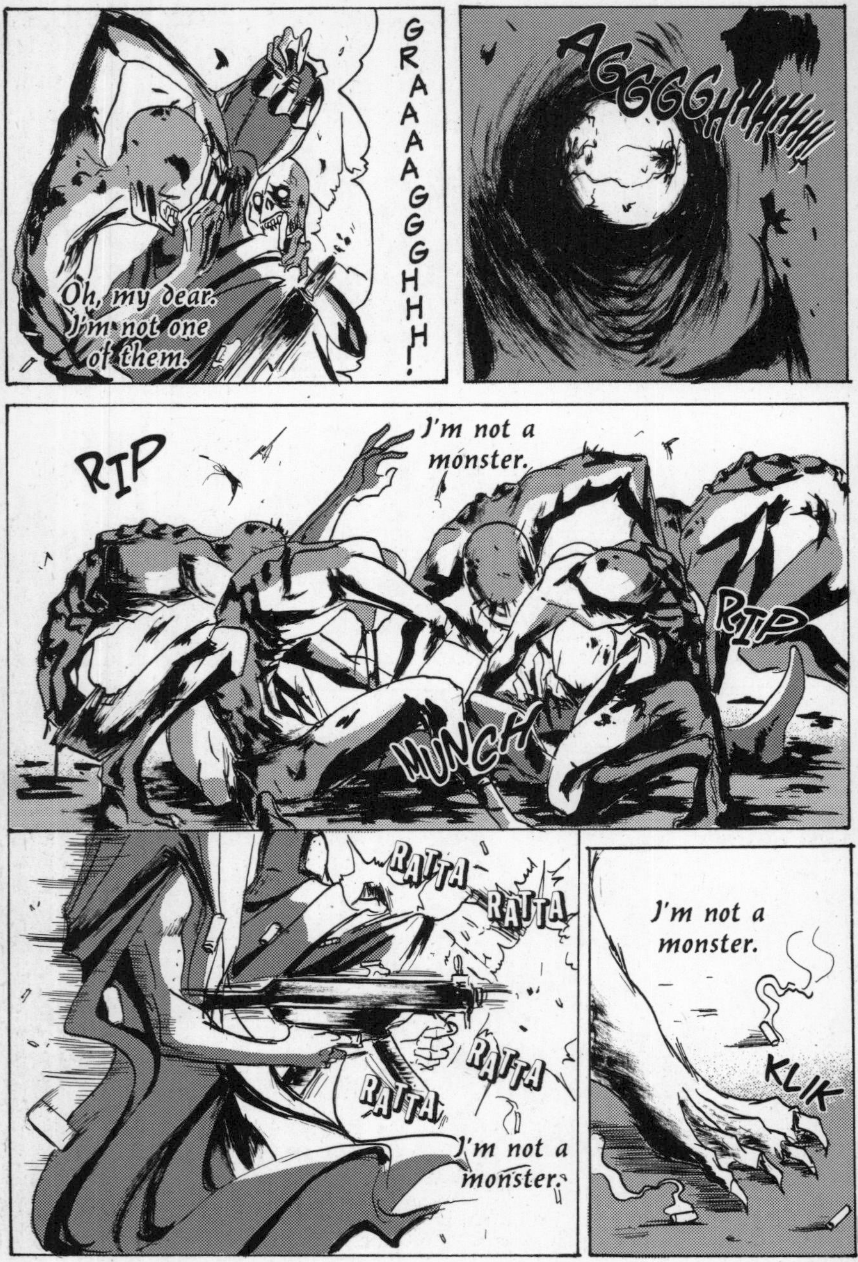
Oh, my dear. I'm not one of them.
GRAAAAGGGHHH!
AGGGGHHHHHH
RIP
I'm not a monster.
RIP
MUNCH
RATTA
RATTA
RATTA
RATTA
I'm not a monster.
I'm not a monster.
KLIK

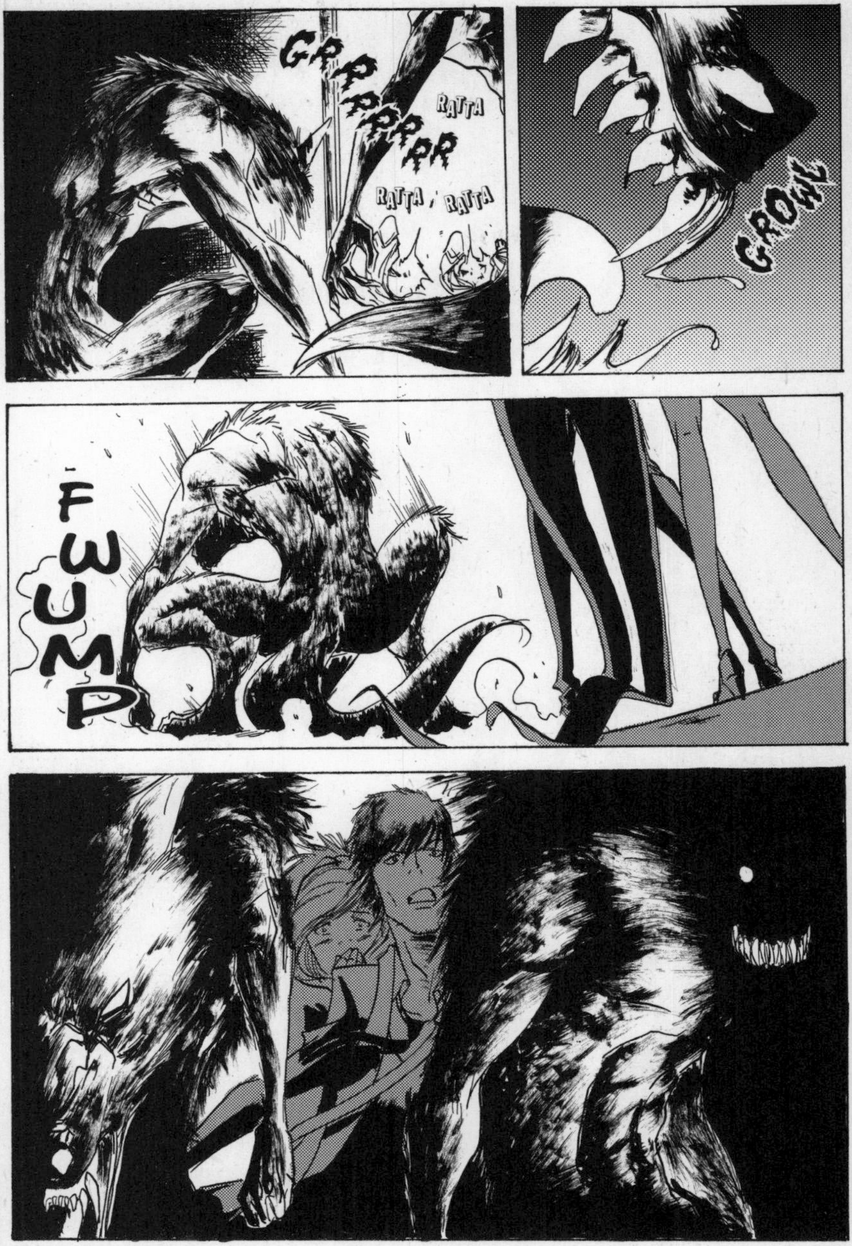
GROWL
GRRRRRRR
RATTA
RATTA, RATTA
FWUMP

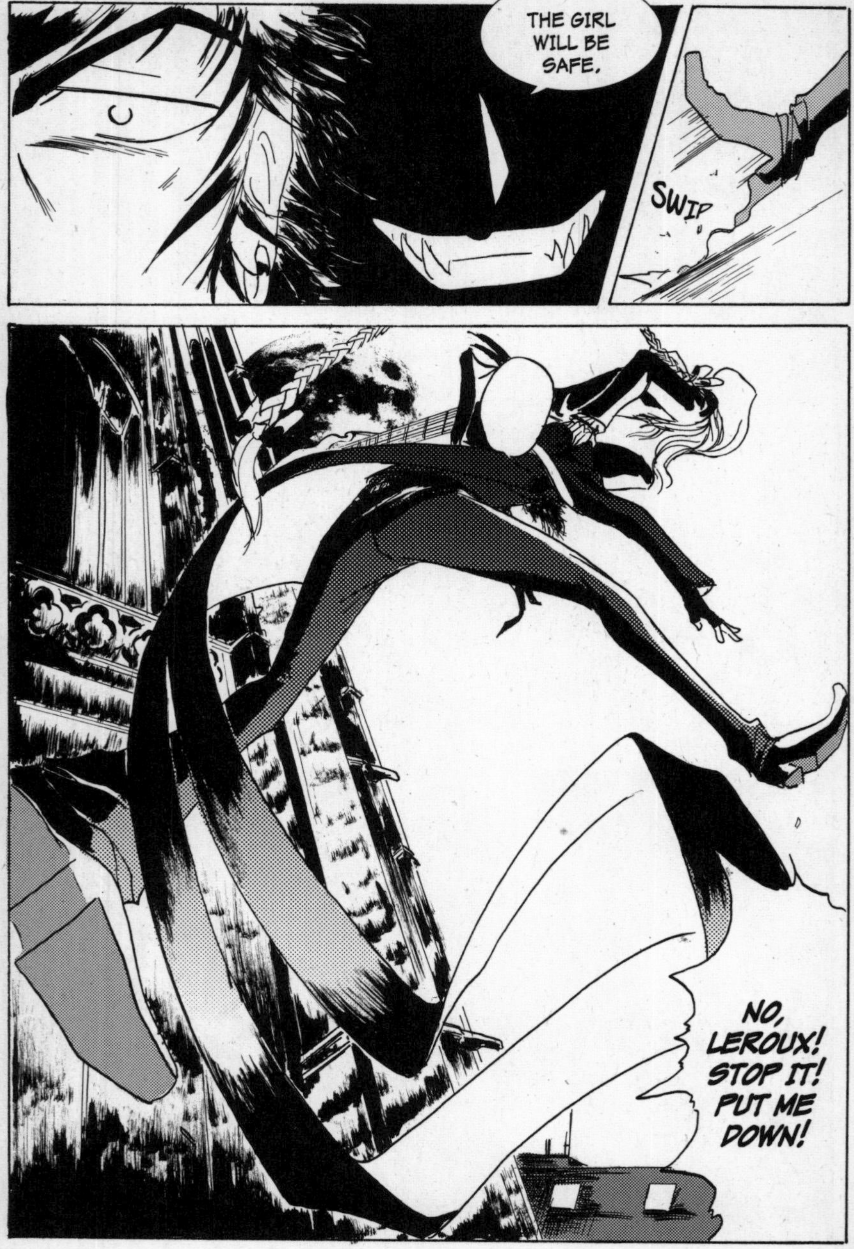
SWIP
THE GIRL WILL BE SAFE.
NO, LEROUX! STOP IT! PUT ME DOWN!

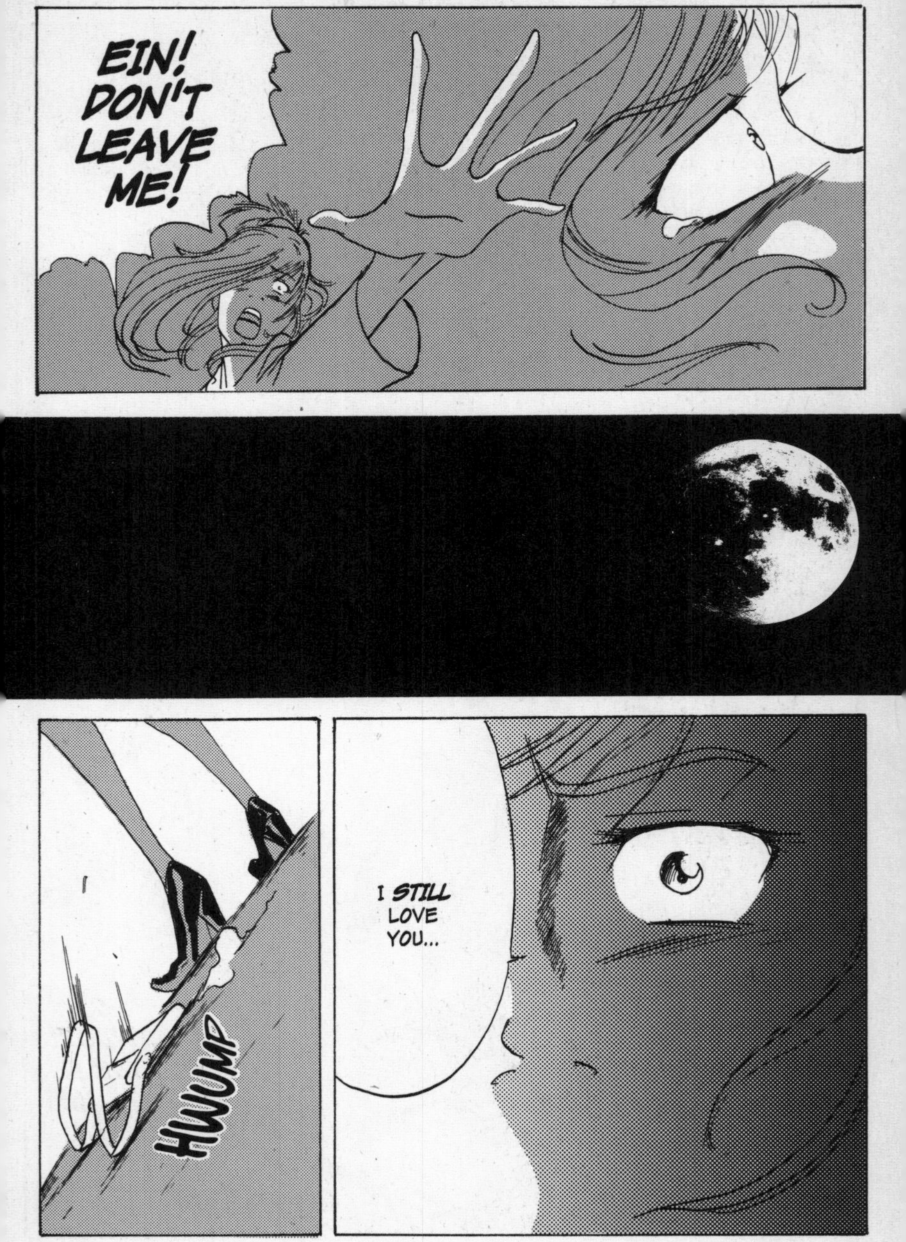
EIN! DON'T LEAVE ME!
I STILL LOVE YOU...
HWUMP

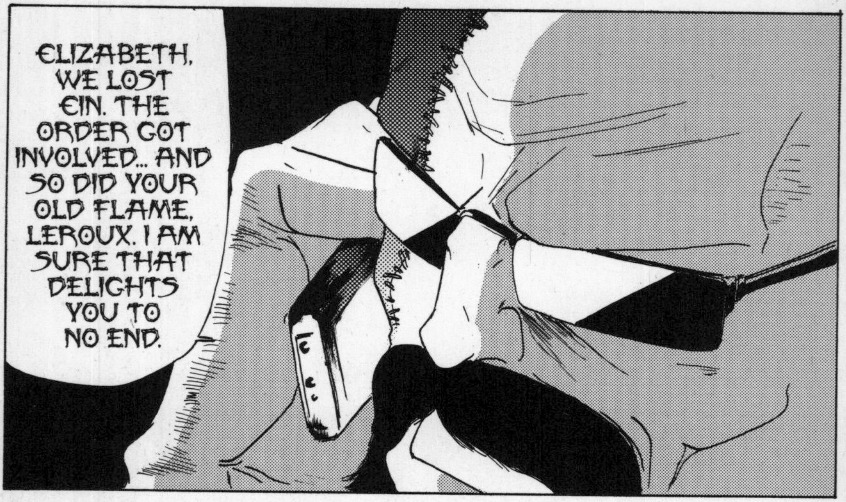
ELIZABETH, WE LOST EIN. THE ORDER GOT INVOLVED... AND SO DID YOUR OLD FLAME, LEROUX. I AM SURE THAT DELIGHTS YOU TO NO END.

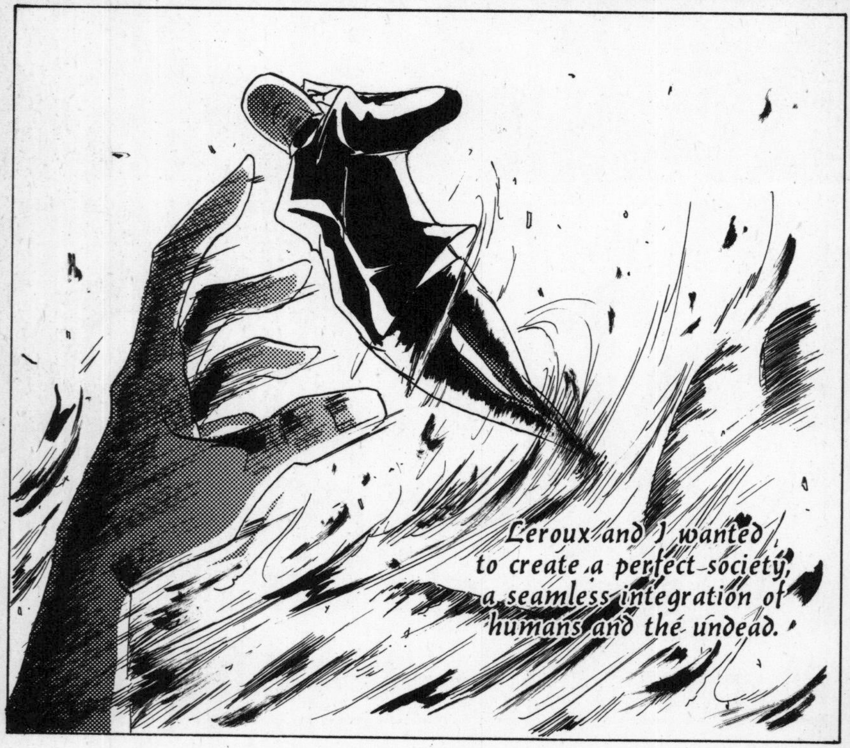
Leroux and I wanted to create a perfect society, a seamless integration of humans and the undead.

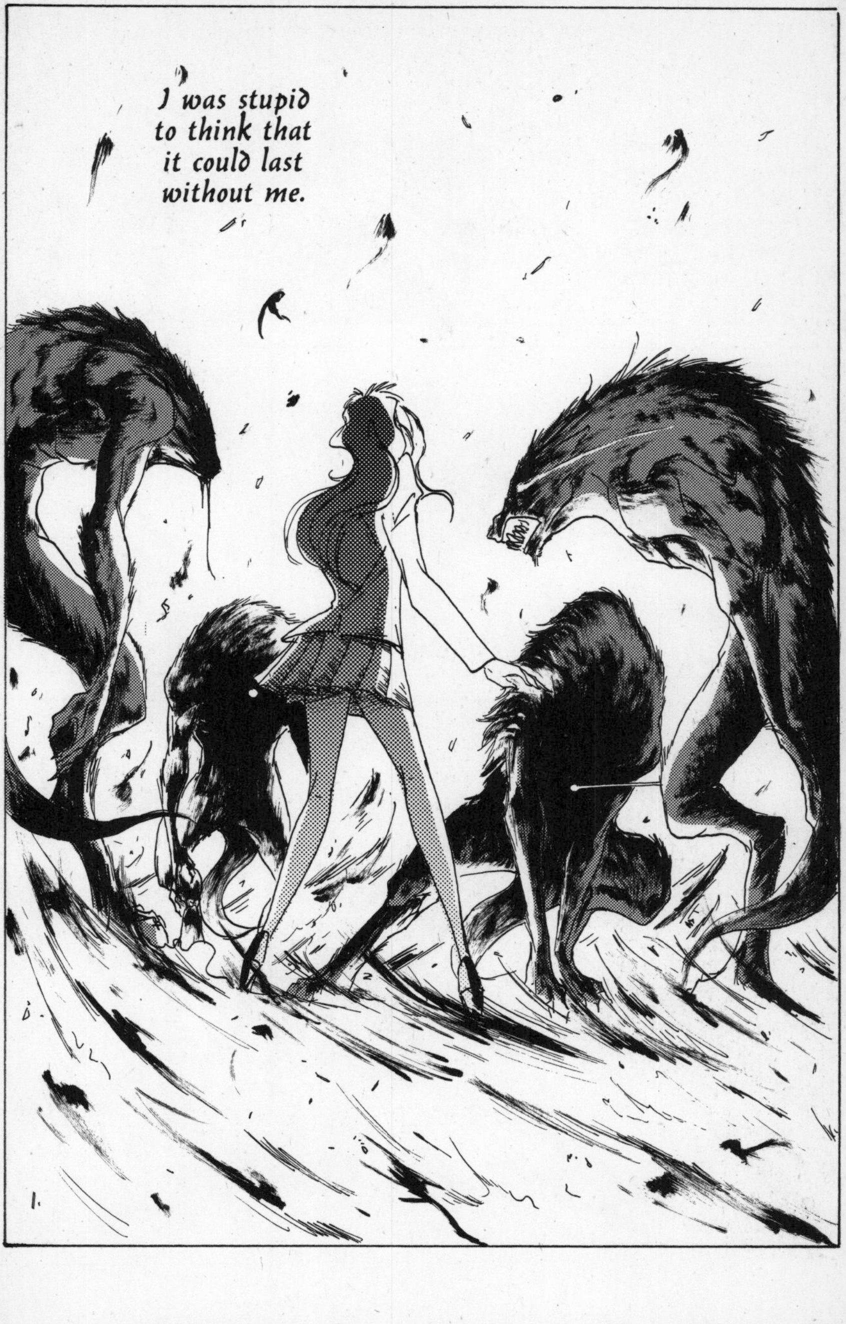
I was stupid to think that it could last without me.

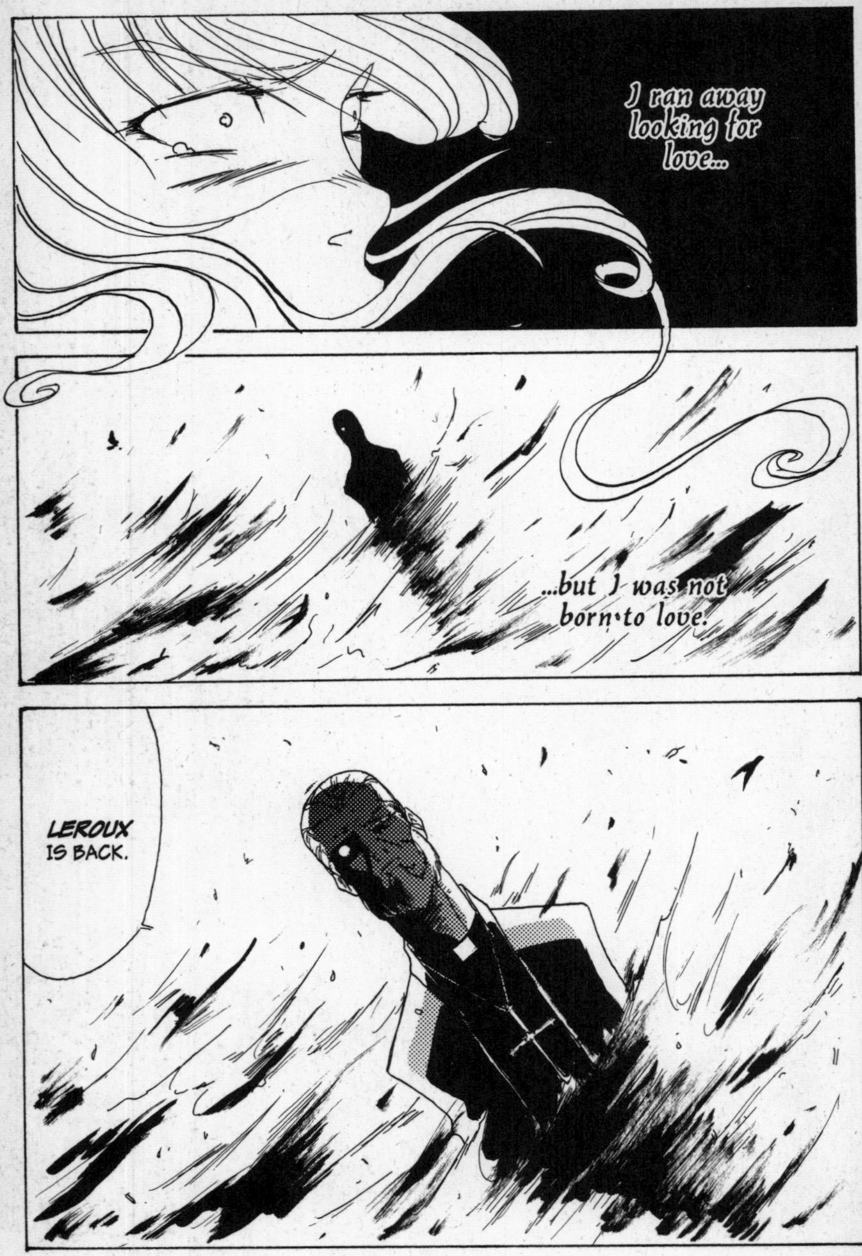
I ran away looking for love...
...but I was not born to love.
LEROUX IS BACK.

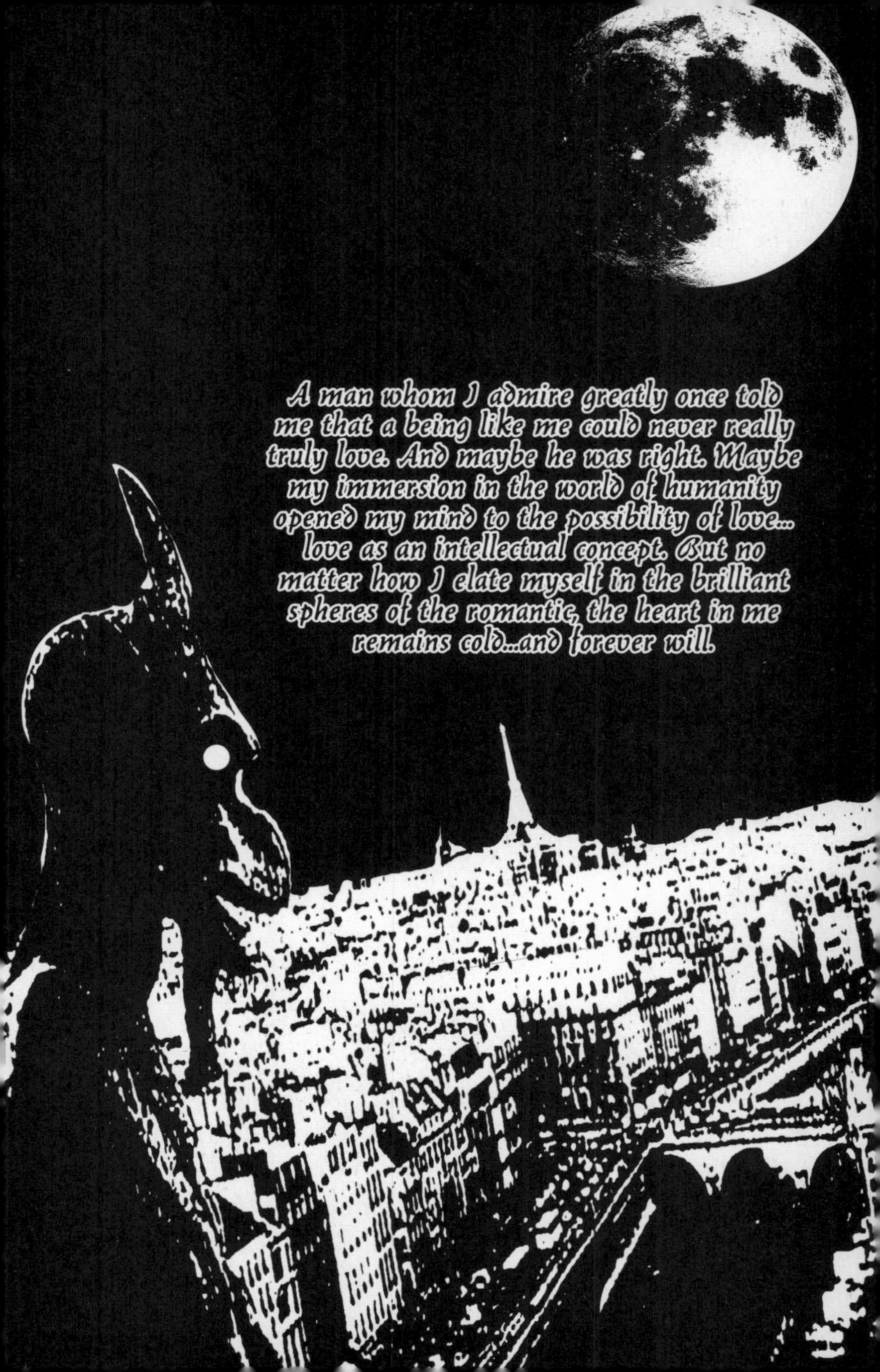
A man whom I admire greatly once told me that a being like me could never really truly love. And maybe he was right. Maybe my immersion in the world of humanity opened my mind to the possibility of love... love as an intellectual concept. But no matter how I elate myself in the brilliant spheres of the romantic, the heart in me remains cold...and forever will.

IN THE NEXT VOLUME OF

# A MIDNIGHT OPERA

Reunited under the direst of circumstances, the brothers DeLaLune now face challenges from all around: on one side the ghoulish creatures of the undead under the control of the witch Elizabeth Bathory, and on another side, Cardinal LaCroix and the soldiers of The Order. And with everything he built over the last four hundred years now either usurped or destroyed, Einblick must now rebuke the enlightened philosophy that has guided him for so long and embrace the very warrior's savagery he has always worked to abolish.

## COMING APRIL 2006

# Hans Steinbach

came to us in the fall of 2004 with an idea for a different kind of gothic horror story, one steeped in history and lore and rich in character. He presented us with some of the most incredible character designs and sequential art we had seen in the fledgling days of our foray into original English language manga. Hans' artistic style is influenced greatly by European and American artists. But his storytelling style-- contemplative, stirring musings on the human condition--has been shaped primarily by exposure to Japanese manga. The following pages feature his original submission to TOKYOPOP, the first glimpse we had of an artist we are now proud to herald as one of our original creators.

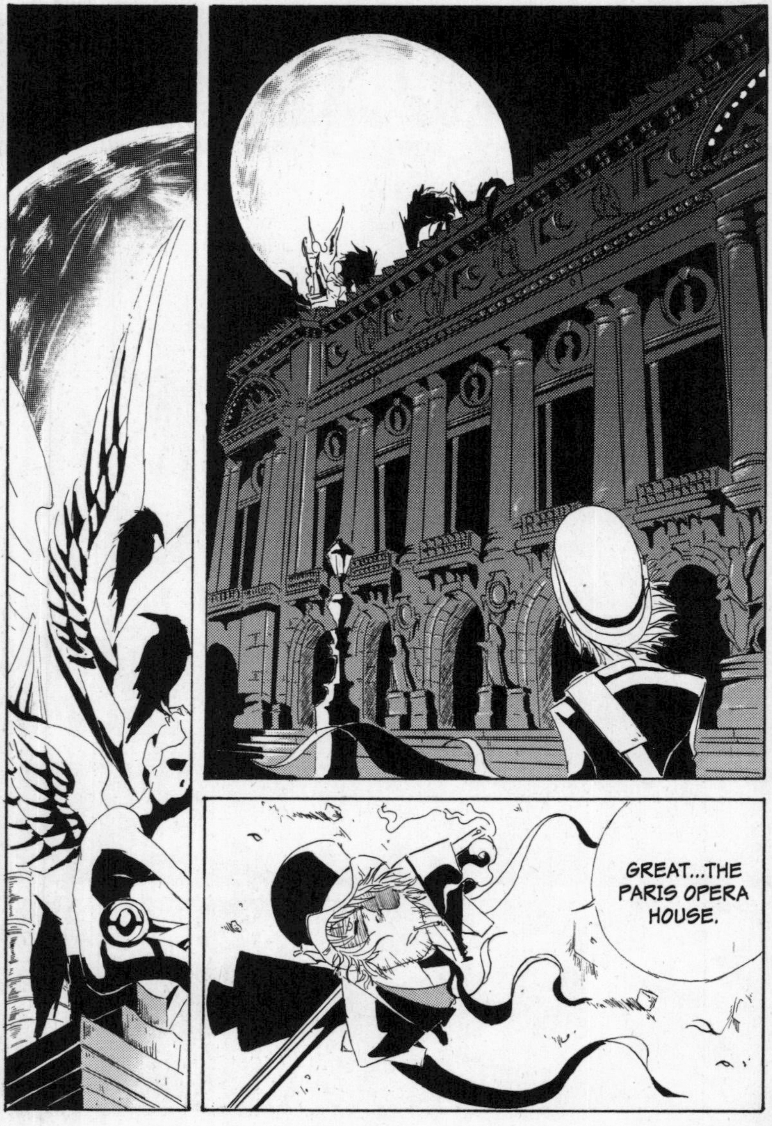
GREAT...THE PARIS OPERA HOUSE.

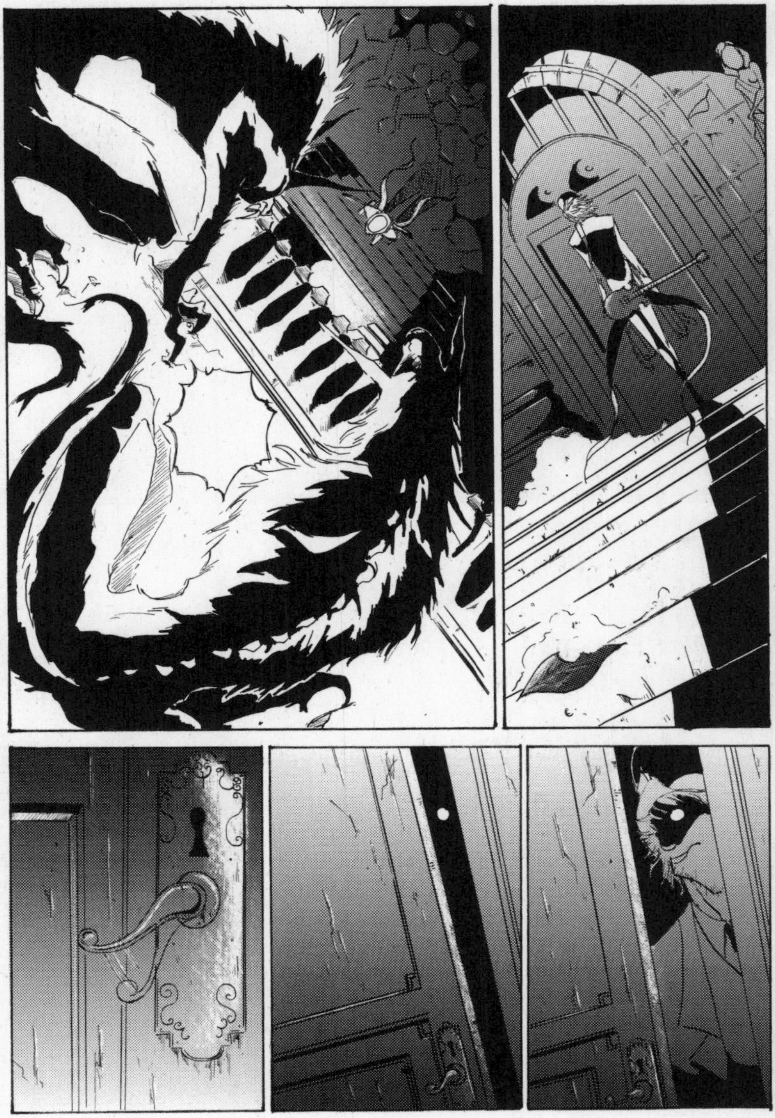

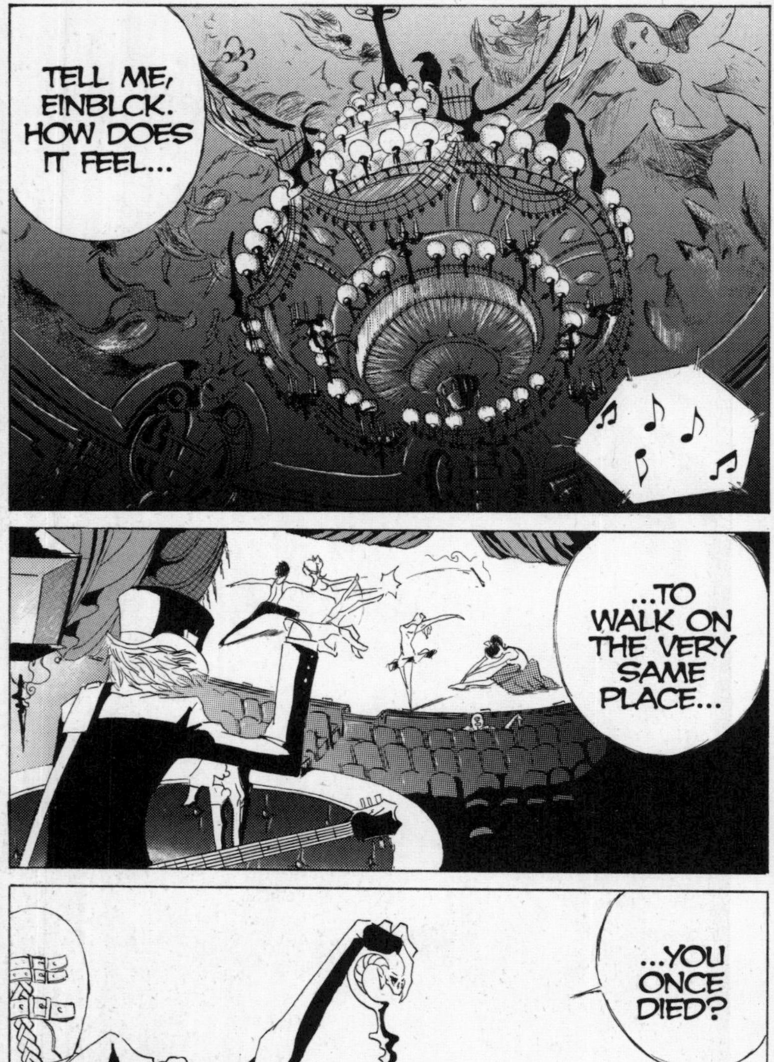
TELL ME, EINBLCK. HOW DOES IT FEEL...
...TO WALK ON THE VERY SAME PLACE...
...YOU ONCE DIED?

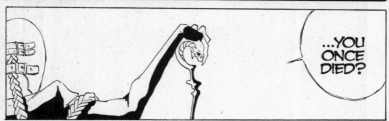

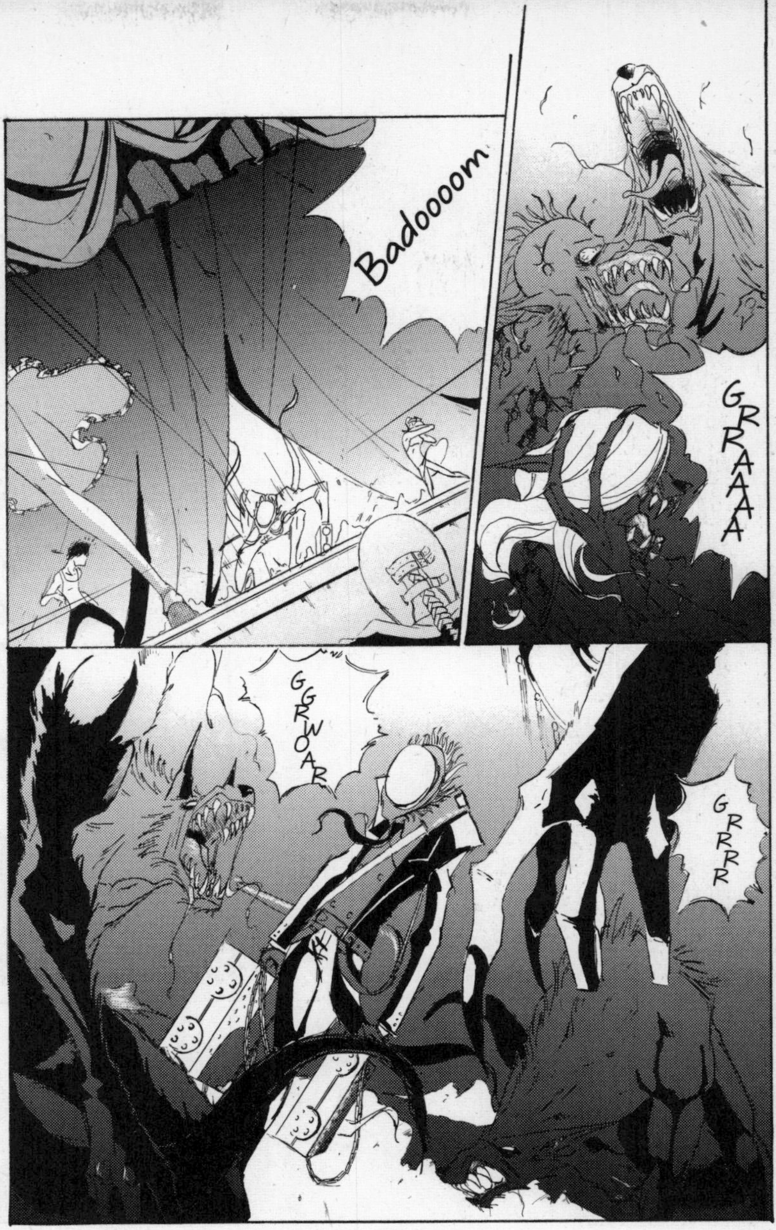
GRRAAAA
Badoooom
GRRRR
GGRWOAR

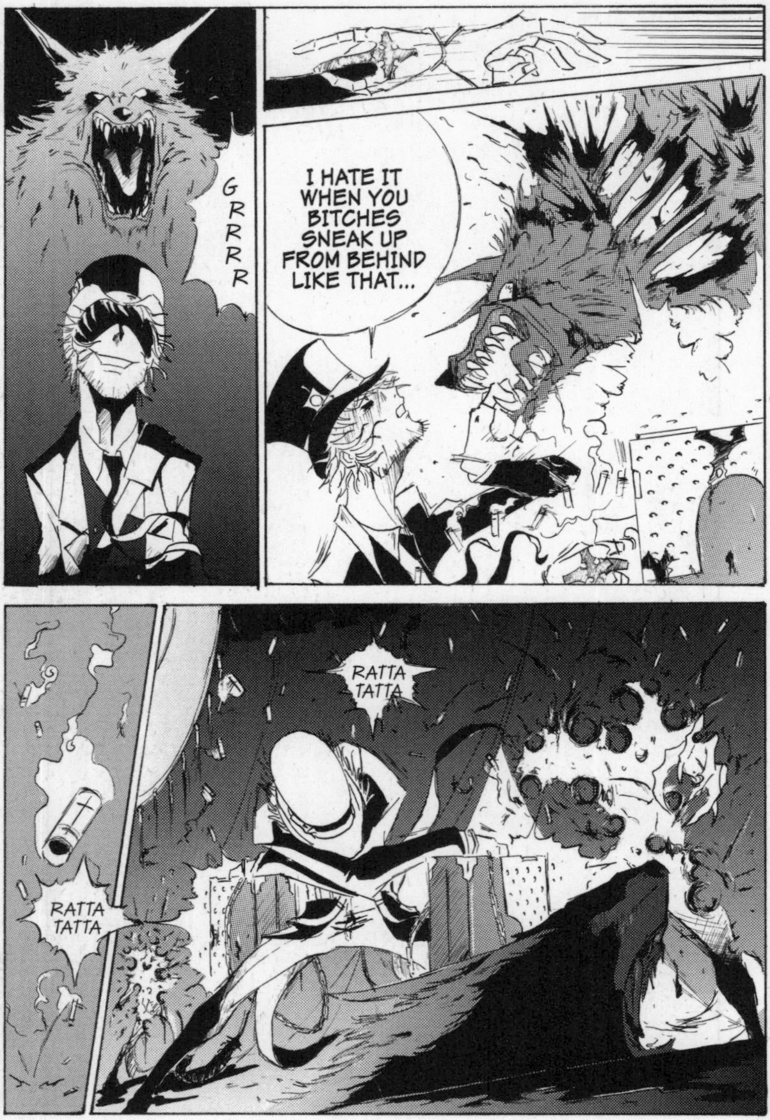
GRRRR
I HATE IT WHEN YOU BITCHES SNEAK UP FROM BEHIND LIKE THAT...
RATTA TATTA
RATTA TATTA

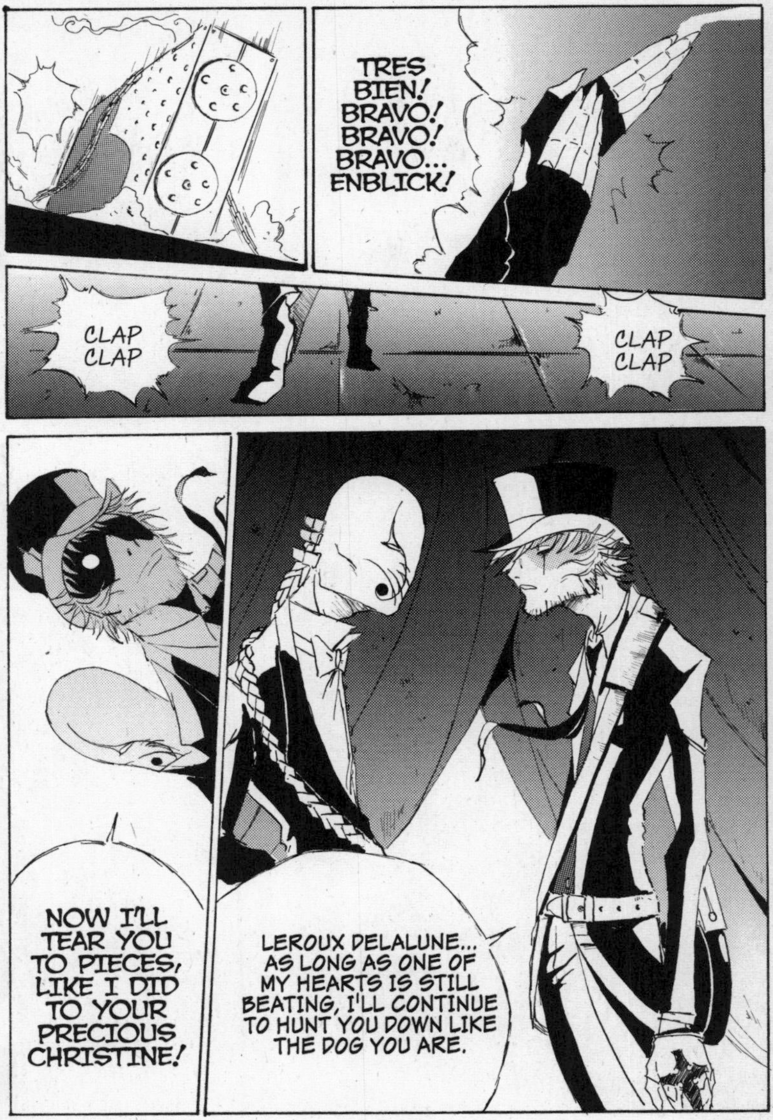
TRES BIEN! BRAVO! BRAVO! BRAVO... ENBLICK!
CLAP CLAP
CLAP CLAP
LEROUX DELALUNE... AS LONG AS ONE OF MY HEARTS IS STILL BEATING, I'LL CONTINUE TO HUNT YOU DOWN LIKE THE DOG YOU ARE.
NOW I'LL TEAR YOU TO PIECES, LIKE I DID TO YOUR PRECIOUS CHRISTINE!

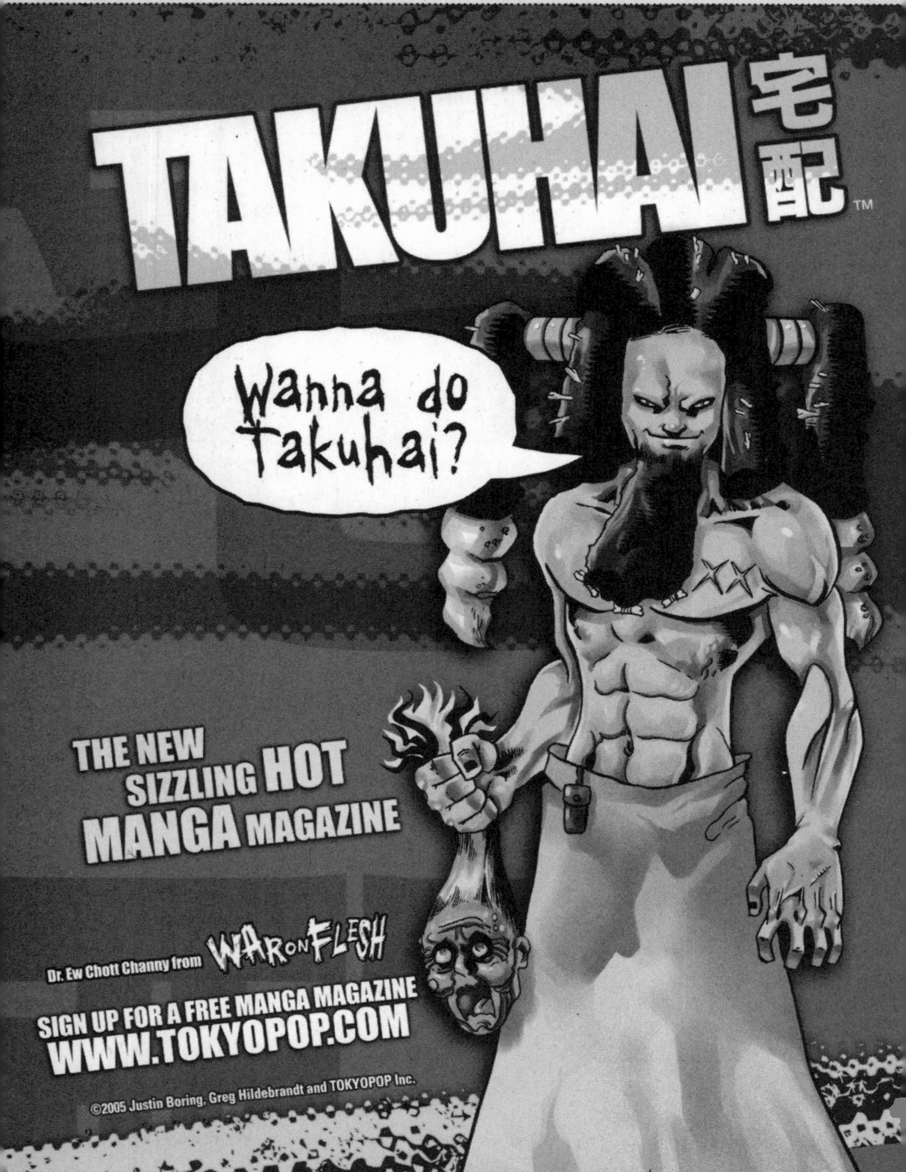
TAKUHAI 宅配 ™
Wanna do Takuhai?
THE NEW SIZZLING HOT MANGA MAGAZINE
Dr. Ew Chott Channy from WAR ON FLESH
SIGN UP FOR A FREE MANGA MAGAZINE
WWW.TOKYOPOP.COM
©2005 Justin Boring, Greg Hildebrandt and TOKYOPOP Inc.

# TOKYOPOP SHOP

## WWW.TOKYOPOP.COM/SHOP

### HOT NEWS!

Check out the TOKYOPOP
SHOP!
The world's best collection of
manga in English is now
available online in one place!

### SAMURAI CHAMPLOO

### KINGDOM HEARTS

## DRAMACON

WWW.TOKYOPOP.COM/SHOP

- **LOOK FOR SPECIAL OFFERS**
- **PRE-ORDER UPCOMING RELEASES**
- **COMPLETE YOUR COLLECTIONS**

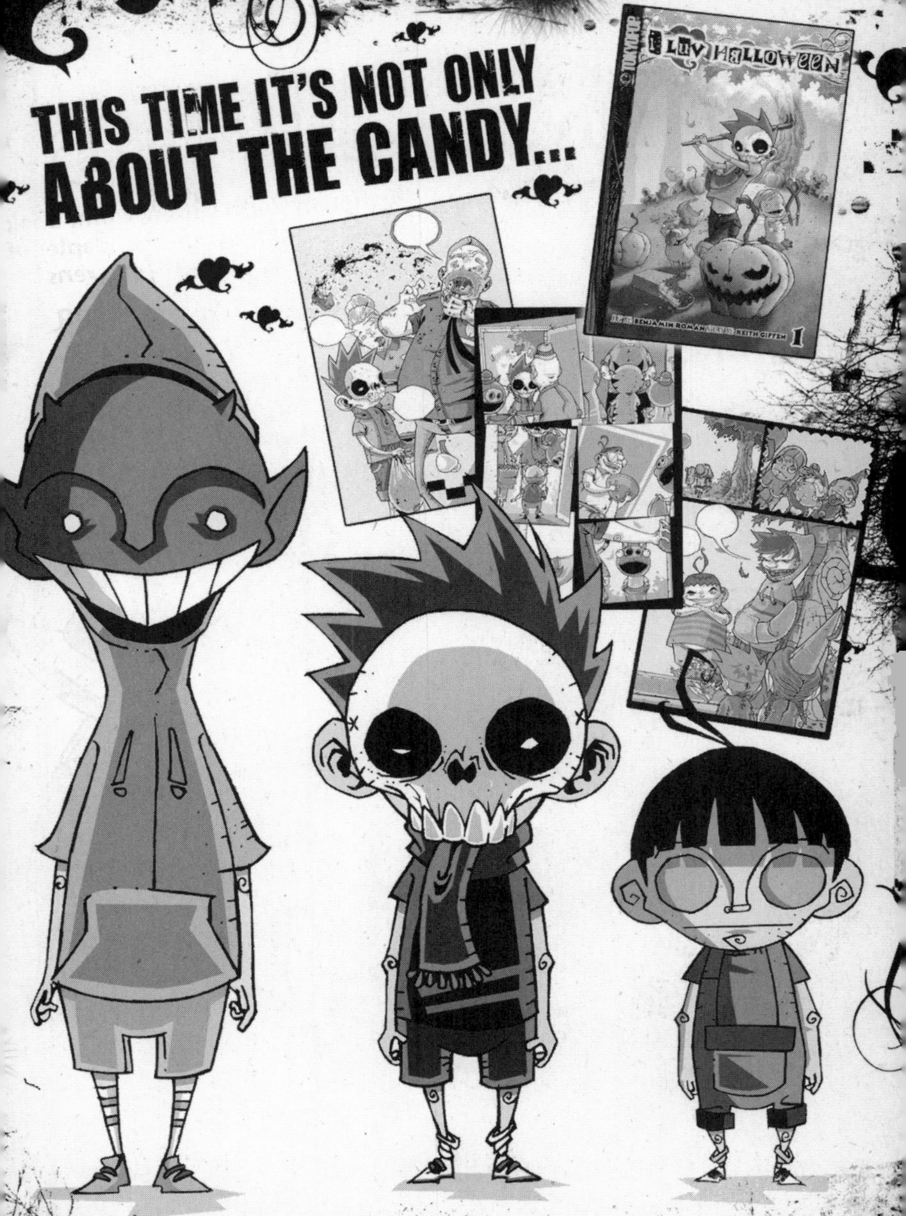
I LUV HALLOWEEN
BENJAMIN ROMAN
KEITH GIFFEN
1

## MARK OF THE SUCCUBUS
BY ASHLY RAITI & IRENE FLORES

Maeve, a succubus-in-training, is sent to the human world to learn how to hone her skills of seduction. But things get complicated when she sets her sights on Aiden, a smart but unmotivated student at her new high school. Meanwhile, the Demon World has sent a spy to make sure Maeve doesn't step out of line. And between Aiden's witchy girlfriend, his nutty best friend, and Demon World conspiracies, Maeve is going to be lucky to make it out of our world alive!

Here is a Gothic romantic fantasy set in one of the most menacing worlds known to humans: high school.

TEEN
AGE 13+

FOR MORE INFORMATION VISIT: WWW.TOKYOPOP.COM

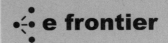

MARS
1
by Fuyumi Soryo

BY FUYUMI SORYO

## MARS

I used to do the English adaptation for *MARS* and loved working on it. The art is just amazing—Fuyumi Soryo draws these stunning characters and beautiful backgrounds to boot. I remember this one spread in particular where Rei takes Kira on a ride on his motorcycle past this factory, and it's all lit up like Christmas and the most gorgeous thing you've ever seen—and it's a factory! And the story is a super-juicy soap opera that kept me on the edge of my seat just dying to get the next volume every time I'd finish one.

~Elizabeth Hurchalla, Sr. Editor

DEAD END
SHOHEI MANABE
01

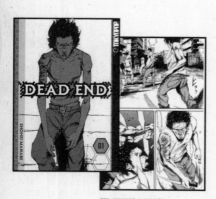

BY SHOHEI MANABE

## DEAD END

Everyone I've met who has read *Dead End* admits to becoming immediately immersed and obsessed with Shohei Manabe's unforgettable manga. If David Lynch, Clive Barker and David Cronenberg had a love child that was forced to create a manga in the bowels of a torture chamber, then *Dead End* would be the fruit of its labor. The unpredictable story follows a grungy young man as he pieces together shattered fragments of his past. Think you know where it's going? Well, think again!

~Troy Lewter, Editor

© Rivkah and TOKYOPOP Inc.

## STEADY BEAT
### BY RIVKAH

"Love Jessica"... That's what Leah finds on the back of a love letter to her sister. But who is Jessica? When more letters arrive, along with flowers and other gifts, Leah goes undercover to find out her sister's secret. But what she doesn't expect is to discover a love of her own—and in a very surprising place!

**Winner of the Manga Academy's Create Your Own Manga competition!**

**T** TEEN AGE 13+

© MIN-WOO HYUNG

## JUSTICE N MERCY
### BY MIN-WOO HYUNG

Min-Woo Hyung is one of today's most talented young Korean artists, and this stunning art book shows us why. With special printing techniques and high-quality paper, TOKYOPOP presents never-before-seen artwork based on his popular *Priest* series, as well as images from past and upcoming projects *Doomslave*, *Hitman* and *Sal*.

**A spectacular art book from the creator of *Priest*!**

**T** TEEN AGE 13+

© 2003 Liu GOTO © SOTSU AGENCY • SUNRISE • MBS

## MOBILE SUIT GUNDAM SEED NOVEL
### ORIGINAL STORY BY HAJIME YATATE AND YOSHIYUKI TOMINO
### WRITTEN BY LIU GOTO

A shy young student named Kira Yamato is thrown in the midst of battle when genetically enhanced Coordinators steal five new Earth Force secret weapons. Wanting only to protect his Natural friends, Kira embraces his Coordinator abilities and pilots the mobile suit Strike. The hopes and fears of a new generation clash with the greatest weapons developed by mankind: Gundam!

**The novelization of the super-popular television series!**

**T** TEEN AGE 13+